'We are men of honour, we're the elite of the crime world . . . We're the worst of all'

Antonino Calderone

WHITE SHOTGUN

THE SICILIAN MAFIA IN THEIR OWN WORDS

ATTILIO BOLZONI

Translated by Shaun Whiteside

MACMILLAN

First published 2008 by RCS Libri S.p.A., Milan

First published in Great Britain 2013 by Macmillan
an imprint of Pan Macmillan, a division of Macmillan Publishers Limited
Pan Macmillan, 20 New Wharf Road, London N1 9RR
Basingstoke and Oxford
Associated companies throughout the world
www.panmacmillan.com

ISBN 978-0-230-75216-0

Originally published in 2008 as *Parole d'onore* by RCS Libri S.p.A., Milan.

1 3 5 7 9 8 6 4 2

A CIP catalogue record for this book is available from the British Library.

Typeset by Ellipsis Books Limited, Glasgow
Printed and bound by CPI Group (UK) Ltd, Croydon, CR0 4YY

CONTENTS

GLOSSARY OF TERMS

Commissione or *Cupola* – the body of leading Mafia members that regulates the actions of the Cosa Nostra.

Commissione interprovinciale – a governing body made up of the representatives of various provinces of Sicily.

Consiglieri – the adviser or advisers, appointed by the *capo*, or elected in the case of large families.

Capo – the head of the individual family, elected by the men of honour. The *capo* of the family is called a *rappresentante*, a representative.

Capomandamento – the chief of a Sicilian jurisdiction, voted for by three families to represent them in the *Commissione*.

Capodecina – the 'head of ten', a man of honour in charge of a number of Cosa Nostra foot soldiers.

Soldati – the 'soldiers', the lowest level of the Mafia hierarchy.

Sottocapo – the 'underboss', or second-in-command, appointed by the *capo*.

Soldati – Mafia foot soldiers

INTRODUCTION

They are voices that reach us from another world. They rise up threateningly, they are bewildering. Sometimes they are fleeting, innocent-sounding, sometimes they are deliberately freighted with omens. They always hide something, they always deliver a message. Everything in their language is message – even the most apparently irrelevant details, the gestures that go with the voices or take their place. The silences, too. It's an unsettling chorus that I've found in my notebook. Those words, those 'speeches', have become my notes.

In this book the Mafiosi tell the story of the last half-century of their Sicily. They talk about morality and family, about business and crimes, rules, loves, friendships betrayed, religion and God, money and power, life and death. About their relationship with prison and the law, endless periods spent in hiding, the state.

In some circumstances they reveal their fragility, in others they demonstrate a startling constitution. And they recall with regret ancient privileges; they describe the symbolic places of their authority. The Ucciardone* above all. They confess their past and defend their present. They talk about wives and children, about fathers, about renegade sisters or brothers. They explain who they are and where they come from. One of them says, 'Because in

---

* The prison in Palermo, historically home to many Mafiosi.

Sicily, the one thing you can't do without is the consideration that other people have for you.' That's what they call *dignitudine*. The book is the account of a journey into Mafia territories. It is a collection of their thoughts and their *ragionamenti*.* Words of honour.

Sometimes it seems like an inventory of madness. A combination of insanity and the most implacable logic, halfway between paranoia and a terrifying rationality. Mafia language is more than just a language, more than just a code: it's an exercise of the intelligence, a permanent exhibition of power. Every reflection is a calculation, every turn of phrase reveals the nature of these unique criminals. Their words open a door into their world and, as we pass through it, we recognize other signs, catch its smells and humours.

As the murdered judge Giovanni Falcone once explained to Marcelle Padovani in *Cose di Cosa Nostra*, 'Knowing the Mafiosi has had a profound influence on my relations with other people, and also on my principles. Strange though it might seem, the Mafia has taught me a lesson in morality.' With the rigour of a magistrate and the civic passion of certain great Sicilians, Falcone was the first to plumb the depths of the Mafia mentality. He said: 'By knowing the men of honour, I have learned that Mafia logic is always either outmoded or incomprehensible. In reality it is the logic of power, and it always works towards a purpose. Sometimes those Mafiosi strike me as the only rational beings in a world populated by madmen. Sciascia† also maintained that the worst Cartesians‡ are to be found in Sicily.'

Here you will find the words of Mafiosi big and small, well known and less well known, the ones from Palermo and the others from the internal provinces, *pentiti*§ and non-*pentiti*. Underground

---

* 'Reasonings'.

† Leonardo Sciascia, twentieth-century Sicilian writer and politician.

‡ Followers of the rationalist philosophy of René Descartes (1596–1650).

§ 'They who have repented', the name used for Mafia members who collaborate with the police and state.

or forgotten. Leonardo Messina, Tommaso Spadaro, Giuseppe Di Cristina and Pino Marchese, Masino Buscetta, Totò Riina, Nino Salvo, Pietro Aglieri, Stefano Giaconia, Luciano Leggio, Giuseppe Joe Cambino, Tano Badalamenti, Vito Ciancimino, Calogero Ganci, Gioacchino La Barbera, Giovanni Brusca, Aurelio Neri, Nino Rotolo, Francesco Inzerillo, Bernardo Provenzano, Gaspare Mutolo, Totuccio Contorno, Giovanni Bontate, Michele Greco, Matteo Messina Denaro, Antonino Giuffrè, Nino Calderone, Angelo Siino. And many, many others. Each chapter is a self-contained story, but never one that is separate from the others. It is like an underground river that has run through events in Sicily over the last fifty years. The book moves back and forth in time, following an order dictated by their arguments. Always the same, always identical. Eternal. Each chapter is built on direct quotations from the Mafia, whether given in testimony to a trial or a public prosecutor, apprehended by a bugging device or shouted or whispered in the street. There are many voices, but only one plot. As in life, everything here stays within Cosa Nostra.

My job as a journalist has allowed me to meet many of them. In the Palace of Justice. In the suburbs. Sometimes even in their houses. I have bumped into them in the streets of Palermo, where the Mafia war was raging a quarter of a century ago. Among the last kitchen-gardens in Brancaccio and past the ruined houses on the Mare della Bandita, behind the great blocks on Passo di Rigano and in L'Uditore, in the alleyways of L'Acquasanta and L'Arenella. I saw them again a few years later, locked up in their cages in the bunker courtroom. A unique observatory in which to understand their way of thinking.

I have seen them from the Palermo Maxi-Trial in the winter of 1986 (though their story goes back much further than that) to the last forays in the spring of 2008. From the Buscettas and the Leggios – via Totò Riina and the massacres – to the 'ten commandments' found in the hideout of the Lo Piccolos, father and son, the makeshift *capi* of a Cosa Nostra with an uncertain future.

One final note: on some pages you will find quotations from individuals who are not Mafiosi. But they talk about Mafia and Sicily. With their unease and distaste, they too somehow convey a message.

The idea of this book was born a long time ago, in 1993. Over the weeks that followed the arrest of Totò Riina I spent some time in Corleone; on more than one occasion I was able to meet his brother Gaetano. I was there to reconstruct the lives of those Sicilian 'peasants' – the Corleonesi – who had held the Italian state hostage in the 1980s. Gaetano Tanuzzu Riina and I talked about lots of things. Not least, about the *pentito* Tommaso Buscetta. About what he had confessed to Judge Falcone. About what he had done in his life between Sicily and America, Palermo and Brazil.

As we talked about Buscetta, Gaetano Riina said something that I have never forgotten. I had asked him why Buscetta had turned *pentito*. He said: 'He saw the world, and his brain exploded.'

Attilio Bolzoni

Corleone, a Sicilian village fifty-six kilometres from Palermo. The most famous Corleonesi: Bernard of Corleone, saint; Francesco Paolo Nascè, man of letters; Bernardino Verro, socialist mayor murdered by the Mafia; Mother Terese Cortimiglia, founder of the Order of the Franciscan Sisters of Santa Chiara; Pippo Rizzo, painter; Francesco Bentivegna, patriot killed by a Bourbon firing-squad; San Leoluca, abbot and patron saint; Placido Rizzotto, trade unionist killed by the Mafia. And Salvatore Riina, Bernardo Provenzano and Vito Ciancimino, Mafiosi.

Mario Puzo, the author of The Godfather, *called the protagonist of his novel Vito Corleone. Vito like Ciancimino, Corleone like the village.*

'He saw the world and his brain exploded'*

Gaetano Riina, known as Tanuzzu

Corleone, the spring of 1993. The Sicilian village is in a state of siege, under military occupation by police units, isolated. On every street there's a van with an aerial sending and receiving signals; every other house is full of bugs. Corleone is one big microphone.

Only a hundred days has passed since the arrest of the Cosa Nostra boss Salvatore 'Totò' Riina, and among the dusty alleyways that come down from the Rocca del Mascaro a great manhunt is on for all the other fugitives. They are looking for them in the farms behind the Montagna dei Cavalli and down in the valley, towards the walls of a monastery. Totò Riina's family has just come back to the village. His wife Ninetta, his sons Giovanni and Salvo, his daughters Maria Concetta and Lucia. They all live at 24 Via Scorsone, in the upper part of the village, where a narrow street climbs to the old ice factory. Every morning in the little square in front of the village hall, Gaetano Riina appears like a ghost, the younger brother of the *capo dei capi* of Cosa Nostra. He is a man of humble appearance: short, squat and ungainly, always wrapped up in clothes that are too long and too wide.

His old economy car is parked in a courtyard, the engine roaring, belching out smoke and leaking oil. His family is the most powerful in Sicily. He has treasures hidden in strongboxes halfway

---

* Interview by the author with Gaetano Riina, Corleone, May 1993.

across Europe, but Tanuzzu looks like a pauper. He still looks like the peasants of fifty years ago who hoed the land on the estates of the counts and barons. But for the Riina family it's always been a mantra: never display your wealth, never show off your possessions.

In the square in Corleone Tanuzzu meets his fellow villagers. These are long days, waiting for everything and nothing, in the growing heat of the Sicilian sun. There are long conversations consisting of looks, nods and silences. It's a contorted, exhausting way of talking. Every now and again a phrase is left hanging, a pause, then another half-word.

The armoured vehicles dart along the village streets. Some people remember the previous night's raid, others the one the previous month, the *carabinieri* closing all the routes in and out and then leaving at dawn. Empty-handed, without a wanted man.

A *pentito* had brought them to Corleone. Someone like Tommaso Buscetta, whose name has just been murmured in the square. Tanuzzu pretends not to hear it, but his lips form a grimace. Then he turns slowly and hisses: 'That man's mad.' He repeats it again – 'That man's mad' – without changing the tone of his voice, without moving a muscle, never looking into the eyes of the others.

And yet Tommaso Buscetta, the biggest enemy of Cosa Nostra, doesn't inspire Gaetano Riina's rage. It's as if Tanuzzu, when he speaks of him, no longer bears him any rancour, as if he had buried all resentment in the depths of his heart. Then Tanuzzu begins to draw up a list. He remembers all the men who left Corleone and Prizzi and Piana degli Albanesi in his youth, to travel far away from Sicily. Men who chose no longer to live in this closed, distant, different land. Away from the corral. From the tribe.

'Tommaso Buscetta travelled,' Gaetano Riina says to his fellow villagers. He went to the mainland, to Milan and Turin. He went to New York. And then to Brazil. In the square in Corleone, Gaetano

Riina reveals to himself and the others the origin of Tommaso Buscetta's madness. In a resigned voice he whispers: 'He saw the world and his brain exploded.'

TRADITION

THE COMMISSIONE, 1960

Capo: Salvatore Greco known as Cicchiteddu
Capimandamento:
Antonino Matranga (Resuttana family)
Mariano Troia (San Lorenzo family)
Michele Cavataio (L'Acquasanta family)
Calcedonio Di Pisa (La Noce family)
Salvatore La Barbera (Palermo Centro family)
Cesare Manzella (Cinisi family)
Giuseppe Panno (Casteldaccia family)
Antonio Salamone (San Giuseppe Jato family)
Lorenzo Motisi (Pagliarelli family)
Salvatore Manno (Boccadifalco family)
Francesco Sorci (Villagrazia family)
Mario Di Girolamo (Corso Calatafimi family)

In the late 1970s, after the war between the Greco and La Barbera familes, Cosa Nostra reorganizes with a 'provisional government', the Triumvirate.

TRIUMVIRATE

Gaetano Badalamenti (Cinisi family)
Stefano Bontate (Santa Maria del Gesù family)
Luciano Leggio (Corleone family)

1975

Capo: Gaetano Badalamenti
Capimandamento:
Antonio Salamone (San Giuseppe Jato family)
Luciano Leggio (Corleone family)
Stefano Bontate (Santa Maria del Gesù family)
Rosario Di Maggio (Passo di Rigano family)
Salvatore Scaglione (La Noce family)
Giuseppe Calò (Porta Nuova family)
Rosario Riccobono (Partanna Mondello family)
Filippo Giacalone (San Lorenzo family)
Michele Greco (Croceverde Giardina-Ciaculli family)
Nenè Geraci, 'the old man' (Partinico family)

In May 2008, looking up 'Mafia' on Google produced 60,200,000 results. The term 'Cosa Nostra' threw up 2,280,000. The request 'Totò Riina' supplied 181,000 sites, and 'Bernardo Provenzano' 197,000. And yet until a few decades ago the Mafia didn't officially exist. Only the Sicilians were aware of it, but even they spoke of it as an old and dying sect. The rest of Italy found out about it in 1961, in Leonardo Sciascia's novel The Day of the Owl.

'As paper I burn you, as a saint I worship you'*

Leonardo Messina

He is a man predestined. His great-grandfather's grandfather's grandfather was a *combinato* – a 'made man' – the first of his clan to be created a man of honour. Blood and Mafia have been passed down for seven generations. In 1980 it's his turn – he being Leonardo, born in San Cataldo, a village seven kilometres and fourteen twists in the road from Caltanissetta. The centre of Sicily.

'I felt as if I'd been born to the trade. My paternal grandfather, who was called Leonardo like me, represented the Serradifalco family; my maternal uncle Cataldo La Marcia was *capodecina* of the San Cataldo family; the father of my sister-in-law, Vincenzo Sollami, was *sottocapo* . . . I have the rank of *capodecina*.'

Leonardo Messina is thirty-two years old when he tells his story.

'It's not like you get up one morning and say, "From today onwards I'm going to be part of Cosa Nostra." They follow you from babyhood, they bring you up, they observe you, they rear you, they teach you to shoot and kill. Then there are men who join Cosa Nostra with the destiny of being *capi*. And that's just how it is.'

There's an apprenticeship. It can be long or it can be very short.

'The first step is *avvicinato*, being approached, and after a

---

* Examination of the *pentito* Leonardo Messina, Parliamentary Anti-Mafia Commission, Rome, 4 December 1992.

period of assessment that can last one, five or twenty years, depending on the individual, someone tells you the time has come to join Cosa Nostra. But by the time they call you, you already know you're joining, not least because you've served these men already. You talk the talk perfectly. And yet there's always someone guiding you.'

That's the godfather, the *pipino* in the dialect of the island's internal provinces.

'Everyone chooses his own. My *pipino* was Vincenzo Burcheri, he was the one who pricked my finger. It was him and not *capodecina* Luigi Calì because a short time before, on 16 November 1980, Calì had been killed and the San Cataldo family had lost its head. They'd killed Liborio Terminio as well. Usually the meeting to join is like a party with loads of people at it. They explain all the problems to you, but no one explains the rules of Cosa Nostra. You have to work those out for yourself, *then* they'll explain them to you piece by piece.'

The man predestined in San Cataldo remembers the moment he'd been waiting for all his life.

'Behind me I had Vincenzo Burcheri. There was the whole *Commissione provinciale*. They pricked my fingertip with a needle and handed me a holy picture of the Madonna of the Annunciation. They stained it with my blood, they set fire to it and I passed it from one hand to the other. Then they whispered the words I was to say. They told me to repeat: "As paper I burn you, as a saint I worship you, as this paper burns so my flesh must burn if I one day betray the Cosa Nostra."'

Leonardo is now a man of honour. Everyone hugs him, everyone kisses him.

The *punciuta*. Initiates are asked for the index finger of their right hand, the shooting hand. In some villages they used to use the thorns of the wild orange tree. In Riesi it was a gold pin, always the same one.

The holy picture that every Mafioso venerates is the one of the Madonna of the Annunciation. She is the patron saint of Cosa Nostra. Her saint's day is 25 March.

'The oath is like the Ten Commandments'*

Salvatore Contorno, known as Totuccio

'If you find me here it's because I'm trying to save my life. My family's taken care of, if I die I don't care. And I'm also here because Cosa Nostra has turned into a bunch of cowards and murderers. They're the real *pentiti* of Cosa Nostra. Everything's changed now, they even kill women and little ones. They're a wretched bunch, and they dare to call me a *cornuto*.† There are no *cornuti* in my family, but there are in theirs. So I'm not a *cornuto*, but they are *cornuti*.

'It was in 1975 that I was called to make the oath. It was my late friend Mimmo Teresi who brought me to the house of the late Stefano Bontate. One way or another I was forced to stay in Cosa Nostra. The oath is like the Ten Commandments: don't look at the other guy's wife, always tell the truth, anyone who betrays Cosa Nostra will be burned like a holy picture. First you're *frequentato* – they hang out with you – to work out whether or not you're a cop, then they want to check whether there are any bastards in the family, in other words if they're good people.

'Michele Greco is a traitor. The corpses piled up in Palermo, and he's to blame for them all. If he wanted to, he could say: no,

* Testimony of the *pentito* Salvatore Contorno at the Maxi-Trial in Palermo, hearings on 11 and 17 April 1986.

† A cuckold, but used as a more generally disparaging term: 'bastard'.

you don't do these things. I can tell you some very old stories about Michele Greco, from when I was a little boy. Michele Greco is the son of Piddu il Tenente – yes, a real lieutenant in the *carabinieri*. Between 1940 and 1945 there'd been a feud between the Grecos of Ciaculli and the Grecos of Croceverde Giardina. There had been a village fête and it ended with a corpse, Michele Greco's brother. At that point Piddu il Tenente – a total rat, a rotten corpse wherever he is – reported the facts to the police, saying that his son had been killed by Totò Pace di Ciaculli and Paolino Greco and two others. Four poor souls who went down for thirty years apiece. So, according to the custom that I grew up with, when you're the son of such a rotten father you couldn't become a man of honour. That's been the bane of Cosa Nostra. In our circles, in the old days at least, when you have a rotten father or a *buttana*[*] of a mother or a customs officer son, you can't join Cosa Nostra . . .

'I knew they were after me because one day a motorcycle suddenly appeared and Pino Greco[†] fired a Kalashnikov at me from the back of it. I anticipated his move and as I drove I threw my son and the other kid who was with me out of the car. I grabbed my gun, Pino Greco fired at me again. I'm sure I got him in the chest. It was then I knew he was wearing a bullet-proof vest.

'After I escaped the attack I went to Rome to look for Pippo Calò. Not to ask him for help, but to kill him. Calò had all the drug channels under his control. He's no fool, he owned a stack of properties, but not a square inch registered in his name. While I was in Rome they killed a few of my relatives, to put the wind up me . . . me, who's never been scared of anyone. These are the men of honour we have in Palermo today: it's me they should have been killing, not those innocent people.

'Along with my late friend Mimmo Teresi and four others I was

---

* 'Whore'.

† Michele Greco's nephew.

invited by Rosario Riccobono for a *mangiata*,* a peace-making. I said to Teresi: "Mimmo, watch out because this is a cage, watch out, it's a trap." They went off and they didn't come back. I waited for them for hours and hours. That's how I got away the second time.'

* Literally, an 'eating', a meal, but in Cosa Nostra it is often the occasion for an assassination.

'He's like us'*

Tommaso Buscetta

'I was made a man of honour in 1946. I was very young, I'd say I was a child. In those days they used to send out bits of paper out to all the families all over Sicily to find out if anyone had anything to say against the boy who'd been proposed. So it was more about moral issues. A man of honour didn't have to know how to shoot, though there also had to be men who did know how to shoot.

'Lawyers, doctors, engineers, princes were all made men of honour. But men like that aren't going to shoot and they didn't shoot. They were made men of honour because they served the common cause, some because they had an estate, some because they were needed to tend to injuries. All of those people joined up very willingly. Cosa Nostra wouldn't have made a man of honour without testing, testing, testing him.

'They told me it [Cosa Nostra] was born to defend the weak from the abuses of the powerful, to affirm the values of friendship, of respect for the given word. In a nutshell, the sense of honour. Cosa Nostra made the law on our island . . . Because we Sicilians felt ignored, abandoned by foreign governments, and by the government in Rome.

'The word Mafia is a literary invention. The true "Mafiosi" were

---

* Examination of the *pentito* Tommaso Buscetta at the Parliamentary Anti-Mafia Committee, Rome, 17 November 1992.

just called men of honour or soldiers. Each of them is part of a family. In the family you have the *capo*, elected by the men of honour, who in turn appoints the *sottocapo* and one or more *consiglieri*. But if it's a big family, the *consiglieri* are elected as well, never more than three at a time. Then there are the *capidecina*. The *capo* of the family is called a *rappresentante*. The families are brought together three by three, and nominate a *capomandamento*, who is the person voted for by the three families to represent them in the *Commissione*. The members of the *Commissione*, in my day, lasted in the job for three years, but I don't know if those rules are still respected. The profound degeneration of the rulers of Cosa Nostra has meant that that these rules are now respected only in theory, because in reality the *Commissione* is the instrument through which the man or the men in charge impose their will.

'After the *Commissione* comes the *Commissione interprovinciale*, which is made up of the *rappresentanti* of the provinces of Palermo, Catania, Caltanissetta, Agrigento and Trapani. The *Interprovinciale* deals with problems that go beyond small-town interests. If, and this is just an example, a decision had to be made about a coup d'état, then the *Commissione interprovinciale* would be convened. In the *Interprovinciale*, between one and ten are in charge: Palermo ten, Trapani eight, Agrigento eight, Caltanissetta six, Catania four.

'When men of honour talk to each other about anything to do with Cosa Nostra, they are always under an absolute obligation to tell the truth. People who don't tell the truth we call *tragediaturi** and then they undergo punishments which range from expulsion – in that case you say the man of honour is *posato*† – to death. The man of honour never stops being one for as long as he lives. A man of honour can't introduce himself to another man of honour all by himself, because neither of the two would ever be sure that they

---

* 'Tragedians', or 'actors'.

† 'Placed'.

were actually talking to another man of honour. There always has to be a third man of honour who knows both and introduces them to each other, saying: "He's like us," or "He's the same thing." That's Cosa Nostra.'

'We are men of honour, we're the elite of the crime world . . . We're the worst of all'*

Antonino Calderone

'Every man of honour feels like one. He knows it, and he repeats it to himself continuously, and he feels superior to any other criminal. When he sees the ordinary common criminal guys he studies them carefully, he cultivates them with a view to bringing some of them into the association, but he always looks at them with a certain detachment because they're coarse, immature elements who might start doing things that a man of honour shouldn't do. The exploitation of prostitution, for example, which the Mafia doesn't allow . . . The clever thing about Cosa Nostra has always been that it's an association of men of honour, a secret thing for the few, while at the same time staying connected to normal life; with the trades and professions of the people. The Mafia has a bit of everything. Apart from judges and policemen, there are all kinds of people. The Mafioso is like a spider. He constructs webs of friendships, of acquaintances, of obligations . . .

'We are men of honour, the others are just ordinary men. You'll forgive me for the distinction I'm making between the Mafia and ordinary criminals, but I'm sticking with it. We are men of honour, we're the elite of the criminal world. We're pretty superior to common criminals. We're the worst of all.

---

* The *pentito* Antonino Calderone speaking to Pino Arlacchi in his book *Gli uomini del disonore* ('*Men of Dishonour*').

'Most people become men of honour down the family line, but not like in the aristocracy, where the father passes on the sceptre of command and the title of prince or marquis to his son. No, in the Mafia it's more complicated. They observe, they study things . . . In my day, for example, people knew nothing about this Mafia that everyone's talking about today. In Catania they actually used to talk about the Mano Nera, the Black Hand. They had adopted the Mafia mentality without knowing it. And there are things that fire a child's imagination: this guy comes and kisses your father, this other guy comes and he kisses your father as well.

'Now it's normal. Absolutely normal for two men who know each other well, who are intimate, to kiss each other on certain occasions. For example, when they meet, two men today can kiss each other if they're very good friends or relations. But in my day . . . this never happened. When people used to greet each other, they shook hands, they bowed, they smiled to one another to show that they liked each other. But they didn't kiss each other, at least not in my city. That "kiss" wasn't a normal thing . . . When two men kissed each other, the thing had an ambiguous flavour about it, no one thought it was all that . . . normal. I first got to know the Mafia when I saw Pippo, my big brother who was a man of honour, kissing other men of honour. Men of honour kissed each other when they met. They were the only ones who did it.

'Pippo had other friends, young men like himself, who knew each other and had socialized with each other all their lives. They had grown up together, they had played together, they had worked together. And yet, when they met, when they were older, they didn't kiss each other. They greeted each other. They said, "*Ciao, ciao, come stai?*" Then they joked, they teased each other, but they didn't kiss. Then I, when I saw men of honour kissing – but I didn't yet know that they were men of honour, I found out afterwards – I stood there open-mouthed, and I wondered, I racked my brains.'

'We mustn't talk about Mafia: we talk about friendship'

Giuseppe Genco Russo

Paolo Campo, Ribera family, 1970s: 'I protest my innocence to the crime of Mafia association because I have never been a criminal. But I must say that I was born and will die a Mafioso if by Mafia is meant, as I take it to mean, being good to your neighbour, giving something to those who need it, finding work for those who don't have it, giving help to people in need. In this sense I have been, and am, considered and consider myself to be a Mafioso. I have never sworn an oath to join the Mafia. I was born a Mafioso.'

Giuseppe Genco Russo, *rappresentante* of the Caltanissetta family, 1950s and '60s: 'We mustn't talk about Mafia: we talk about friendship. People say I'm a very powerful and very famous man: I say I'm just the head of my family. I'm not ambitious and I'm not vain. People ask me who to vote for because they feel a duty to ask advice to show a sign of gratitude, of acknowledgement; they feel they're in the dark and they want to do right by people who have done good things for them. I was born like that. I act without intent. If anyone asks me a favour I think about doing it because my nature tells me to. Things are said, one after another. When someone has come and I've done him a favour, then that's how things have gone, a kind of habit. That's how the circle of my name has spread.'

Calogero Vizzini, the head of the agrarian Mafia, immediately after the Second World War: 'In every society there has to be a category of people who correct situations when they get complicated. In general they're functionaries of the state. Where there is no state, or the state isn't strong enough, there are deprived people . . . I'm nothing. I'm just an ordinary citizen . . . People think it's out of discretion that I don't talk much. No, I don't talk because I don't know much. I live in a village, I don't come to Palermo that often, I don't know many people. And yet I'm a bit of a grandee now, I'm over seventy.'

Giuseppe Joe Bonanno, boss of the Castellammaresi clan in New York, 1970s: 'I've helped a lot of people. There isn't a man who can say I've cheated him or defrauded him of what belonged to him. I've led a productive life, I've never been a parasite. I've had to protect myself and my people, I've made a lot of mistakes but I've always remained faithful to my name and my principles. I was born in a world that had a tradition of its own. I was born among people taught by experience to cultivate certain values. That tradition was the flower of our culture. It taught us the right things and the wrong things, it guided the young men along their path to maturity, it drove men onto the straight and narrow and punished those who deserved it. Out tradition showed us the way to live. I've learned that true wealth is born out of a united family and true friends. When a man betrays his friends by *singing* to the police, he betrays himself as well.'

'Did you see him in the paper today, that Gina Lollobrigida?'*

Antonino Calderone

'Without a doubt, one of the best men of honour I've known was Totò Greco Cicchiteddu. He was a real powerhouse, he had tons of charisma. And he was very different from that fake, his cousin Michele, who was nobody: he was mothballed till 1975, until Totò Greco, the engineer, made him *rappresentante provinciale* and *capomandamento* . . .

'Reputation and notoriety within Cosa Nostra don't necessarily coincide with the actual position of a man of honour within the association. Everybody knows Calogero Vizzini, Don Calò, and everybody knows about Giuseppe Genco Russo. They were famous; all the newspapers were always talking about them. And yet Calogero Vizzini has never been a *rappresentante* of the whole of Sicily. The head of the *Commissione regionale* in his day, in the 1950s, was actually Andrea Faio, a Mafioso from Trapani that nobody knew. And Giuseppe Genco Russo was just the *rappresentante* of the province of Caltanissetta.

'The notoriety of Giuseppe Genco Russo and Calogero Vizzini wasn't looked upon too kindly in Cosa Nostra. They put themselves too much on show, they gave interviews, they even had their pictures taken. They'd become names on posters, like singers and

* Speaking to Pino Arlacchi in *Gli uomini del disonore* ('*Men of Dishonour*').

dancers. People were very sarcastic about them in those days, in Cosa Nostra. Referring to Giuseppe Genco Russo, Totò Minore used to say, "Did you see him in the paper today, that Gina Lollobrigida?"

'The best men of honour weren't well known. They were people who shunned publicity, like old Giovannino Mongiovino, to whom my brother offered the job of *rappresentante regionale.* He asked Mongiovino to take on that job because his authority was such that it guaranteed the respect of all the families, and he refused, saying he didn't want to represent people who didn't deserve to be in Cosa Nostra.

'The regard that a Mafioso enjoys within Cosa Nostra has nothing to do with his profession or his academic title. Stefano Bontate – a great man of honour, a real leader who is capable of commanding and ruling a family, sure of himself, elegant – had a very modest level of education, for example. The very opposite of his brother Giovanni, who had a degree but was a more pallid and indecisive figure, and much less highly regarded than him within his own family and also outside it. Not least because, when Stefano or someone else treated him roughly, he always went and cried on Michele Greco's shoulder.'

Among the mirrors and stucco ceilings of an art nouveau dining room, the Mafia decides its future. This is the room where, at the beginning of 1881, Richard Wagner composed the third act of Parsifal *at the piano: cream-coloured walls, floral stained glass, elegant decoration. Around a big round table, in the corner furthest from the kitchens, the Sicilian and American bosses sign a pact which will make them the wealthiest criminals in the world. It's Cosa Nostra's first step into the international drugs trade. The summit begins on 10 October 1957 and ends four days later at the Grand Hotel et Des Palmes, a patrician house built a century before by the English Ingham-Whitaker merchant family and then turned into a splendid hotel in the heart of Palermo.*

At the 'Palme' in the early days of autumn, all the capi *meet up. From America come Frank Garofalo, Giuseppe Joe Bonanno, Vito Vitale, Santo Sorge, Lucky Luciano, Charles Orlando, Nicola 'Nick' Gentile and Carmine Galante. They kiss and hug Vincenzo Rimi from Alcamo, Cesare Manzella from Terrasini, Giuseppe Genco Russo from Mussomeli. The Palermitans are represented by Mimì La Fata, Calcedonio Di Pisa and Rosario Macino.*

Twenty years later, Palermo is the heroin capital of the world.

'You Feds take care of the citizens' virtues, I'll look after their vices'*

Salvatore Lucanio, aka Lucky Luciano

He's a Sicilian that the other Mafiosi never really think of, deep down, as a true Sicilian. Not so much because he grew up practically on the other side of the world, a long way off, taken to Brooklyn by his parents when he was barely nine years old. More because of what he does, and the way he does it. Too far ahead of everyone else. And too rich. And too lucky. Even as a boy on the East Side they give him that name. In the archives of the FBI his file number is 62920. His ID calls him Salvatore Lucania. But everyone knows him as Lucky Luciano, and between the two World Wars he's America's king of crime.

In the 1930s he lives in the most opulent suite in New York's Waldorf Astoria, and brings in several million dollars a month. On 1 April 1936, in Arkansas, the agent of the Federal Bureau of Narcotics who arrests him in Hot Springs can't contain his rage. He shouts: 'You've drugged America!' Lucky replies: 'You Feds take care of the citizens' virtues, I'll look after their vices.' His men are dealing drugs coast to coast, and Lucky is running 50,000 girls in twelve different states.

If there's one thing more than any other that distinguishes the

---

* From the FBI/Drug Enforcement Administration files on Salvatore 'Lucky' Luciano.

American Mafia and the Sicilian Mafia, it's this: the prostitutes.* The heads of the Palermo families see prostitution as an 'unworthy' activity, not respectable for men of honour. While the Americans make loads of money out of the ladies from Atlantic City to Las Vegas, the Sicilians despise that kind of business, and take a dim view of anything to do with sex for money. But America is America and Lucky is Lucky: the boss who modernized Cosa Nostra.

He was born in 1897 among the sulphur mines and olive trees around Lercara Friddi, the last village in the province of Palermo before the district of Agrigento. He becomes famous at the end of the Second World War when he is released from Sing Sing† on parole 'for giving assistance to the Allies'. He leaves the States as an 'undesirable'; in fact he's the first to have made contact with the Sicilian bosses before the Sicily landings. In 1946 he spends the winter in Cuba, the Cuba of the casinos, he goes to Caracas, to Casablanca, to Rio and to Bogotà. He goes back to Italy. Naples, Palermo, Capri, Taormina, Rome.

In the last years of his life Lucky Luciano moves to Naples. He has a regular room at the Hotel Vesuvio with a view of the Gulf; he's surrounded by hitmen and starlets. Evenings with Orson Welles and Ava Gardner, dining at Giacomino's, betting on the ponies at Agnano. He's extremely popular. In the streets of Naples, the marines from the US fleet on leave ask for his autograph. A lifestyle unpopular with the men of honour of Lercara Friddi, of Palermo, of Bagheria, of Alcamo. But then he isn't just anybody; he's Lucky.

---

* *Buttane* in Sicilian, *putane* in Italian.

† A New York prison.

'I'm the Gianni Agnelli of Palermo'*

Tommaso 'Don Masino' Spadaro

There's a district of Palermo that's all his. La Kalsa. Courtyards, alleyways, baroque churches, bastions and a fortification that was once the residence of the Emirs. There's still something oriental about it, it's Palermo at its most sensual and disfigured. Don Masino's in charge here. Don Masino Spadaro.

He becomes a man of honour out of necessity. Not his own, the necessity of the other men of honour. It's the end of the 1960s and Cosa Nostra is trying to rise again after its first big internal war: the car bombs, the '*ammazzatine*'† between the Greco and La Barbera families, the police round-ups, the trials in Catanzaro and Bari, the first Parliamentary Anti-Mafia Commission. The bosses are almost broke. The open building sites of the 'sack' of Palermo remain an eyesore, but the business of the day is cigarettes. The smuggler with the most ships is Tommaso Spadaro, 'the king of the Kalsa'.

He's extremely rich. Brazen, and loquacious. 'I'm the Gianni Agnelli‡ of Palermo,' he would repeat on every street corner. He lacks the 'qualities' that a man of honour ought to have. Discretion,

---

* Quotations from the trial against Abbate Giovanni + 706, Palermo. 8 November 1985.

† Literally 'little killings'.

‡ Italian businessman famed for his style and wealth.

apparent meekness, modesty. He seems to have come from another world. But rules are made to be broken. Even inside Cosa Nostra.

But the bosses need money and they need Don Masino Spadaro. His fleet, safe routes in the Tyrrhenian Sea, his contacts with the Neapolitans.

The Porta Nuova family agrees. The family of Tommaso Buscetta. The family of Pippo Calò. So does Zaza, the Neapolitan. Another thing never seen before: a non-Sicilian man of honour. But by the end of those twitchy 1970s 35–40,000 cases of cigarettes are landing every night in the Gulf of Naples. A very valid reason to elevate even someone like Don Masino to the rank of man of honour.

It's the *Commissione* that now regulates the Tyrrhenian 'traffic'. One ship at a time. And one cargo at a time. The first to the *Commissione*. The second to the Porta Nuova family. The third to Nunzio La Mattina, another Palermitan smuggler. The fourth to the Neapolitans.

The Sicilian Mafia has been involved in smuggling for five or six years. The men of honour come and go from Naples, staying at the Hotel President in Santa Lucia, dining at the restaurant Ù Cafone, going to the 84 night club. It's their first contamination. They meet Michele Zaza and his associates, in Marano they *fanno pane* – break bread, or make friends – with the brothers Lorenzo and Ciro Nuvoletta. After the ready-made foreign cigarettes comes morphine base. With the same smuggling fleets, the same men.

Antonino Calderone remembers the period: 'It must have started in about 1978, when the drugs came in. That was life-changing for Cosa Nostra, it turned the heads of the men of honour.'

Masino Spadaro suddenly winds up in jail. Thirty years for drug-trafficking. Eighteen apartments and four warehouses in Palermo are confiscated, as well as three villas in Santa Flavia, four farms, fifteen current accounts, fifteen deposit books and two safety deposit boxes full of gold. In Spoleto jail Don Masino signs up for university. Faculty of Letters and Philosophy: he studies Kant, Schopenhauer and Saint Augustine. When his sentence is almost completed in 2008, he is informed of another arrest warrant. He is accused of the homicide of Police Marshal Vito Ievolella. More than a quarter of a century previously, the marshal had investigated the affairs of the King of the Kalsa.

'The smuggling milieu was . . . not respectable enough for a man of honour like me'*

Francesco Marino Mannoia

The chemists come from a long way away, they're known as '*Marsigliesi*'.† In fact they're all Corsican. Bousquet and Doré, Rammen and Bozzi. They teach the Mafiosi how to turn the base morphine into heroin. They are hidden in houses around Trabia. Or on the other side of the province, towards Cinisi and Carini. Day and night they move around between phials and alembics, they breathe in smoke, they manipulate acids. They treat the *pasta*‡ and the Bontate and Inzerillo families sell it to their cousins in America. The Tyrrhenian traffic in cigarettes is dead and buried. Palermo is now a big refinery.

'The smuggling milieu was dreadful, not respectable enough for a man of honour like me. I remember my first kilo was at the end of 1978. Giovanni Bontate had received a considerable quantity from Nunzio La Mattina, and he planned to give it to the *Marsigliesi*. But then Nino Vernengo, who had studied at university and was interested in this problem, actually managed to produce heroin . . .'

---

* Record of the questioning of the *pentito* Francesco Marino Mannoia by the deputy state prosecutor of Palermo, Giovanni Falcone, 9 November 1989.

† '*Marseillais*', from Marseille.

‡ 'Paste', morphine base.

Those are the first words, on 9 November 1989, of the confession of Francesco Marino Mannoia about the drugs that are bringing in the *piccioli* – the money – for the men of honour. Listening to him is the deputy state prosecutor, Giovanni Falcone. He writes down the minutes of the questioning with a fountain pen, interrupting with a question every now and again. The first *pentito* of the Corleoni clan is scrupulous, almost fussy, about the reconstruction of his account.

'Stefano Bontate got hold of the tropein, the benzoiltropein, that is, which has a very high melting point: about 270 degrees . . .'

Between the end of 1978 and 2 December 1980 – when he's arrested for the first time – Francesco Marino Mannoia refines 700 kilos of morphine. In a stable in Baida. Behind a bar in Pagliarelli. In a warehouse at La Guadagna. In a small villa on the Via Messina Marine. In a kitchen at Ponte Ammiraglio. Some days he looks like a ghost – all those vapours make his skin white. Sometimes his skin is covered with spots.

He is on a salary. First they pay him three million lire a kilo, then five million. All the families bring him morphine every month. Forty kilos for Gerlando Alberti, eighty kilos for Stefano Bontate, seventy-nine kilos for Pippo Calò, 293 kilos for Antonino Rotolo. Morphine arrives all over Sicily. By plane to Punta Raisi. By ship to Trapani. By truck across the Strait. The Sicilians no longer need the Marsigliesi to take charge of world traffic. Now they have their chemicals. And above all they have relatives on the other side of the Atlantic.

It's John Gambino – of the American Gambinos, one of the five big New York families – who comes to the island to negotiate agreements. He comes with his uncles from Torretta, the Di Maggios, and with the others from Passo di Rigano, the Inzerillos. He meets Stefano Bontate. They have big projects, they do big business together. It's a happy season for Cosa Nostra.

In twenty-four months – from the end of 1978 until the start of

1981 – the Bontates and the Inzerillos bank between thirty and thirty-five million dollars. The Gambinos of America bank between eighty and ninety million. Just with the *pasta* that passes through the hands of Mannoia, the finest chemist in Palermo.

'For me four kilos is a modest amount'*

Gaspare Mutolo

His world lies within the confines of Resuttana, his suburb. He burns a few cars, he's let loose on the streets of Palermo to scare the shopkeepers. He 'recovers credit': extortion. He's a Mafioso like many others until the day he meets a Chinese man from Singapore. That is the day that Gaspare Mutolo becomes the biggest drug importer in the whole of the West.

In 1993 he tells the story of his life.

'I started trafficking modest amounts . . .' The president of the Court of Assizes† stops him and asks: 'Mutolo, what do you mean by a modest amount?' He replies: 'For me four kilos is a modest amount.

'From that unimportant stuff I moved on to the most significant trafficking that Cosa Nostra has ever organized. The plan was to get the base morphine in Thailand and have it refined while it was being transported across the sea.'

By 1982 Gaspare Mutolo is in Teramo jail, on part-time detention. He is let out in the morning, climbs into his Ferrari, speeds

* Hearing of the *pentito* Gaspare Mutolo, Parliamentary Anti-Mafia Commission, Rome, 9 February 1993.

† An Italian court comprised of two professional judges and six lay judges. It has the jurisdiction to judge the most serious crimes, and can issue life sentences.

off towards Fiumicino, takes the plane to Palermo, meets the people he has to meet in Sicily, comes back to Rome on the last flight and goes back into Teramo jail. He is a modern prisoner. The Surveillance Court judge thinks he's selling furniture on behalf of a small factory in Abruzzi – in fact he's buying tons of heroin.

Fabulous deals with the Gambinos of Cherry Hill, with the Caruanas and the Cuntreras, who are split between Montreal and Caracas. And with Koh Bak Kin, the Chinese man from Singapore.

The drug that Gaspare brings to Cosa Nostra is like manna falling from heaven. Dizzying profits.

'After a while, I told Koh Bak Kin to send me all the drugs he wanted because I was calmly giving it all away. I bought it for 50 million a kilo; on the street in Rome it was already about 110 or 120 million. Talking about Thai heroin, the white stuff – we knew the Americans went nuts for that stuff . . . For cargoes of 400 or 500 kilos, I had the chance to buy it for 13,000 dollars a kilo and you could sell it in the United States for 120,000 or 130,000 dollars.'

All the Sicilian families are involved, for larger or smaller quotas. First his boss, Saro Riccobono, whose territory stretches from Partanna Mondello to Cardillo. And then the others. The Palermitans like Pino Savoca. The Corleonesi of Totò Riina. The Catanesis, the ones from Santapaola and the ones linked to the Pillera family. There isn't a single boss who wants to stay out; they all want a seat on the merry-go-round.

'During those years the only people I knew in Palermo dealt in heroin.'

It's the Mafia's new El Dorado. After three refineries were discovered by the police in Sicily between 1980 and 1981 and after the arrest of the 'chemist' Marino Mannoia, Gasparino's Thai channel makes everybody rich.

'The quotas were only fixed for the first cargoes, 300,000 dollars. It wasn't yet known whether the transportation was going well or badly. Of those first 300,000 dollars my share was 50 or 55 million lire. But at first we weren't looking at profit, we Sicilians had to break a market run by other people, so even if it meant getting 10,000 dollars less we had to be competitive with all the other nations. We wanted to take the whole of the market.'

90 . . . 91 . . . 97 . . . 100 . . . These numbers are headlines on the front page of the daily newspaper L'Ora, *August 1982 – red ink on the black-and-white photographs of the corpses. Every day two or three more murders. They are counting, Cosa Nostra style.*

'That's it, that's what I'm saying: the damage'*

Salvatore G.

It's noon in the houses of Oreto, in Palermo. Outside the general hospital there's the usual Sunday traffic jam, the Maghrebi street-vendors are selling their knickknacks on the pavements, the *stigghiolaro*† is roasting the innards of a kid on hot coals. There's also a crowd in the bar on the corner. A man with his back to the wall is drinking a coffee; the woman with him has gone up to the till to pay. Two young men push their way through the throng. One of them draws his revolver and fires.

Five shots. Five bullets in the head of Nenè Geraci, known as 'the young one',‡ the *capomafia* of Partinico, who has just got out of jail. His freedom scares Vito Vitale, the new ruler of the village. Nenè has come down to the city to recuperate in hospital. He allows himself one coffee. His last.

There's a witness who gets a good look at the guy with the revolver, and also the one who's waiting outside, behind the glass. He's the barman. His name is Salvatore G.

In the early afternoon of Sunday 23 November 1997, Salvatore

---

* Testimony of Salvatore G. to the trial in the Court of Assizes for the murder of Nené Geraci, 'the young one', Palermo, 6 November 1999.

† Maker of *stigghiola*, a kebab-like Palermitan dish based on lamb or goat tripe.

‡ The cousin of 'old' Nenè Geraci.

is in the offices of the mobile squad to provide identification. He's confused, retching. Salvatore faints. Two years later, on 6 November 1999, he's summoned to a court to testify.

Counsel: 'Do you by any chance remember if in the time that passed after you served the coffee you also served a bottle of water to anyone?'

Salvatore G.: 'I couldn't say.'

Lawyer: '*Presidente*, may I? Just one question: I'm sorry, you spoke of a general stampede in the bar. Why would that have been? Did you hear any shots being fired?'

Salvatore G.: 'Because people from outside were coming in, the rumour spread. So I was at the bar . . .'

Lawyer: '"The rumour spread" – what does that mean?'

Salvatore G.: 'That people were . . . talking, you know?'

Lawyer: 'So someone outside came in and said . . .'

Salvatore G.: 'He warned those of us inside.'

Lawyer: 'He warned you about what? What did he say?'

Salvatore G.: 'What had happened.'

Lawyer: 'And what had happened?'

Salvatore G.: 'What happened was that there was . . . this thing that happened. Let's say, let's say . . . the damage'.

Lawyer: 'The damage?'

Salvatore G.: 'That's it, that's what I'm saying: the damage.'

Judge: 'Someone from outside comes in and says, "There's been some damage"?'

Salvatore G.: 'No.'

Judge: 'Was there a shoot-out?'

Salvatore G.: 'Ex . . . excuse me. OK, then, I'll say it again: I was at the bar serving coffee. Because the bar is always crowded on Sunday morning. People outside, talking about the football. And people inside eating from the rotisserie . . . outside they knew what was going to happen, and they came in and then they all went away.'

'Strangulation, what they usually did'*

Giuseppe Marchese

Counsel: 'So, were the corpses on the floor?'

Giuseppe Marchese: 'Yes, yes, strangled, by these people . . .'

Counsel: 'Did you recognize them?'

Marchese: 'No, I really didn't know them, but . . . but they were tied up, tied up on the floor. Strangulation, what they usually did . . .'

Counsel: 'On the floor . . . *incaprettati*† . . . '

Marchese: 'Because first they strangled them, and then they put the rope around their necks; they folded their legs, and the rope was passed between the neck, pulled tight, to the legs, so that if they were still alive they couldn't move, they had no way of moving . . . and, what's more, when they're being strangled, they do their business on them, they shit on them . . . and they piss on them . . . and then, when they start decomposing, you chuck them . . .'

Counsel: 'And take them where?'

Marchese: 'Out into the countryside . . .'

Counsel: 'The Prestifilippos' land?'

---

* From the questioning of the *pentito* Giuseppe Marchese, trial of Mariano Agate + 51, fifth penal session of the Palermo tribunal.

† Literally: 'tying up like a kid'. A form of ligature associated with the Mafia.

Marchese: 'There, they start digging on farmland. It isn't easy to find spots in advance because it's so big . . . it's . . . let's say, it's enormous. There are corpses there, right in the middle. Sometimes we used to joke, we used to say: there's as many corpses out there as there's cowpats, and cows . . .'

Counsel: 'Yes, that's fine, we know what cowpats are . . .'

Marchese: 'When Mario Prestifilippo came to take my uncle with Pino Greco . . . OK, while they were talking, they were laughing, they were joking, because afterwards, when you were doing a murder, it was always . . . it was always a laugh, they were carrying out these murders day after day, and it was practically like going for a stroll . . .'

Counsel: 'OK, let's get back . . .'

Marchese: 'Let's get back . . .'

Counsel: 'Let's get back to the moment when you arrived.'

Marchese: 'Pino Greco was there and I learned from them that Franco Mafara had started crying in front of my uncle Fifo, my uncle Filippo, saying, "Fifù, I have nothing to do with it, I have nothing to do with these things . . ." He started crying, he wanted to be forgiven: "Please don't kill me . . ." But Antonino Grado said to Franco, "Act like a man of honour, ignore these bastards." Because he knew that once he had the rope around his neck, there wasn't much . . . there wasn't much you could do . . .'

Counsel: 'They were talking?'

Marchese: 'Yes . . . And then Salvatore Cocuzza says, "Then I'm royally fucked." Like I said before, when you're involved in one of these things it's like going for a stroll, seeing people enjoying murder, so they sat him down in the chair, and they interrogated him, they gave him a few slaps . . . and after all that the two of them are loaded onto a Lambretta . . .'

Counsel: 'A Lambretta? What does that mean?'

Marchese: 'An Ape* . . . gardening model . . .'

Counsel: 'And they were loaded on there by whom?'

Marchese: 'The one who loaded them on was Mario Prestifilippo with . . . a guy known as Minnone . . .'

Counsel: 'Will you please tell us the exact name of this Minnone?'

Marchese: 'Giuseppe Greco.'

Counsel: 'Giuseppe Greco.'

* Ape, pronounced *ah-pay* – 'bee'. A three-wheeled light commercial vehicle.

'Kill the puppy'

Giovanni Brusca

The child has been a prisoner for 779 days. He's a skeleton, he weighs barely thirty kilos. A man puts him with his face to the wall and lifts him from the floor, the little boy doesn't understand, he doesn't resist, not even when he feels the rope around his neck. His voice is barely a whisper: 'Are you taking me home?' It's two different men who are holding him. By the arms and by the legs. And then off little Giuseppe goes.

A month and a half later, a Mafioso appears in front of a Palermo deputy attorney, who asks him, 'Do you intend to collaborate with the forces of law and order?' Giuseppe Monticciolo replies, 'I intend to make a declaration of homicide.'

He starts with the end, the last one. He starts with Giuseppe Di Matteo, eleven years old, the son of Santino Mezzanasca, one of Capaci's hitmen. They kidnap the child to make their turncoat father retract his statement. Mezzanasca refuses to retract, and his son disappears into a barrel of muriatic acid, his remains buried in a ditch beyond the mountains of Palermo.

Giuseppe Di Matteo was kidnapped on 23 November 1993, and killed on 11 January 1996. He was taken to the riding ground belonging to the Villabate family, the butchers of Brancaccio. He was tied up and taken beyond the plain of Buonfronello, to Lascari. There he was handed over to Giovanni Brusca, the man known in San Giuseppe Jato as *ù verru*, the pig. He was hidden in the boot of the car, and moved halfway across Sicily, from one hideout to another. To Misilmeri, near Palermo. To Villarosa, to the gates of Enna. To Giambascio in the countryside, behind San Giuseppe Jato. Always bound and blindfolded, always in chains. Giuseppe never cried. He never asked anything from his jailers.

They kept him prisoner for two years. And waited for a signal from his father, that *infamone*.* They made Giuseppe write letters to his grandfather. They wanted to force Mezzanesca to eat his words. Weeks pass, nothing happens. It's the evening of 11 January 1996. Giovanni Brusca is watching television; it's time for the news. He hears a headline: 'Thanks to the revelations of the collaborator with the forces of law and order Santino Di Matteo, Giovanni Brusca and Leoluca Bagarella have been sentenced to life imprisonment.'

Giuseppe Monticciolo is there, beside Brusca, who glares with rage. Then *ù verru* tells him: '*Uccidere il cannuzzu.*' Kill the puppy.

Vincenzo Chiodo is the one who bangs his face against the wall and lifts him up. Enzo Brusca and Giuseppe Monticciolo hold him by the arms and legs. It's Chiodo who pulls the rope. 'He strangled him,' Monticciolo confesses. The magistrate asks him, 'Didn't the child react?' Monticciolo lowers his eyes: 'No, nothing, he wasn't a child like the others any more, he was weak, weak.'

The barrels of acid have been got ready. Soon all that is left is Giuseppe's feet. The three Mafiosi kiss each other.

Some time later Giovanni Brusca will say: 'We were used to keeping the acid to hand, even if there was no immediate need to use it. It takes 50 litres of acid to break down a body in about three hours. The body dissolves slowly, the victim's teeth are left, the skull becomes distorted. At that point you take the remains and throw them somewhere. In San Giuseppe Jato they threw them in the river. We Palermitans didn't care because we were rough

---

* That 'informer', that rat.

peasants, we did what was asked. As for you lot, lovely water you drink in Palermo . . .'

The water from the river in San Giuseppe Jato ends up in a reservoir. The one that quenches the thirst of the whole of the city.

'Always fire two or three shots . . . then you can spray him in the head'*

Antonino Rotolo and Gianni Nicchi

Antonino Rotolo: 'One revolver each.'
Gianni Nicchi: 'Yes'.
Rotolo: 'And try these revolvers.'
Nicchi: 'Yes.'
Rotolo: 'You can see that they're . . . good, I mean . . .'
Nicchi: 'I know that, we've talked about these things before.'
Rotolo: 'You have to try them.'
Nicchi: 'You have to try them.'
Rotolo: 'Who are you going to do this job with?'
Nicchi: 'Me? There's two of us, we don't need anybody, just the two of us.'
Rotolo: 'Which two?'
Nicchi: 'Me and Enzo and me and Totò. We don't need anyone, they don't have to reinforce the streets for me. The road's clear all the way to Via Roccella.'
Rotolo: 'Always fire two or three shots . . .'
Nicchi: 'There's just one more thing . . .'
Rotolo: 'And don't get too close.'
Nicchi: 'I know.'
Rotolo: 'And don't make too much noise.'

---

* Recording of conversation played during the detention of suspects, 20 June 2006.

Nicchi: 'No, no . . .'

Rotolo: 'One . . .'

Nicchi: 'One to get him on the ground.'

Rotolo: 'When he's on the ground one in the head and that's it. Then you can spray him in the head, and immediately . . .'

Nicchi: 'Immediately I'm off, shoes . . . that are nothing like mine, oilskin trousers, as soon as you pull them they come off straight away, the ones with buttons and an oilskin k-way jacket, hood up, and that's it.'

Rotolo: 'And your gloves?'

Nicchi: 'The gloves I've got. Latex, the kind nurses wear.'

Rotolo: 'But what I mean is, have you tried it?'

Nicchi: 'Of course.'

Rotolo: 'You've tried holding the revolver in latex gloves?'

Nicchi: 'Yeah, I've done all that, to see if they slip.'

Rotolo: 'Then you have to burn everything you've worn, or else bury it . . .'

Nicchi: 'One thing . . .'

Rotolo: 'You know when you do something like this . . .'

Nicchi: 'Two or three days . . .'

Rotolo: 'You've got to hide away, because a trace . . .'

Nicchi: '. . . is left . . .'

Rotolo: '. . . the powder . . .'

Nicchi: '. . . is left.'

THE TRAGEDY

THE COMMISSIONE, 1979

Capo: Michele Greco
Capimandamento:
Salvatore Inzerillo (Passo di Rigano family)
Bernardo Brusca (San Giuseppe Jato family)
Stefano Bontate (Santa Maria del Gesù family)
Salvatore Scaglione (La Noce family)
Giuseppe Calò (Porta Nuova family)
Rosario Riccobono (Partanna Mondello family)
Francesco Madonia (Resuttana-San Lorenzo family)
Nenè Geraci, 'the old man' (Partinico family)
Calogero Pizzuto (Castronovo di Sicilia family)
Ignazio Motisi (Pagliarelli family)

THE CORLEONESI LEADERS, 1958 ONWARDS

Luciano Leggio
Salvatore Riina
Bernardo Provenzano
Leoluca Bagarella

24 Via Scorsone. If anyone knocks at the door, it's always a woman who answers: 'Signora Bagarella doesn't live here any more.' But it's her, it's Ninetta, the wife of the Cosa Nostra capo dei capi. *It all started in this house in Corleone, in the late 1950s. It all started here. The love between Ninetta and young Totò. The blood pact between the Bagarellas and the Riinas. The power of the Corleonesi.*

‘This is how tall Salvatore Riina is’*

Salvatore ‘Totò’ Riina

‘I’m 1 metre 61 according to my ID. When I was measured in jail the other day it was 1 metre 59. If someone says he knows me, and then he’s ten, fifteen or sixteen centimetres out, those are slanderous accusations, scandalous accusations, aberrant accusations. Fifteen centimetres for a man is like a metre. Forgive me, my lord, if I get up – this is how tall Salvatore Riina is.

‘I didn’t give anyone an order to kill *indirectly* because no one has ever done me any harm, I’ve always worked for myself and my family. I’ve never had any involvement with these people.

‘Counsel, let’s not say I was in hiding . . . The fact is, no one has ever come looking for me. I went to work every morning, no one ever stopped me, I took the train to go to Trapani, I took the bus, no one ever said anything to me.

‘In the cases of La Torre, Reina and Matarella,† well, these things are political . . . You have to look somewhere else. You have to look up, you mustn’t look for me, I’m not *political*, and I didn’t want to take the place of La Torre or Reina or Matarella.

‘I was a farm labourer when I was young. Lately I’ve been

---

* Transcription of the questioning of Salvatore Riina on 1 and 4 March 1993 in the trials for ‘cross-linked crimes’ and ‘political crimes’, bunker court, Rebibbia, Rome.

† Three politicians murdered by the Mafia in 1990.

working for a construction company and I've provided for my family. There was an old person there who'd been giving me work for over twenty years. First she gave me 300,000 lire a month, then the same amount a week. My family, your honour, is a modest one. My wife and my children aren't used to going to restaurants and living the good life. And all through those years my mother never abandoned me; she always sent me money when I needed it. My mother has three pensions, and my brother Gaetano also has an invalidity pension.

'I was acquitted in a trial in Bari for association. I was acquitted in Genoa in the trial for killing the prosecutor Scaglione. I was acquitted in Reggio Calabria for killing the judge Terranova. I've been acquitted in lots of trials. If, instead of having two, three, four, five, six or ten trials, I'd only had one, like Judge Prinzivalli got, I'd be a free citizen now.

'I don't know Michele Greco, I don't know Bernardo Provenzano, I don't know Francesco Madonia, I don't know Antonino Geraci, I don't know anyone called Ciancimino, I've never met Stefano Bontate, I've never met Salvatore Inzerillo, I don't know Salvatore Contorno, I don't know Antonino Calderone, I don't know Giuseppe Marchese, I don't know Giovanni Drago. I know Leoluca Bagarella because he's my brother-in-law.'

'I love him because the *Corte de Assise* in Bari told me that Salvatore Riina . . . did not have blood on his hands'*

Antonina Bagarella, known as Ninetta

'I chose him, first because I love him, and love doesn't look at things that way. Then because I respect and trust him, just as I respect and trust my brother Calogero, who is unjustly accused of involvement in so many crimes. I love Riina because I think he is innocent. I love him in spite of our age difference; me twenty-seven, him forty-one. I love him because the *Corte de Assise* in Bari told me that Salvatore Riina, having been fully acquitted of many crimes, did not have blood on his hands.

'I'll start with my official engagement. It took place in July 1969, two years ago, after Totò Riina was acquitted and released from prison. When he was released one evening he came to Corleone, but I didn't see him that night. After twenty days he was sent back to jail, he was given permission to spend forty-eight hours in Corleone. That was when we got engaged. I haven't seen him since then.

'They judge me harshly because I, a teacher, fell in love with, and got engaged to, someone like him. I met him in the 1950s, when the things that happened in Corleone happened, and involved many families, including mine and Riina's. And that was the atmosphere of my early childhood, a sad atmosphere that turned

* Interview with Antonina Bagarella by Mario Francese, in *Il Giornale di Sicilia*, 27 July 1971.

Via Scorsone in Corleone into a police barracks. Salvatore and I had known each other as children. I felt I loved him. But perhaps – am I not a woman? Don't I have the right to love a man and follow the laws of nature?

'My legal problems began on 16 December 1969, when I went to police headquarters to get a passport. I had to go to Venezuela, for the christening of a little girl that my sister had had the previous November. They released my passport, and a month later they withdrew it again. From Easter 1970 until 17 April I was literally kept under guard at home. They'd sacked me from my teaching post by now.

'I moved to Frattamaggiore, where my father lived . . . Every night for three nights, at the most impossible times, policemen came to the house on the pretext of keeping my father under surveillance and checking on the people who were helping him. I was at my wits' end. I came back to Corleone.

'I can say in all sincerity that from the day of my engagement, that is, for two years, I haven't seen Salvatore Riina or heard from him either directly or indirectly. It's not true that I went to see the Archbishop in Aversa to try to have a secret wedding with Totò. After everything that had happened, I could only get married in broad daylight. I'm not a character in [Manzoni's novel] *I Promessi Sposi*. I'm not interested in playing the part of Lucia in her secret wedding with Renzo.'

The interview is conducted on 27 July 1971 by Mario Francese, legal correspondent of *Il Giornale di Sicilia*. Mario had met Antonina Bagarella in court on the morning of the previous day. Ninetta was in Palermo because the judges wanted to place her under 'obligatory residence': 'Four years in a northern town to cut off her communication with Luciano Leggio's *cosca*.'*

She's wearing a floral dress; she's beautiful, dark, with big

---

* 'Gang'. The word literally means the heart of an artichoke.

black eyes. The journalist talking to her – a sleuth, who's good at his job in a Palermo that doesn't see or hear a thing – will be killed eight years later, on 26 January 1979. At home, in the evening. On the orders of Totò Riina.

'I've never seen him angry'*

Gaspare Mutolo

'He's a very polite person, Totò Riina, with such a kind face, when he talks to you he's like a preacher, that handsome face . . . but sadly some faces deceive. Another face that deceives belongs to Michele Greco, who ran rings around the most dangerous people in Palermo, him with his kind face too. He used to say, "No, because as soon as the first shots are fired, there's a massacre in Palermo" . . . those faces that deceive . . .

'Totò Riina is a very calm, apparently humble person. I've never seen him angry. Sometimes I saw him with his colour up, but never bad-tempered or aggressive. In 1973 we went from being led by an arrogant person like Luciano Leggio to Salvatore Riina, who often used to say, "I trust the young guys. You've got to make way for the young guys." He had a strategy. Until then, he'd made sure that all the families put one or two people at his disposal on the grounds that he was in hiding. At any time and in any town he could find someone to go with him, let him in, find him a place to sleep. With his nice manners, he had managed to create a whole group around him.

'If somebody talks to Totò Riina, he'll wonder: is it really possible that this is Salvatore Riina? So kind! He's the first person who

* Hearing of Gaspare Mutolo, Parliamentary Anti-Mafia Commission, Rome, 9 February 1993.

came up with this system of inviting a man to dinner before killing him. After dinner he would strangle him and that was that. He didn't shout, "You've done this! You've done that!" No, no, you ate, you enjoyed yourself a bit, and then you killed him. That was the new thing that Totò Riina introduced.

'I know Luciano Leggio very well, just as I know Salvatore Riina well. Leggio knows that Salvatore Riina was angry with him and is still angry with him, not least because Leggio once told all the *capifamiglia* to go not to Riina but to Provenzano, and by way of justification he cited the fact that Salvatore Riina drank and then talked too much. Because Salvatore Riina has always had trusted people in the various families, he always opened up about what was happening, and that talk was reported to Leggio. Lucianio Leggio was a bloodthirsty person; it was scary just talking to him. Not Riina. Leggio, over time, started working out that this boy he'd known for so many years was much more intelligent than he thought. If Luciano Leggio didn't get out of jail it's because Salvatore Riina didn't want him to. I remember that, immediately after 1974, when Luciano Leggio had been arrested and was in prison in Lodi, I and some others told Salvatore Riina that we could get a little team together and go and get him. But Riina told us, "Mind your own business, this is my concern, I'll bother you if I need to." From that point Luciano Leggio never got out of jail again.'

'They look like two people but they're just one person'*

Salvatore Cancemi, aka Totò Caserma

The Corleonesi. One of them is on the Interior Ministry's list of wanted men for July 1969; the other disappeared in September 1963. They're the sons of peasants, poor, hungry. They lead the troubled lives of the Sicilians who, in the years around the Second World War, broke their backs in the countryside: sun-scorched hills, fields of grain and the odd olive tree. At Contrada Frattina, le Rocche di Rao, la Venere del Poggio, Strasatto. The estate. With its barons and its marquises, with its *campieri*† on horseback. Salvatore Riina was born in 1930, Bernardo Provenzano in 1933. Salvatore Riina, known as Il Corto – Shorty – or Zio (Uncle) Totò. Bernardo Provenzano, known as Bino or Binnazzu, but also called the Tractor or the Accountant. The former will spend twenty-four years and five months in hiding, the latter forty-two years and seven months.

The Corleonesi. They come down from their village in the late 1960s, and in the early 1980s they take charge of Palermo. They wipe the 'cream' of the Sicilian Mafia from the face of the earth. They launch an assault on the state. For the first time in its existence, they make the Cosa Nostra declare war on the Italian state.

The Corleonesi. 'They're the lords of Sicily and there was no,

* Documents from the trial of Giuseppe Agrigento + 17, Capaci massacre, 10 October 1993 and 2 November 1993.

† 'Estate managers'.

shall we say, difference between the two. What one had the other had, the potential that one had the other had too – they swapped and shared everything, they were the same,' Salvatore Cancemi, man of honour of the *Commissione*, explains in the Court of Assizes. Then he gets even more explicit: 'They look like two people but they're just one person.'

The Corleonesi. They kill magistrates, policemen, politicians, prefects, generals, journalists, businessmen, doctors, witnesses, women, children. And all the other Mafiosi. A thousand people die between 1979 and 1983 in the four western provinces of the island. The Corleonesi sow terror. They plant bombs and plan terrorist-style attacks. This is a Cosa Nostra which is altering its DNA, which is no longer insinuating itself into Sicilian society but instead raising its head and seeking to dominate it. This is the Cosa Nostra of Totò Riina and Bernardo Provenzano. It's *Cosa Loro* – no longer 'our thing', but 'their thing'.

The Corleonesi. At first the others contemptuously dubbed them the *picciuttanazzi*, the low, 'rough' boys who come from the fields, the *peri incritati*, the ones whose boots are always covered with soil. Peasants. In the end the others all become their servants. The Madonias of Resuttana, the Galatolos of the Acquasanta, the Gancis of La Noce, Michele Greco of Croceverde Giardina, Antonino Rotolo of Pagliarelli, Pippo Calò of Porta Nuova, the Bruscas of San Giuseppe Jato, Mariano Agate of Mazara del Vallo, Nitto Santapaola of Catania, Giuseppe Piddu Madonia of Caltanissetta. They have all become Corleonesi.

The Corleonesi. Toto is arrested in circumstances that have never been explained on 15 January 1993. In Palermo, on the ring road. Special *carabinieri* units. Bernardo Provenzano comes out of hiding on 11 April 2006 in a cottage on the Montagna dei Cavalli, two kilometres from his old house down in the village. He is arrested by state police.

The Corleonesi. Two men who hold Sicily and Italy hostage for almost twenty years.

The Corleonesi. Are they acting entirely on their own? Are they – Totò Riina, aka Shorty or Uncle Totò, and Bernardo Provenzano, known as Bino or Binnazzu, also known as the Tractor or the Accountant – doing everything?

The Corleonesi. Two men who are one single man.

'*Monsciandò*[*] for everybody'

Totò Riina

The water in the pot is saturated with aromas designed to soften the strong smell of the meat. Carrots, celery sticks, potatoes, sun-dried tomatoes, onions, parsley. The water is changed three times; the last one is for the cooking of the soup that reaches the table before the pieces of *picurazza*. An ancient dish made by the shepherds of the Belice Valley, boiled sheep, a dish that requires lengthy preparation, recurs frequently in the stories of the men of honour about their *mangiate*.

The *picurazza* is served by the owners of a farm in the countryside near Trapani in early 1992, when Totò Riina summons the *capi* and *sottocapi* of the families of Mazara del Vallo and Marsala to decide on the killing of Carlo Zicchitella and Leonardo Marino. Uncle Totò barely tries it, sips a finger of wine, then one of his fellow diners peels an orange and hands it to him.

When they need to meet and discuss someone or something, the Mafiosi always organize this event, the banquet – in Sicilian the *schiticchio* or the *schiticchiata*. The table is a sacred place for the men of honour. Eating is a ritual.

There are years when they all meet up in the *baglio*[†] of Stefano Bontate, on his land in Magliocco. And years when they move to

---

* Moët et Chandon.

† Sicilian-style farm.

Cinisi, to Gaetano Badalamenti's little villa at the foot of the Montagnalonga. Then it's Michele Greco who opens the doors of his estate, La Favarella. Artichokes and lamb roasted on the grill, caponata, peperonate, pecorino with red peppercorns, mandarins, cassata and *cannoli*.

And, finally, it's the years of the Corleonesi. The torture of the 'dinner invitation' from the Brusca family of San Giuseppe Jato, at their farm at I Dammusi. It's the nightmare of every man of honour.

'Uncle Totò wants to eat with you, he has to talk to you,' warn Salvatore Riina's messengers. Whoever receives the invitation trembles with fear. He's in a trap. If he doesn't go, his fate is sealed. It means that he isn't 'trustworthy' or, worse, that he has something to hide. If he does go, he knows what his fate might be: never to return.

Totò Riina always sits at the head of the table at I Dammusi. On his right he has Bernardo Brusca, on his left 'old' Nenè Geraci. Sometimes Mariano Agate is there too. Or Raffaele Ganci or Francesco Madonia. They eat, they laugh and they joke, and then someone slips behind the guest's back and strangles him with a length of cord.

'*Monsciandò* for everybody,' orders Uncle Totò as the corpse is taken away. There are always cases full of Moët et Chandon, even at I Dammusi.

Murders, blow-outs, food as a sign of power and perhaps also as compensation for an ancient hunger – *schiticchiate* that begin at midday and end at sunset. A Mafia world is wiped away at table by the moderate eating habits of the latest godfather. Bernardo Provenzano introduces a gastronomic revolution to Cosa Nostra. His diet is extremely strict: fresh milk, honey, ricotta. And chicory.

The Mafia wars as told by the Mafia. When Cosa Nostra is silent and at peace no one knows what's happening among the men of honour, but when it shoots it reveals itself.

1958–63

Corleonesi against Corleonesi (Leggio, Riina, Provenzano and Bagarella on the one hand, old Michele Navarra on the other).

1962–3

Palermitani against Palermitani (the Greco family against the La Barbera family).

1981–3

Corleonesi against everyone.

‘The tax-collectors aren’t monsters’*

Nino and Ignazio Salvo

There are two of them, Nino and Ignazio. Nino is fiery and extrovert, with a love of luxury. On his yacht, anchored at La Cala, there are paintings by Van Gogh and Matisse on the walls of the cabins. His guests include the powerful men of Italy. Ignazio is closed and silent; every now and again his shadow is glimpsed behind the windows of the armoured car that darts along the streets of Palermo. He’s the only person in Sicily with a car like that, both armoured and ‘official’. Sometimes the police ask to borrow it when ‘personalities’ come to the island and need an escort. Nino and Ignazio are cousins, originally from a village at the end of the Belice Valley: Salemi.

Unni viditi muntagni di issu, chissa è Salemi, passatici arrassu; sunnu nimici di lu crucifissu e amici di Satanassu. It’s an old Sicilian saying: where you see chalk mountains, that’s Salemi: stay well away; they’re enemies of the crucifix and friends of Satan.

Nino and Ignazio Salvo are famous. And untouchable. Social Democrats, the chief financiers of the ‘Andreottian’ trend in western Sicily. They are the best friends of the former mayor of Palermo, Salvo Lima. And they are men of honour. Closely linked to Stefano Bontate, the prince of Villagrazio, the boss who more than any other embodies the Mafia aristocracy.

---

* *Panorama*, 5 July 1982.

The Salvos are extremely wealthy. They have land from one end of Sicily to the other, three investment companies, a bank, travel companies, hotels, vineyards. Above all they are the bosses of Satris, the tax-collecting companies. In the rest of Italy a premium (*aggio*) of 3.5 per cent is paid, in Palermo the rate is 6.72 per cent, and in some years it even reaches 10 per cent. A feudal system. They are the lords of the realm: Nino and Ignazio. Laws and by-laws of the region grant them the privileges of caliphs. When their authority is questioned they roar: 'Let's stop this once and for all: the tax-collectors aren't monsters sucking the blood of the Sicilians.'

Everyone pays. Friends and enemies. Majority and opposition. When they sense that the people in Rome want to bring some order to the Sicilian tax-collecting companies, the cousins from Salemi mobilize all the parliamentary troops at their service. They are alleged to control between sixty and seventy deputies in Parliament, plus a number of regional MPs. And it's said that – on 5 August 1982 – the first Spadolini government falls at the behest of Nino and Ignazio.

In 1976 the first Parliamentary Anti-Mafia Commission calls them 'one of the most serious polluting factors in the province of Trapani'. In 1986 they are two of the 474 defendants called to court for the Maxi-Trial set up by Giovanni Falcone.

It's an uneasy time for the tax-collectors. Symbols of Sicily, they are subjected to the most serious of insults. Someone is doing something that no one has ever done between Palermo and Trapani: kidnapping. They abduct Luigi Corleo, Nino's father-in-law, and demand a ransom of twenty billion. Old Corleo will never be found. It wasn't just any old thugs who took him, it was Totò Riina's Corleonesi. It's a sign, the first that the peasants of Corleone give to the men of honour giving the orders inside Cosa Nostra.

When the Mafia war breaks out in Palermo, Nino Salvo disappears to Greece for a few months. Ignazio vanishes for a few weeks as well. They try to work out what's happening after the killing of Stefano Bontate, after the ambush of Totuccio Inzerillo. Ignazio Lo Presti, Nino's brother-in-law, has the job of contacting Tommaso Buscetta in Brazil. They want him to come back to Sicily. Don Masino Buscetta has charisma; they want to get him to talk to Totò Riina and his men. But it's too late. The Corleonesi have already decided to take no prisoners.

'Too much envy, too much betrayal, too many *cose tinte*'[*][†]

Ignazio Lo Presti

A voice carries the corpses of Palermo to the other side of the world. They are whispered words, words that become an epigraph for the big Mafia war of the 1980s.

Stefano Bontate is already dead. So is Salvatore Inzerillo. Mimmo Teresi is dead, along with about ten men of honour of the family of Santa Maria de Gesù and l'Uditore. The Corleonesi are killing all the *capi* of the old guard. Santino is dead too, the brother of Totuccio Inzerillo. But the *pentito* Tommaso Buscetta doesn't yet know anything about Santino when, one evening in June 1981, he calls his friend Ignazio in Palermo. Ignazio Lo Presti, the brother-in-law of the Salvo cousins of Salemi, the powerful *esattori*, or tax-collectors. Buscetta is in Brazil; he goes by the name of 'Roberto'.

Ignazio: 'Hello, hello?'
Roberto: 'Ignazio?'
Ignazio: 'Eh . . . good evening, Roberto.'
Roberto: 'How are you?'

---

* 'Murky things'.

† Intercepted conversation, 12 June 1981, in the files of the legal judgement against Abbate Giovanni + 706, Palermo, 8 November 1985 (investigating magistrates Antonino Caponnetto, Giovanni Falcone, Paolo Borsellino, Giuseppe Di Lello and Leonardo Guarnotta).

Ignazio: 'Well, how are you . . . hello?'

Roberto: 'Fine, fine . . . you know . . . life . . .'

Ignazio: 'Life is . . . a wonderful thing.'

Roberto: 'I know.'

Ignazio: 'We're going mad here . . .'

Roberto: 'Is something up? . . . The cruellest thing in the world is that there's no going back.'

Ignazio: 'Sure . . .'

Roberto: 'But tell me something, can I talk to my brother?'

Ignazio: 'I, let's say, I haven't seen him . . . I haven't seen him and I haven't seen anyone for a month . . . there's some murky stuff going on here, Signor Roberto.'

Roberto: 'Yes . . .'

Ignazio: 'Too murky . . . you no longer know who you're supposed to be looking to . . .'

Roberto: 'Ah . . . I see . . .'

Ignazio: 'Things are serious, very serious . . .'

Roberto: 'That's life . . . the hand of fate . . .'

Ignazio: 'Too much envy, too much betrayal, too many *cose tinte*.'

Roberto: 'But I'll call again in three or four days, if you have the chance to talk. It'll have to be very confidential.'

Ignazio: 'Of course, I understand that.'

Roberto: 'And can you tell me something . . .'

Ignazio: 'But . . . if you are thinking of coming . . . we'll, we'll organize it all.'

Roberto: 'Yes, yes . . .'

Ignazio: 'But no one must know anything . . . I, I talked to Nino [Salvo] . . .?'

Roberto: 'Huh?'

Ignazio: 'I told him you would call . . . he told me he's thinking of coming, that nobody knows anything. Let's try and get him over.'

Roberto: 'I'd have liked to hear him.'

Ignazio: 'He doesn't know anything because he hasn't been here . . .'
Roberto: 'Then don't look, don't look . . .'
Ignazio: 'That is, I know how to get hold of him . . .'
Roberto: 'No, no . . . don't look for him . . .'

Ignazio Lo Presti disappears a few weeks after the phone-call with 'Roberto'. No trace left: a style of murder known as *lupara bianca*. White shotgun. Tommaso Buscetta prepares to go back to Sicily. To meet Nino and Ignazio Salvo and discuss the *cose tinte* that are happening in Palermo.

'That magistrate did some crazy things'[*]

Nino Salvo

'No one has ever been able to say: the Salvos are Mafiosi. Or: Nino Salvo is a boss. I grew up with Christian Democracy;[†] there's no money in being loyal. We are suffering personal attacks from both those who are seeking to exploit the whole of Sicily's business activity and those who want to strike at the Christian Democrats and the men who are close to it . . . some political forces, especially within the left, often use dirty, aggressive tactics, consisting of winks, insinuations and gossip.

'They said all kinds of things about us, even that we recycle our dirty money in the heroin racket. But we Salvos earn so much of that money from tax-collecting that we're looking for someone to recycle our billions. We're the richest people in the island; we're the biggest Sicilian finance company; we have a huge amount of liquidity. If they don't award us the ten-year tax-collecting contract in 1983, we'll run riot.

'I don't know what the Guardia di Finanza fiscal investigation into our tax-collecting will throw up, but as far as I'm concerned my conscience is clear. But I would be very sorry to discover some day

* *L'Espresso*, 4 July 1982; *Panorama*, 5 July 1982; *Corriere della Sera*, 17 September 1982.

† An Italian political party founded in 1943. Ideologically it sits roughly in the centre.

that somebody, taking advantage of the assassination of Pio La Torre, the MP, had wanted to use the opportunity for their immediate political advantage. This raid has occurred at a particular moment, and in order to understand it all you have to do is think back to a few dates. The Communist MP La Torre was killed on 30 April 1982; the central committee of the Italian Communist Party met on 10 May. The next day, the newspapers published an extract of Ugo Pecchioli's speech suggesting that the tax-collection system is the source of all wickedness, past, present and future. So, two days later, the Guardia di Finanza turn up at our offices. Just a coincidence?

'It's true, I've been hauled in or investigated lots of times. And, I'd say, with particular persistence. But who by? Certainly not the judiciary, or by any other investigating body. I challenge anyone to find even the slightest trace of evidence against me. My name has been dragged in by some local rag that's been over-zealous in getting some literature together about the Salvo cousins to distribute to all the other papers. There's a lot of tired old nonsense about my relations with the Mafia. In the twenty-five years of my career, I've never been involved in a Mafia trial, I've never been accused of a crime. If I was a Mafioso, would any of that be possible?

'I know that when people talk about lobby groups they mention lots of things . . . corrupt practices or nepotistic cliques . . . but we don't use methods like that. Which is not to say that the Salvo brothers don't carry some weight in everyday Sicilian life. They certainly do. Our co-operatives work, unlike many others, our tourist developments are steaming ahead, and we're the ones exporting wine to the Soviet Union, while the red co-ops only look on. In the light of all this, why shouldn't people trust the Salvos and the ideas, political and economic, that the Salvos represent within the Christian Democrats?

'That magistrate did some crazy things. He went and looked at the banks that the money goes through. Crazy things!'

This is in 1982. The magistrate is Giovanni Falcone.

The Sicilian clergy are divided. A questionnaire distributed among the priests of Palermo reveals that too many parish priests are indulgent towards the bosses. Many of them don't think of Cosa Nostra as an imminent danger. 15 per cent of the priests interviewed showed 'a full awareness of the specificity of the Mafia problem'; 20 per cent had a 'stereotypical awareness, sometimes expressing direct criticism, particularly with regard to the judiciary'; 65 per cent still showed 'a certain ambiguity with regard to the subject, and the Mafia presence on their territory was not experienced as a matter of direct responsibility for the Church . . . it did not seem to appear as a direct threat'. The research was published in 2008.

'Jesus, Jesus, another *parrino* in Cosa Nostra'*

Giuseppe Calderone, known as Pippo

In his habit he looks like a priest, Don Agostino Coppola. He's quick-witted, sly as a fox. He has his parish church in Carini and his farm at Lo Zucco, a heaven on earth wedged in the last ravine of the Conca d'Oro. He entered the seminary at thirteen, at twenty-nine he married Totò Riina and Ninetta Bagarella, at the age of fifty-one he himself was married. Among his many adventurous lives, one winter's night he became a Mafioso. Hardly anyone knows that the Corleonesi 'made' him. Not even the people who should know do. Even Pippo Calderone, the head of the *Commissione regionale*, didn't know.

'You're like us, you're the same thing,' Tano Badalamenti tells him in Ramacca one day in 1969. That's how the ritual introduction is performed between men of honour. Pippo Calderone, known as *Cannarozzu d'argento* – 'Silver Windpipe' – because of the machine that gives him a metallic voice after the operation on his larynx, watches his brother Antonino in amazement: 'Jesus, Jesus, another *parrino* in Cosa Nostra.'

Parrino in Sicilian means priest. There have always been lots of *parrini* who were tolerant of the men of honour, but no made man had ever been seen before that day in Ramacca. Don Agostino was

---

* Attilio Bolzoni and Giuseppe D'Avanzo, *Il capo dei capi*, Milan: BUR-Rizzoli, 2007.

a member of the Anonima sequestri, Luciano Leggio's *cosca*, which was involved in kidnapping in Milan. At the age of twenty-four he is the treasurer for the diocese of Monreale, the wealthiest and most talked-about on the island. He is in charge of the administration of its property. The youngest of the three Coppola brothers of Partinico – there's Domenico and also Giacomo, who is the favourite nephew of Zio Ciccio, the one who is known in the States by another name: Frank 'Three Fingers' – is at ease with money.

Don Agostino has lots of friends. He's a guest at the estates of Peppucio Garda, the patriarch of Montreale. In the sacristy he receives Vito Ofria and Filippo Nania, who are *intesi*, important men in Partinico. And he is always meeting Luciano Leggio.

On 16 April 1974 he sets up an altar in the gardens at Cinisi. Don Mario and Don Rosario serve mass. 'In the name of the Father, the Son and the Holy Spirit, may the Lord be with you.' Totò and Ninetta are husband and wife. In hiding and happy.

The *parrino* has a nose for things. He understands that something disturbing is happening within Cosa Nostra, the Corleonesi are already waging an underground war on the Palermitani. They're organizing kidnappings, one of the actions absolutely forbidden by Mafia rules. And they're doing it even in Sicily. Too much noise. Too many cops in the streets. Too much social alarm.

One morning Luciano Cassino, the son of Count Arturo, the king of construction in Palermo, disappears. Six months later he is freed. Nine months later Don Agostino is sent to the Ucciardone for aiding and abetting a kidnapping. In prison he is given another two arrest warrants. For the abduction of Luigi Rossi of Montelera and that of the industrialist Emilio Baroni. He is given one warrant after another. Extortion, receiving stolen goods, one even for the murder of a petty criminal. Convictions. And miraculous acquittals. In the early 1980s the Sicilian Church can no longer pretend it can't see. And from the Vatican comes the suspension *a divinis* – he is at risk of excommunication.

In his village they still call him Don Agostino. He retires to Lo Zucco. He grows vines. But his health begins to suffer. He ends up in hospital, with kidney problems. There he meets a gynaecologist. She's a beautiful girl with green eyes and flame-coloured hair. Love at first sight. Don Agostino marries Francesca Caruana. The Caruanas of Siculiana.

'Cosa Nostra likes to trace itself back to the Apostle Peter'*

Leonardo Messina

They all have a bible. And they all pray. They always have a picture of a saint in their pockets. Or the picture of a Christ, a Madonna. They're extremely religious. And they make a great display of their devotion. Even when they're far away, on the other side of the world. Like the Cuntrera brothers of Siculiana – Gaspare, Paolo and Pasquale – the masters of drug-trafficking between the 1970s and the 1980s, who, for the Drug Enforcement Administration, are, along with the Caruana family, 'the biggest heroin dealers in the Mediterranean basin'. Originally from that little village in the province of Agrigento, the Cuntrera family became extremely wealthy in Canada and Venezuela. But they don't forget their holy protector: the Most Holy Saviour of the Crucifix. For almost a quarter of a century, on 3 May every year, Gaspare, Paolo and Pasquale venerate the statue of the Black Christ in a little church in Montreal. In return for a generous donation, they wrest it from the faithful of the Matrice in Siculiana to have it all to themselves, and on foreign territory.

'All of us men of honour think that we are Catholic, Cosa Nostra likes to trace itself back to the Apostle Peter,' explains the *pentito* Leonardo Messina.

---

* Questioning of Leonardo Messina, Parliamentary Anti-Mafia Commission.

Benedetto Santapaola is the head of the family of Catania. As a student in the Salesian institute in San Gregorio, he attends the oratory of Santa Maria delle Salette, dreams of becoming a priest and then chooses to become a murderer.

Calogero Vizzini, the patriarch of Cosa Nostra when the Americans disembarked in Sicily in 1943, had two brothers who were priests: Don Giovanni and Don Salvatore. And one cousin who was a parish priest, Don Angelo. And two bishop uncles, Monsignor Giuseppe Scarlata and Monsignor Giuseppe Vizzini.

The 'Pope' of Croceverde Giardina, Michele Greco, always clutches a gospel and two breviaries; in his cell he recites the Divine Office: 'The Psalms, Prime, Terce, Sext, None, Vesper and Compline, which is the prayer of the night.'

Another man who is devout is the fiery Luciano Leggio of Corleone. So is Giuseppe Piddu Madonia of Vallelunga, who has a suitcase full of sacred images when he is arrested. And so is Filippo Marchese, who always makes the sign of the cross before strangling someone. And Bernardo Provenzano, holed up in a wretched cottage in the countryside behind Corleone, where the Holy Spirit hovers in every corner.

But the most religious of all, the most mystical of all the Cosa Nostra bosses, is the one that the *Guardian* puts at the top of its list of the most famous Italians in the world: Pietro Aglieri, known as *ù signurinu.** A former paratrooper from La Folgore, a former seminarian in Monreale, holder of a classical graduation certificate from the dioscesan grammar school, son of a fruit-dealer, one aunt a nun, he is the head of the family of La Guadagna and extremely loyal to the Corleonesi. He is one of the bosses who decide to kill the magistrate Paolo Borsellino.

Ù signurinu – a nickname inherited from his father who inherited it from his grandfather – is arrested on 7 June 1997, when he

* '*Il signorino*', the little gentleman.

is thirty-eight and has been in hiding for almost nine years. His refuge looks like a chapel. Inside are benches lined up as if in a church: there is a little altar, there is a candlelit statue of the Madonna. The chairs are scattered with books by Kierkegaard, novels, an introduction to the philosophical thought of Sister Edith Stein, who died in Auschwitz. The head of the family of La Guadagna is wearing jeans and a sweater; a heavy wooden cross hangs from his neck. Pietro Aglieri is unrepentant. And he too, in the name of God, begins a slippery negotiation with the state. He calls it the 'way of active silence'.

'A lot of confusion . . . between sins and crimes'*

Pietro Aglieri

'I prefer to linger over my thoughts, where I feel much more at ease talking to God. Hence my silence. Not the silence of *omertà*† as some people suppose, or the silence of someone who has nothing to say, but "active silence", where you make your personal actions talk, as opposed to all that chitter-chatter when you're free.

'It strikes me as fairly easy to guess why no one even wants to try to prepare a pastoral line appropriate to current problems. No controversy, for pity's sake. Even if I don't share it, I understand the apparent lack of interest of that part of the Church hierarchy that is intent on protecting itself against hypothetical accusations of aiding and abetting criminals.

'But I continue to believe, and experience supports me in this, that it is better and more productive to remain, with the help of God's grace, in the context within which I find myself.

'I don't think that the administration of justice creates a good impression at the moment, and to describe certain trials as fair is a complete contradiction in every sense. So, taking the aspect of the Gospels which invites us to side with those who suffer, I greatly

---

* Interview with Pietro Aglieri by Salvo Palazzolo, *La Repubblica*, 14 March 2004.

† A refusal to cooperate with the state.

prefer the rigours of 41-bis* to the ambiguity of "collaborative'" positions.

'Obviously, I have no certainties, let alone any advice to dispense. On the other hand, I have never sought to be labelled as a Catholic, I've never sought certificates of conversion or safe-conduct passes for personal benefit, so I think that to tell the story of a fundamental part of my life, particularly of those periods when there was a lot of confusion going on between sins and crimes, and when only that which is indictable under law was considered evil, would be rather pointless. I am not after free publicity.

'The common denominator drawn from the opinions of many observers is that jail, as currently structured and conceived, does not improve anyone, because it contains no moral teaching. If you add to this the fact that regulation 41-bis is seen as jail within a jail, anyone can draw the conclusions that he will find most appropriate to the state of things. Unfortunately, in an age full of conflicts and contradictions, in which the predominance of aesthetics over ethics is everywhere, people believe that they can drive out social anxieties by incentivizing repression, and think of prison as the panacea to heal the ills of society. Perhaps, but sometimes legality bears illegality within it . . . Not only the "good" are right.'

---

* A prison act which prevents criminals from communicating with their associates. 41-bis are generally lifted if the prisoner agrees to collaborate with the law.

'Don Pino smiled and said, "I've been expecting this"'*

Salvatore 'Totò' Grigoli

'We weren't supposed to kill Father Pino [Puglisi] that evening, but then we saw him on his own. He was making a call from a phone-box near the church of San Gaetano, in Brancaccio. He was calm, Don Pino was. We went and got the gun, a 7.65 with a silencer. When we came back near to the phone-box, Don Pino wasn't there any more. So we went and waited for him outside his house. He showed up. He was opening the door and Gaspare Spatuzza put his hand in Pino's hand to take his bag, and then he said quietly: "Father, this is a robbery."

'They told us that the murder mustn't look like a Mafia murder, but the work of a drug addict or a thief. That was why a small-calibre pistol was used, and the priest's bag was taken. I was shooting, Don Pino smiled and said, "I've been expecting this." That smile has been imprinted on my mind for ever. It was a smile full of light, Don Pino Puglisi's smile: I will never forget it.

'Padre Pino had been left alone in Brancaccio. He went on preaching against the Mafia; he tried to tell the young people to be careful. Some people, people who associated with him, passed on everything that Don Pino did to the Graviano brothers. Cosa Nostra always knew everything. It was a crime foretold; Don Pino was

* Interview with Salvatore Grigoli by Salvo Palazzolo, *La Repubblica*, 8 September 1999.

more and more alone. People were convinced that the Padre Nostro Centre he had set up was a den of police informers. Then they found out it wasn't true . . . In my opinion Don Pino could have been saved if the state had protected him . . . and then what happened happened . . .

'We began to understand that the killing hadn't been useful to us. In fact it had made the situation worse. At that point we opted for silence. And that was when the problems started, and we all started talking to each other about it as a curse . . . For Cosa Nostra the church was what hid you if you were in hiding. Not because it was in collusion, but because it helped those in need. A neutral territory. The very thing we've lost over the past few years . . . Don Pino Puglisi's church had always been a different church . . .

'The pardon I was given by Pope Wojtyla was my hope, my relief. He will always be my guardian angel, he will help me even more than he already has on earth. I'm sure he will meet Don Pino in heaven and he will talk about me, and together they will boast about how I've changed because it was those two, it was just those two who gave me a reason to change.

'But I maintain that what happened between me and God must remain locked in my soul. I was acting on the orders of the Graviano brothers, the bosses of Brancaccio, when the Pope launched his anathema against the Mafia from the Valley of the Temples in Agrigento . . . I don't remember all the words the Pope said in Agrigento that day, I was still a man of honour . . . but I remember that from that day people in Cosa Nostra started saying that the Church was starting to be very different from before . . .'

'These are the murders that give you satisfaction'*

Salvatore 'Totò' Grigoli to Pasquale Di Filippo

'Basically Salvatore Grigoli, early in 1995, got accidentally shot in the foot with a rifle by another of our companions, so he spent several months with bullets in his foot . . . He couldn't move, so I spent most of my time taking care of him. Afterwards, when he got better, we were together in the villa again . . . we were at war with other people, so we kept out of things a little bit, because we were afraid that someone might do us harm in some way. But if necessary we were always at the disposal of Nino Mangano, to be called on to carry out murders. It was during those weeks that he first told me about Don Pino . . .

'There was still so much about the murder of Father Puglisi in the papers and on television. Every now and again when that murder came up Totò said to me, "Look, you see, these are the murders that give you satisfaction." He was proud because they were murders that people talked about a lot. They were always boasting about doing that murder, about killing Don Pino Puglisi.

'It was in Casteldaccia that he really confided in me about that murder, at Casteldaccia in a little villa that we own, where I was on holiday. He came to see me there very often. One evening we were watching the television news and we thought that the judicial

* Quotations from the trial of Gaspare Spatuzza + 4, second Court of Assizes of Palermo, 14 April 1998.

authorities had discovered who it was who had killed the priest. At which I said to him, "Look, Totò, they've identified the killers of Father Puglisi," because I was worried, because I knew it was him . . . But we must have misunderstood the news, because we were wrong: they'd identified the killers in another murder, so we'd got it all wrong.

'And then I said to him, "Totò, I'm sorry, are you worried because they might identify you?" And he says . . . he says, "No, no, they haven't identified me, because when I did the murder no one knew a thing." And I remember I said to him, "But did you go with your faces covered or uncovered?" And Totò replied, "No, faces uncovered, but there's no problem because there was no one there, so no one could have seen me." So that was what was said, for good or ill that's what I remember about that murder.

'Out of personal habit, Salvatore Grigoli always had a 7.65 in his hand, a pistol of that calibre and with the silencer. He was actually always holding it, I remember when we were in the Room of Death.* Totò always let you see it. But I don't know if that 7.65 was the same one he used to kill Father Puglisi . . .'

---

* A small apartment on the Piazza Sant'Erasmo where the Corleonesi murdered many of their victims. It was run by Filippo Marchese.

It was the Bourbons who built the fortress, between the sea and the humble dwellings of the Borgo Vecchio. They chose a plateau where les chardons *grew, the spiny thistles that the pack animals ate. The name Ucciardone comes from* 'chardon'. *When its dungeons filled up with the prisoners of the old Vicariate, between 1832 and 1850, Palermo prison was the most 'modern' in Europe. In the next century the Sicilians called it Villa Mori, after the prefect – Cesare Mori – whose mandate under the Fascist Party sent hundreds of rogues from the Madonie Mountains into its arms. It was only after the Second World War that it became the Mafia's Grand Hotel della Cupola. Its address was known to just about everyone in Palermo: 3 Via Enrico Albanese.*

'An unforgettable *mangiata* in Section Seven'*

Giuseppe Guttadauro

Men of honour aren't scared of jail. It's never final for them, it's always temporary. Even if you're given life, sooner or later you'll have your freedom. That much is certain for men of honour. But first you have to do time inside. And with *dignity*. The Mafia jail is the Ucciardone.

'It was Easter Sunday, 1984, and we had an unforgettable *mangiata* in Section Seven. The van came from La Cuccagna restaurant, the guards were open-mouthed: there were cases of Dom Perignon, we were guzzling down lobsters.'

Giuseppe Guttadauro, a man of honour of the Brancaccio family and star of the Palermo health service, is talking to three friends in his sitting room at home, unaware that he's being bugged. He's recalling his time in the Ucciardone.

'They prepared me a place at the head of the table – there was a hierarchy. At the time the man in charge was Totò – Salvatore Montalto. But the really powerful man was Nardo, Leonardo Greco. He could have corrupted God the Father. Nardo always gave me his ear. Need to draw up a list of special meetings, fifty meetings for the Saturday before Easter? Totò and Nardo would put the list together . . .'

---

* Files from the trial of Giuseppe Albanese + 54, penal court of Palermo, Section 4, 1 December 2005.

Number Seven is the section of the men of honour. Seven's on the third floor, out of bounds for all the other prisoners. A prison within a prison. The cells are always open, the prison guards mingling with the inmates, and the exercise hour lasts a whole morning. The sick-bay is where the summit gathers. The Mafiosi don't go to the canteen: prison food is 'government grub'. They never touch it. They book meals from the best restaurants in Palermo. The Ucciardone is divided into classes. The bottom of the heap are locked up in the Sixth, the section devoted to the *froci*, the *pedofili*, the *marocchini*, the *scafazzati*, the *spiuna*.*

At the Ucciardone, the Mafiosi are in charge. They are in charge of the prison warders, the doctors, sometimes even the governors. In return they guarantee order. Between the end of the 1960s and the beginning of the 1970s there were revolts in every Italian prison. Except the Ucciardone. Never a protest, never a complaint. It's a 'model' prison. These outstanding prisoners don't want to hear so much as the buzzing of a fly. They are the bosses in there. Pietro Torretta, patriarch of the Uditore district of Palermo. And Tano Badalamenti, Tommaso Buscetta, Gerlando Alberti, Paolino Bontate.

And Giuseppe Guttadauro.

'The Saturday before Easter we turned up in the meeting room: me, Montalto and Leonardo Greco. But once we got there . . . complete and total mess. My aunt Mariella picks a fight with my wife and asks her, "How come your husband gets a meeting and my husband doesn't?" So I say, "Take me out and put in my uncle Ignazino." What was I supposed to say? That ball-breaking aunt of mine . . . So I went off to have a good *mangiata* and a workout. I had a sauna, too.'

---

* Homosexuals, paedophiles, Moroccans, the 'crushed', police spies.

'Talking about cells is just a manner of speaking'*

Gaspare Mutolo

'Drugs were the only thing you couldn't get. We didn't take drugs. We had a store that had everything, a cell turned into a warehouse. There was money, whisky, champagne. There was nothing but our food. This was 1978, 1979 . . .

'The meetings weren't recorded, that was how things were in those days. Various people came to see me at the Ucciardone. Including fugitives. Gaetano Badalamenti. Rosario Riccobono was a major fugitive. Vernengo came too, Ganci, Scaglione. I can't remember everyone who came. I don't think anyone even asked them for their papers.

'The prison guards are the people who have most contact with the inmates. It's hard to find one who isn't decent and who won't do you a favour. Not so much now perhaps, but before. I'm talking about that time when the guards were still at the mercy of the inmates, who were more in charge than they were. There was one brigadier who had been in Palermo for many years and knew everybody. I don't know if the orders came from the governor, but the prison officers knew everybody's habits. This brigadier would call the porter's lodge and say, "Tizio's family's turning up in ten minutes."

* Questioning of the *pentito* Gaspare Mutolo, Parliamentary Anti-Mafia Commission, Rome, 9 February 1993.

'Then somebody came down and said, "Roll call." Sometimes we went on our own, other times they sent a guard. Then the brigadier and the marshal could say, "Mutolo's family's coming." If I didn't see her and my wife turned up at the porter's lodge, my wife would say to the guard, "I've got to have a special meeting." It was called a special meeting.

'Changing cells was an insignificant matter. Talking about cells is just a manner of speaking because there was a corridor with cells leading onto it on either side. They were always all open – we only closed them in the evening when we went to sleep. Then there was the sick-bay. Some people had bad hearts, others asthma, others hernias. Apparently we were all sick, we all had medical files on us so we were all sick. There was a doctor who was fired on the spot, poor guy. Then the various specialists came and backed us up. Some of them were friends of ours. We lived together, some brought coffee, others brought biscuits . . .

'That's not to say I was actually sick. We chose the experts for their abilities. The expert was there because another three experts had to come and say, "This man is sick, this one's schizophrenic." The high-profile experts could involve the official experts sent by the magistrate. If he's a high-profile doctor, it's easy for him to say the inmate is ill.

'Oh, madness . . . If someone gets twenty or thirty years in jail and there's a way for him to get only five or eight. I knew that, thanks to the experts, there are ceilings, that is, if you get a twelve-year sentence you get let off two, for twenty-five years it's five, while with a life sentence the maximum you can be let off is ten years – then you know that half the crime is discounted. I was also in the judicial asylum of Barcellona Pozzo di Gotto. You were even better off there than in Palermo: that was why we went there.'

'I had half the *Cupola* in hospital'*

Giuseppe Guttadauro

He never loses his asthma. The treatment isn't working, his doctors are worried. They want to 'keep an eye on him' at all times, right there in hospital. For the allergy tests, the blood tests. For a case this big they will also need the opinion of international specialists. The prisoner, Giuseppe Spina, a man of honour of the Noce family, isn't getting any better. He has a bad cough, fever, he feels as if he's suffocating. For 424 days his cell is no longer on the first floor of the seventh wing of the Ucciardone, but on the third floor of the Pulmonary Department of the City Hospital. A big, bright room. Giuseppe Spina is solicitously tended to by the nurses, pampered by relatives, fed and refreshed by friends, who turn up every evening with sea urchins and boiled octopus from Mondello.

Strangely, all the bosses in Palermo are ill. Pippo Calò is ill. Renal disturbances and 'cerebral lesions'. Giuseppe Giacomo is ill, complaining of 'bad leg pains' for four months. Cesare Ciulla is in hospital too, 'to undergo skin sensitivity tests'. Also ill are Salvatore Montalto and old Bernardo Brusca, Antonino Rotolo, Pino Savoca, Pietro Porcelli, Francesco Cicio Madonia, Giuseppe Olivieri. All hospitalized. All together. They come together for 'meetings' in

* Recorded in the files from the trial of Giuseppe Albanese + 54, Penal Court of Palermo, Section 4, 1 December 2005.

a big room at the City Hospital, deciding on men, issuing orders, organizing the drugs trade.

'I was a surgeon at the hospital. I had special permission to talk to everyone. I was untouchable, you know?' Dr Giuseppe Guttadauro, man of honour of the Brancaccio family, reminded his pupil Fabio Scimò. He told him, 'Besides, there was a time when there were no problems: I had half the *Cupola* in hospital. I went to see Beppe Lima, the MP's brother, his door was always open, but when I turned up he closed it, he sent everybody away, and I was left there on my own.'

In 1987 the hospitalized prisoners at Palermo's Civic Hospital spent a total of 2,839 days in bed. Across the whole of Sicily the number was 5,634. This scandal was created by a mixture of fake certificates, threats, warnings. Favours that had to be repaid. Colonel Mario Mori's *carabinieri* investigated, the public prosecutor's office of the Republic launched two inquests, the senior police commissioner Domenico Sica prepared a file on 'easy hospital admissions'. The accused were the surgeons at the City Hospital, but also certain judges in the Court of Assizes. The allegation was that they had placed too much trust in the medical files, in the diagnoses of the star doctors. Claudio Martelli, the Justice Minister, was also furious about the Mafiosi on life sentences who were all out of prison.

The scandal becomes a farce one evening when Pietro Vernengo puts on a silk dressing-gown and says goodbye to everyone on his ward. Undisturbed, he leaves hospital to become what he was before. A *latitante*, a fugitive.

It is an easy escape, unimpeded. Pietro Vernengo is from the Corso dei Mille family, accused of ninety-nine murders at the Maxi-Trial. He was acquitted of ninety-eight, but received a life sentence for the last one. He has a second conviction for association in Naples, a third for drug-trafficking in Lecce. His lawyers issue a special hospital arrest warrant 'on grounds of serious health issues', as granted by the second Court of Assizes in Palermo. Location: the tumour treatment centre at the City Hospital, urology department, ward 26, first bed on the left.

'The land draws us Sicilians, fugitives or non-fugitives'*

Gaspare Mutolo

'I've been a *latitante* for many years and I've always lived with my wife and children. If you go up Montepellegrino you can see that Palermo is a plateau. It isn't like Rome or Milan: Palermo's small. Totò Cancemi and other characters, you might imagine they're in America or something, but no, no – they're here. Cancemi built a seven billion lire villa; Giovanni Brusca's at San Giuseppe Jato every Saturday, calm, peaceful . . .

'We fugitives were in Partanna Mondello, in Valdesi, in Pallavicino. Sometimes we moved for a week or two because there was a murder, or because we knew there were police investigations under way. So instead of being in Via Ammiraglio Cagni I was in Via Patti, a hundred yards away. Maybe the fugitives aren't at number 25, they're at number 30. The police were doing their duty when they went to 25. When they went in search of me, they went to Via Catalano . . . I hadn't lived at Via Catalano for twenty years. The land draws us Sicilians, fugitives or non-fugitives; we're there and no one bothers us much. That's how things are done in Palermo.

'We went out normally, we knew what time the patrols came back. When a corpse or a drugs cargo had to be transported, for example, we knew that you could walk from half-past one until

* Questioning of Gaspare Mutolo, Parliamentary Anti-Mafia Commission, Rome, 9 February 1993.

half-past three or four and that it was quiet in the evening from half-past six until half past eight or nine . . . Sometimes we knew when there was an arrest warrant in the *Catturandi** office. There was a guy at the *Catturandi* office who received monthly payments, and also got extra presents when he brought us information in time. Some others did it just to get paid, but usually you don't . . . It's vulgar to say, "You give me this much, I'll give you this much"; you can always find a different way to ask for a gift.

'Until a cop or some kind of official tells me, "Look out, there's an arrest warrant for you," it's all done quite calmly. It makes for a quiet life in a way, in return for some favours you've done. But as soon as I find out from a cop who gives me a tip-off, and afterwards we organize a massacre . . . and that's why I, we Mafiosi, are concerned that the guy who gave the tip-off might have known about a potential massacre. Until that happens it's all idle chat, I'm not risking a life sentence, it doesn't matter if the cop or the bailiff or whoever knows it . . . but if I risk a life sentence I'll kill that policeman fifty times.

'At that time [in the police squad] it was Boris Giuliano, Tonino De Luca, Bruno Contrada, Captain Giuseppe Russo, the ones who caused the most problems for Cosa Nostra. The bar where Boris Giuliano was killed belonged to a cousin of mine, and I had the job of checking when Giuliano came out of the house. We were also able to identify where De Luca lived, where Dr Contrada went . . . In 1981, when I got out of jail, I asked how come some of them – and I'm referring to Dr Contrada – still hadn't been killed. I was amazed that Dr Contrada was still alive. But Saro Riccobono told me not to worry because: "Contrada is in our hands; in fact, if they arrest you, call him and if they take you to the station make sure he knows about it." If De Luca hadn't left Palermo, he'd be dead too. I know for certain that he's one of the ones who just made it by the skin of his teeth.'

* The elite police force devoted to rounding up Mafia members.

'When you're in the middle of that stuff, the more you eat the more you like it'*

Giuseppe Marchese

'For me, Cosa Nostra was a bit like a game of cops and robbers. What I saw most of all was the respect they gave my uncle Filippo, and then the hierarchies, the power. When my father knew my uncle wanted to make me a made man he got really angry. He said, "Leave him alone, he's just a kid." My brother had already become what he was. Riina and my uncle decided to get me to join anyway, but I had to be discreet. I was seventeen, eighteen years old.

'At that age seeing certain things makes you sky-high. When they tell you secret things like: "You've got to go to Totò Riina's," you don't stop to think about it. Now, thinking about it properly, I say: I wasn't aware of it. But when you're in the middle of that stuff, the more you eat the more you like it.

'In our territory everything was quite calm; my uncle even went to the bar with the cops. This is Cosa Nostra: you move the way you move, everything comes out into the open. If there was a theft, you knew straight away who had done it. Then our income came from construction companies, drugs-trafficking, cigarette-smuggling and the occasional big robbery. But to do a robbery you always had to ask permission from my uncle. For example, at Corso

* Interview in *Gruppo Abele*, 'Dalla mafia allo stato. I pentiti: analisi e storie', Turin: Ega, 2005.

dei Mille there was a bank, but my uncle never gave anyone permission to rob that bank, because he knew the director.

'On 15 January 1982 I was arrested for carrying an offensive weapon. And for the first time I ended up in the Ucciardone prison. For me it was like acceptance, and they'd prepared my cell perfectly.

'While I was in jail my uncle Filippo sent a message to me, saying, "Act crazy." So I did and I got diminished responsibility. Then they did another psychiatric examination in Milan and the examination went well. During that time my uncle Filippo was killed, I was told by my brother. If you make a mistake in Cosa Nostra you pay for it; they don't care if you're a father, uncle or brother. My uncle was killed by Riina with a white shotgun. But we nephews couldn't do anything, we just had to sit quietly in jail.

'I've spent twenty years in jail altogether. In 1982 I was in the asylum in Reggio Emilia, then I come back to the Ucciardone. Early in 1984 they send me to the asylum in Aversa. I come back to Sicily, to Termini Imerese. From Termini Imerese to Trani. From Trani to Trapani for the Maxi-Trial. Then back to the Ucciardone and back to Termini Imerese, Voghera and Cuneo . . . In the jails they only talked about murders . . .'

Giuseppe Marchese is betrayed by Cosa Nostra on 11 May 1989. He's locked up in the Ucciardone, they order him to kill his cellmate Vincenzo Puccio, a man of honour suspected of 'plotting' against Totò Riina. They explain to him that the murder has to look like the result of a violent argument. Giuseppe is already on a life sentence. He obeys.

He picks up a cast-iron grill and smashes Vincenzo Puccio's skull. 'He wanted to see one television programme and I wanted to watch another one,' Marche confesses to the prison police.

But the Mafioso of Corso dei Mille doesn't know what's happening outside the Ucciardone on the same day and at the same time as he's killing Vincenzo Puccio. At I Rotoli, the closed cemetery between Montepellegrino and the sea of Vergine Maria, Totò Riina's hitmen also kill Pietro Puccio, the brother of Giuseppe Marchese's cell-mate. The pretext suggested by the Corleonesi – Giuseppe's lie about his motives – is unsustainable. The murder of the Puccio brothers is a perfect Mafia crime. Only Giuseppe Marchese is left in a trap. Betrayed, used by his Cosa Nostra.

'That day I understood that I was dead meat,' he would say as soon as he turned *pentito*.

Anxiety, sexual insecurity, depression. Distress and irritability. The wives and family members of the Cosa Nostra capi *end up on the psychiatrist's couch. As the* pentito *C. says: 'When the two Brancaccio brothers talk about their relationship with their wives, they tell you, "You have to respect her," and respect doesn't refer to normal respect but respecting her in bed, which for them means: "Be careful, don't do things that . . . because there are things you do with whores that you don't do with wives."'*

They talk about their fears. In the consulting rooms and mental-health departments of late 1990s Palermo, witness statements are collected from the brothers and sisters of murdered bosses, from widows and women with husbands in jail, from pentiti *and their families. The data from these confessions becomes 'medical cards'.*

‘[They] had lovers . . . they had no morals’*

Gaspare Mutolo

‘We’ve always stuck to the image. If I’m going to rebuke a boy, try to kill him or force him to marry a woman just because he was engaged to her, I have to be the first in the district where I live – and where the man of honour is looked upon well by all the men and all the women – to set an example.

‘There are women, wives or *mamme* of men of honour, worthy of admiration for the sacrifices they make for their sons and husbands. If you’re a murderer but you’re faithful and in love, your wife is willing to make any sacrifice for you. If someone had told my wife they’d seen me in Mondello with some girl or other, my wife would have told him that it must have been the wife or sister of some friend in hiding; she certainly wouldn’t have thought of anything else.

‘I remember that Gaetano Badalamenti and, for a certain period of time, Totò Scaglione too, were both dogged advocates of total dedication to the family. That gives a wife a lot of security.

‘But there are rules which were observed more strictly in the past than they are now. And yet they aren’t fixed rules . . . In the Porta Nuova family, the family of Pippo Calò, for example, there were two or three people – I’m talking about men of honour – who

---

* Questioning of Gaspare Mutolo, Parliamentary Anti-Mafia Commission, Rome, 9 February 1993.

had lovers. We called the Porta Nuova family "*la famiglia degli spazzini*",* because they had no morals.

'And I remember that Luciano Leggio took a lover, and had a child with her, too. Not just that, but she was a very sick woman, I think she was a spastic. None of that had any consequences, but only because his name was Luciano Leggio. If it had been any other man of honour, he would have been thrown out of the family straight away, or perhaps even killed.

'Having a lover creates lots of problems and Cosa Nostra doesn't want these problems. Besides, a man of honour who takes a lover might also father a child, a child that would bring him new responsibilities. That's not allowed. But . . . but sometimes it happens and in general you pretend not to know.

'It may be that you can't become a made man for family reasons too, it may be that you can't join Cosa Nostra. Obviously if someone has a brother who's a policeman or a magistrate he can't become a man of honour, but I'm also talking about other people, people whose mothers were known to have a lover, or their sisters, or even their wayward daughters . . .

'Lots of stress is given to these things in Palermo but not in other provinces. Like Trapani. Or like Catania. Because inside Cosa Nostra it's always been said that the way they do things in those two provinces is different from the way we do them in Palermo. The origins of some men of honour – well, some of them liked to have lots of lovers . . . For example, there's Nitto Santapaola; he's important. At least, in theory he's important, but he will never be able to become a Salvatore Riina or a Bernardo Brusca. He should be ruled out completely because of what I said about those two provinces. They're not like Palermo.'

---

* 'The family of bin-men'

'I couldn't marry the daughter of a separated couple, but I could marry an orphan'

Giuseppe Marchese

'I'd brought her up, your honour,' he says, his voice dying away.

'Rosaria is my blood, my breath,' he repeats, struggling to get the words out along with the most painful memory of his life. More than all the others.

More than those eyes he still dreams about every night, eyes that stare at him as he's killing somebody. More than Uncle Totò's unchanging face, a wax mask. More than arrest, than the psychiatric prison, than the hell of Pianosa, of *pentimento*, of his dishonoured family.

'Rosaria was the only clean thing I had, I wanted to walk Rosaria up the aisle, I wanted to have her for ever,' says Giuseppe Marchese, the little boy from Corso dei Mille that the *capo dei capi* always had by his side. Salvatore Riina made him a man of honour when Giuseppe wasn't yet eighteen, but discreetly, one of the ones only a very few people know is a 'made man'. He takes him on as his personal chauffeur, a position of maximum trust. He uses him to get rid of Totuccio Inzerillo, one of the most powerful bosses in Palermo, at the start of the Mafia war.

'But I was thinking only about Rosaria, my Rosaria, I knew her when we were both only thirteen.'

Yet even the young Giuseppe Marchese knows it's a hopeless love.

'With this marriage you will destroy yourself,' his brother

Antonino says, 'and you want to destroy all of us, all of your family until the seventh generation.'

Rosaria comes from an ordinary, normal family. Her father is a clerk and her mother is a housewife; they've been separated for some time. Giuseppe sees only her: he wants Rosaria.

'So one day my brother Antonino tells me: "I've found the solution." I couldn't marry the daughter of a separated couple, but I could marry an orphan, so my brother suggested killing her father.

Giuseppe recalls: 'He also told me that, if I wasn't willing to do it myself, he was prepared to do it for me. How could I have looked Rosaria in the eye? How could I have kissed and hugged her? I went to see Rosaria and I was tough with her, nasty: I told her never to come and see me ever again.'

Giuseppe has two brothers and two sisters. The youngest of them, Vincenzina, marries Leoluca Bagarella, Totò Riina's brother-in-law. It's more than a marriage for the Marchese family of Corso dei Mille. It's the deadly embrace of the Corleonesi. They have become one family, and the Marchese family are at their service. They give refuge to their *latitanti*, and from the early 1980s they kill on their behalf.

Corso dei Mille, Viale dei Picciotti, Via Messina Marine and Via Messina Montagne, Ponte dell'Ammiraglio, all streets named in memory of Giuseppe Marchese's namesake, Garibaldi, who passed that way with his red-shirts. All roads which, in the 1980s, are like so many little Palermo cemeteries.

'Bagarella decided to suspend the killings because he was in mourning'*

Toni Calvaruso

'Signor Franco' lives in a flat in the district of Malaspina, through a level crossing and down the road that ends right in the centre of Palermo. In the kitchen there's tripe in tomato sauce boiling away in a pot. Under the bed there's a pump-action shotgun. 'Automatics', five double-magazine pistols, hidden in the wardrobe among the towels. In a drawer, fake IDs, eight of them, all with different names. A jewellery box on the chest of drawers. Three necklaces, two rings and a piece of paper with a message on it.

'My family forgiven everything, my husband deserves a gold statue hugs and kisses for everyone. Luca, the fault was all mine, I didn't want to, forgive me kisses kisses.' It's the last letter from Vincenzina. Then she goes off and takes her life.

Vincenzina Marchese is the wife of the brother-in-law of Totò Riina, Leoluca Bagarella, known in the Malaspina condominium as 'Signor Franco'. He is a fugitive. Vincenzina is also the sister of Giuseppe Marchese, 'the kid' of Corso dei Mille. It is 1995, and Giuseppe has recently turned *pentito* in Pianosa. A source of shame for the Marchese family, a 'family disgrace' for the Bagarellas and Riinas of Corleone. An unbearable weight for Vincenzina.

The woman is desperate. Day after day she is sliding into a

---

* The *pentito* Antonio Calvaruso, quoted in Antonio Di Stefano and Lino Buscemi's book *Signor giudice, mi sento tra l'anguria e il martello.*

hole, the couple are trying to have a child, but there is no sign of conception. Vincenzina decides to take her own life. She hangs herself. On the night of 12 May 1995 her husband finds her dead.

'Signor Franco' is the *capo* of the Corleonesi still at liberty, the hard man of Cosa Nostra, the one who wanted the massacres and still wants them – against the plans of Bernardo Provenzano – to frighten the state with bombs. But for the moment he has other scores to settle in Sicily. To eliminate the men of honour of Villabate who are playing a double game. And then to hunt down the *scappati*, the Inzerillos who fled at the start of the Mafia wars and who have since come back. At the end of spring 1995 the killing starts in Palermo again. Ten dead in Brancaccio. Twelve in Villabate. Three in Corleone. Ten dead in Misilmiri. Then, all of a sudden, the shotguns fall silent.

'Bagarella decided to suspend the murders because he was in mourning,' Toni Calvaruso reveals when they capture both him and Bagarella.

Toni is his shadow, his confessor; he knows all his secrets. He goes with him to his meetings with the Bruscas, he's the messenger for all his '*pizzini*',* he records his outpourings. Even the most intimate of them. Totò Riina's brother-in-law asks him for help to bury his Vincenzina in a secret place. He sets up a little altar in the flat on Via Malaspina, he arranges candles around the framed photographs, he dresses his wife in her prettiest clothes, puts make-up on her, puts her in a car and transports the corpse to a grave that will never be found.

For a month Leoluca Bagarella doesn't shoot, he doesn't kill, he doesn't even leave the house. The last murder in that campaign on the part of the Corleonesi family took place on 28 April. It was only towards the middle of the following June that he talked to his

* From *pizzino*, meaning a 'small piece of paper', and used for Mafia communications.

family about other crimes. In his first interrogation after turning *pentito* Toni Calvaruso reveals that, from that point on, 'When it came to killing, even he wasn't particularly interested in the matter – Bagarella had always done the job with love.'

'Her husband even killed children. That was why God was punishing her'*

Toni Calvaruso

'Leoluca Bagarella was very religious; he always had statues of the saints in the car, and pictures of the Madonna at home. I also remember that there was a picture of a saint, the patron saint of prisoners, that he carried with him wherever he went. Many times I went to church with them, with him and his wife Vincenzina. In Pollina, in San Mauro Castelverde and also in Cefalù.

'In the first few months of 1994 his wife Vincenzina was pregnant and when Bagarella, in March 1994, moved to Via Malaspina, I went with them to the gynaecologist a few times. Bagarella had told me that his wife had had two miscarriages in the past. During her last pregnancy, which had lasted longer than the others, I remember that Vincenzina Marchese sent me to the church on Via Maqueda a few times, opposite the one called Piazza della Vergogna. To offer bunches of red roses as votive gifts to the Madonna, to protect her pregnancy.

'But she miscarried again, if memory serves in March 1994. In hospital. While during the period of her pregnancy she had "blossomed" again, after the miscarriage Vincenzina started undergoing a process of decline that was both physical and psychological. It couldn't be stopped. She got terribly thin, her hair turned white,

---

* Record of the questioning of Tony Calvaruso by deputy public prosecutor of Palermo Teresa Principato, 23 October 1996.

she neglected herself, walking around all the time in a house-coat.

'She stopped leaving the house, and was obsessively frightened of being caught by the police. She was always watching the television news and listening on headphones to her husband's scanner, tuned into the frequencies of the police and the *carabinieri*.

'Leoluca Bagarella tried to distract her by bringing family members home, even at great personal risk. He bought her clothes and other things, but nothing distracted her from her negative thoughts. In fact, her obsession had become so powerful that she even wore wigs at home. To avoid being recognized. I got her two of those wigs myself: one cost 900,000 lire and the other 780,000 lire.

'When I went to the Bagarella house, when he called me to say that his wife was dead . . . he was kneeling in front of the corpse. He was in the darkest despair. He said his wife was reproaching him, blaming him for the fact that she couldn't have children. Vincenzina had known about the kidnapping of the son of Santino Di Matteo and, being aware that that had led to the death of the child, she had convinced herself that she wasn't allowed to have children because her husband even killed children. That was why God was punishing her.'

'Women are drawn to the Mafia, until they're stung by the pain'*

Antonino Calderone

'Women do well in the Mafia. Being the wife of a Mafioso means enjoying lots of privileges, big and small, and it's also, in a sense, demanding. Women are drawn to the Mafia, until they're stung by the pain, by the terrible things that happen in Cosa Nostra; they live very well in it.

'Apart from the fact that many wives of men of honour – almost all the ones I've known, in fact – come from Mafia families, they've breathed the air of Cosa Nostra since birth, so they're very familiar with a Mafioso's way of thinking and acting. You mustn't forget that your own wife ends up guessing everything, and what she can't deduce on her own she has her friends tell her, or her own sisters and in-laws, who are often married to men of honour themselves.

'Nitto Santapaola isn't married to a Mafia woman. His wife comes from a very humble family, and until she got married she worked as a corset-maker. Then she fitted in very well in the Mafia. She's every bit as much a Mafia person as he is. Nitto trusted his wife as much as possible, and then he told me that I was talking too much to my wife. The women of Palermo are very special, of course. They pretend not to know, but they know more than their husbands . . .

---

* Talking to Pino Arlacchi in *Gli uomini del disonore* (*'Men of Dishonour'*).

'My wife, the poor thing, came slowly to understand that she was getting married to a Mafioso. She worked it out for herself, and I didn't notice. After some time we were officially engaged and we went on an outing to the country with a group of families. Pippo and I thought of bringing Luciano Leggio with us too. We had a good *mangiata,* and while I was lying on the grass she came over and asked me all of a sudden, "Hey, Nino, who's that gentleman that everyone's treating with such deference, and calling professor?" "He's a friend. He's been a friend of mine and Pippo's for some time." "What are you telling me? I've seen his picture in the paper. That's Luciano Leggio," my future wife said triumphantly . . . So when she said yes, and when we got married, she knew what she was getting into.

'There's never been a rule that said Cosa Nostra doesn't kill women. A woman who talks, who makes allegations about men of honour, can be killed, and there have been many such cases that you can check, and there still are, even today. But it's true that Cosa Nostra didn't kill innocent women, whose sole crime consisted in being the wives or daughters of enemies. There have been cases in which men of honour have even spared the lives of women who have testified against them in court, doing them significant damage . . . But the tendency to spare the lives of women no longer exists. Either in Catania or anywhere else; if they find out that a woman's talking too much, they kill her without much ceremony. Now it's us men who are talking. Before, it was the women who did that job . . .'

'For a great love I had to do a great thing'*

Giacoma Filippello

'When they came and told me they'd killed Natale, my eyes blurred and my legs started shaking. I was running like mad: I found him in the Campobello supermarket. What a mess they'd made of him. Twenty-five machine-gun rounds, all on target. They chose Kalashnikovs because he'd had his car bullet-proofed and they needed a weapon that would break through the armour. They took him by surprise, defenceless as a bird.

'Natale didn't even notice that he was about to die. He was standing up, he fell like a ripe fruit. I was expecting it, because they'd tried twice before. I knew the bad news could arrive sooner or later. But I couldn't imagine that the pain could be as intense as that. I hugged him, I kissed his forehead. I didn't cry, I didn't shout. I was frozen. I sensed that there was a crowd behind me, but I couldn't see anybody, I couldn't hear voices. I saw his pistol, I touched it, I slipped it out and hid it under my jacket. In front of everybody. And I left, head held high.

'I suddenly thought of avenging him. "Now," I said to myself, "if I meet that worthless Don Alfonso I'll shoot him in the mouth." I didn't see Don Alfonso or the others who, I was sure, could have carried out that killing. I said, "They'll pay for it." When I was with

* Interview with Giacoma Filippello by Francesco La Licata for *Storie di mafia*, produced by the TV station RaiDue.

him I wasn't afraid of anything. He was strong, Natale was. I saw all the others turning towards him with respect and I felt important too. "Aunt Giacomina, you can't live here any more. I've got a grocer's shop and I always have to . . .", "Aunt Giacomina, it's not right that we poor people always have to pay . . .", "Aunt Giacomina, see what can be done . . ."

'I saw the Mafia the way Natale saw it. As a vehicle for justice . . . Women and children were never touched. I didn't think it was bad. But the Mafia used to be something different. I had the same mentality as he did. It would be possible to change something entirely. Now, however, the Mafia has changed a bit, and I've changed a bit. So I said enough to arrogance and blood. Today I wouldn't side with the Mafia, not even the old, losing side.

'I waited for them to avenge him but nothing happened. In fact one of them dared to stop me in the street. He wanted to pay his condolences. And he said, "You're lucky they left you alive. It takes nothing to snuff out a candle." I yelled, "That mistake will cost you dear. I'll do everything to split open the chest and eat the heart of Natale's murderers" . . . Then I had a bright idea. I'll denounce them all, I thought. That will be my revenge. Natale always told me I had to hold my tongue, even if they'd hurt him. But he was a man, a man of honour, and he had his law. Things were different for a woman. Why should I keep quiet? To stay calm, receive visits of condolence from half of Mazara, murderers included? I imagined what my future might be like: surrounded by fake respect due to the widow of a boss, but always prisoner of my secret and maybe destined to switch beds to become the favourite of the new godfather. Giacoma Filippello knows how to react, I said to myself. I called the judge and I started talking.

'I spend my days in a house that is my prison. I live in a city I don't know. I live with the nightmare of opening the door and finding myself looking at lousy Mafiosi who I turned in and

who have got out already. But for a great love I had to do a great thing.'

Giacoma Filipello was the partner of Natale L'Ala, man of honour of the Campobello family of Mazara, killed on 7 May 1990.

The corpse was never found. Mauro De Mauro, journalist for the Palermo daily newspaper L'Ora, *Sicily correspondent for* Il Giorno *and Reuters, disappeared on the evening of 16 September 1970 outside his house on Via delle Magnolie in Palermo. 'I've got a scoop that's going to shake the whole of Italy,' he had confided to his colleagues before he disappeared.*

'All disappeared, disappeared for ever'*

Salvatore Contorno, known as Totuccio

There is no grave for his wife and children to go to mourn him. 'Disappeared', they write on his police file. 'Disappeared', the men of honour repeat fatalistically. In Palermo it's called *lupara bianca* – white shotgun.

White shotgun killings aren't easy. But sometimes they're 'useful'. To slow down investigations into the murder. Or to confuse the members of the other families and throw them off the trail. Where there's no body, there's no crime. Missing corpses tell no tales. With no cartridge cases on the ground, there's always a lingering doubt.

White shotgun means grabbing someone and taking him somewhere, interrogating him, strangling him, then throwing him to the pigs or dissolving him in a vat of acid. White shotgun accounts for a lot of things that happen in Palermo.

'That evening I found myself in a house in Falsomiele with the late Mimmo Teresi, Giuseppe Di Franco and the brothers Angelo and Salvatore Federico. They were talking to each other, they had been summoned by the new *capo* of the family of Villagrazia, Leopoldo Pullarà, to Nino Sorci's farm. They took a walk and they all disappeared, disappeared for ever.'

---

* Records of the questioning of Salvatore Contorno by the investigating magistrate Giovanni Falcone, November and December 1984.

Salvatore Contorno remembers the last meeting with his friend and godfather, 'the late' Mimmo Teresi. It's 26 May 1981. In mid-April they kill Stefano Bontate and four weeks later Salvatore Inzerillo, the two most powerful bosses in Palermo. Mimmo Teresi 'respects mourning' for ten days. Then he starts driving around the city in his armoured car. He is always armed, surrounded by his most trusted men of honour. One is a Judas. He brings him the news that Leopoldo Pullarà wants to see him. He persuades him to go to the appointment, he reassures him, tells him that he too will be at the meeting. In Nino Sorci's *baglio* there are ten Mafiosi waiting for him. They grab Teresi and the other three and strangle them with a rope. The corpses disappear. On 1 June, four women from the village of Santa Maria del Gesù put on black clothes. Their husbands left home and never came back. They are widows.

With white shotgun the traitor is always a friend, or a close family member. An uncle, a nephew, a cousin. Someone who provides a guarantee with his honour, his blood. Someone who is forced to sell the other to save himself. White shotgun is a crime of refined savagery.

'In general it is maintained that the Mafia prizes certain murder techniques over others, but it's a mistake: the Mafia has no fetishistic preferences,' Giovanni Falcone tells Marcelle Padovani, in *Le Cose di Cosa Nostra*. The judge describes the reasoning of men of honour about white shotgun: 'It's logical and simple: if you lure someone into an ambush, arranging to meet him in a garage or a shack or a warehouse – and overcoming his resistance and his suspicions is no small thing – why alarm the neighbours by using a pistol? Strangling's much better. No noise or dirt or traces.'

In Palermo, white shotgun leaves victims in times of peace and in times of war. In times of peace because there's a need for silence. In times of war because you can only slip behind the enemy by subterfuge.

'That day in Palermo we washed our feet'*

Calogero Ganci

The questioning by vice-state attorney Giuseppe Fici is over. The man of honour of the Noce family, Calogero Ganci, tries to reconstruct the mass-disappearance of the Mafiosi of Palermo. He goes back in time, to almost fifteen years before. To 30 November 1982.

'There were people turning up at all hours, they brought them and strangled them and even I didn't know who they were. I even went out . . . unfortunately . . . there have been other murders that I didn't see being carried out. But they all died on 30 November, all that day.

'As far as we're concerned, let's say . . . let's say it was normal for them to have to die. I took part in the killing of Rosario Riccobono, of Salvatore Scaglione, of Salvatore Micalizzi and two or three other people who went with them to I Dammusi, because they died in the very house where Bernardo Brusca lived in the area of Dammusi, outside San Giuseppe Jato. Then there were the ones from the family of Porta Nuova who brought Giuseppe Ficario there, and another, much older man.

'I, along with some others, also had the task of taking people, both from our family and other families, from that warehouse that Gaspare Bellino had in San Lorenzo. In the warehouse I killed

* Record of the questioning of the *pentito* Calogero Ganci by the deputy public prosecutor of Palermo Giuseppe Fici, 13 February 1996.

Salvatore Minore and a certain Miceli Cola. Salvatore Minore was from Trapani, he was 30 November too . . . that's where the strangling took place first . . . There was what we call *la puliziata di pedi*: that day in Palermo we washed our feet . . .

'It was my father who brought Salvatore Scaglione to I Dammusi. That morning my father had had a meeting with him in his butcher's shop on Via Lancia di Brolo, so as not to arouse his suspicions. They had talked there for a bit, and then they bought the fish in the fishmonger's opposite, because they were going to go to I Dammusi. They were going to have a *mangiata*, they'd told Scaglione there was going to be a *mangiata*, you know? And also to explain the new, the new . . . let's say . . districts, the new . . . all those things. And there, after the *mangiata*, we killed Scaglione and the others.

'On 30 November I can say that about twenty or thirty disappeared.'

In fact, forty, fifty, perhaps as many as sixty bosses were killed in a single day. Lured into a trap by their friends, their relations. And then strangled. Slipped into vats of acid and dissolved.

Calogero Ganci's memories are a blur. He can only remember the ones that he killed with his own hands. Up at I Dammusi, in the Brusca family's cottage at San Giuseppe Jato. And the others in San Lorenzo, in the big warehouse behind the abandoned railway station.

He forgets Salvatore Neri and Vinceno Cannella, one Carlo, Salvatore Misseri, Giuseppe and Salvatore Lauricella, Salvatore Cusenza, Francesco Gambino, Giovanni Filiano, three men of honour from Acquasanta and another two from La Vergine Maria, the ones from the village of Pagliarelli, from Resuttana, the others from Falsomiele and La Conigliera. A door-to-door white shotgun. *La puliziata di pedi*, the washing of feet, as the Corleonesi call it. They are getting rid of all the men who had betrayed the Bontates and the Inzerillos at the beginning of the Mafia war, the renegades, the Judas figures on the stronger side. With them, the Corleonesi. But in Cosa Nostra, a traitor is always a traitor.

'We had to take this bitter decision'*

Salvatore Lo Piccolo

'At 7.45 p.m. on 12 January 2006 Monica Burrosi, daughter of Ferdinando and Urso Eugenia, born in Palermo on 12 July 1973, resident at no. 7 Via Ibsen, reported the disappearance of her husband, Bonanno Giovanni, son of the late Armando . . .'

Son of the late Armando. 'Son of the late' – the phrase sums up the story of the Bonanno family of Resuttana.

Twenty-two years previously, Armando Bonanno, hitman, father of Giovanni, disappeared. He left the house one day and never came back. In August 1984, Armando was in hiding, wanted for the murder of the captain of *carabinieri* of Monreale, Emanuele Basile. Yet he was living where he had always lived. In Resuttana, the village that had been swallowed up by the high-rises of Viale Strasburgo, a square suffocated by cars crammed in tightly in both directions, fumes mingling with the scent of late-flowering jasmine. One day Armando Bonanno went to his usual bar, he saw his usual friends. The Madonias. The Di Trapanis. The Puccios. Then, after the mid-August holiday, his wife turns up at the *carabinieri* barracks on Via Belgo and signs a statement: 'At 9.10 p.m. on 22 August 1984 the wife of Armando Bonanno, son of

---

* Evidence at Trial no. 5464/05 of the Palermo District Anti-Mafia Office, requested for the application of custodial measures against Antonino Rotolo, Antonino Cinà and Diego Di Trapani.

Francesco and Caterina Lo Cicero, reported the disappearance of her husband . . .'

Time doesn't pass in Palermo.

The fate of the Bonannos is to die a white shotgun death. The father is killed because he knows too much, the son because he is a thief.

Giovanni's 'death certificate' is found three months after his disappearance. In Corleone, in the hideout at Montagna dei Cavalli, where the police arrest Bernardo Provenzano. It's a *pizzino*, a rolled-up piece of paper with five type-written lines. Dated 10 February 2006, it is signed by Salvatore Lo Piccolo. The boss of the western part of Palermo informs the *grande capo* of the Corleonesi of what is happening in Cosa Nostra, down in the city.

'With regard to the one [Giovanni] who calls himself our fellow countryman, unfortunately we have been unable to find other solutions, as he went off on his own. Many attempts were made to avoid unpleasantness, including keeping someone by his side, but they came to nothing. And at this point we had to take this bitter decision with D . . .'

'D' is Diego Di Trapani, son of Francesco Di Trapani – the man who had Armando Bonanno shot twenty-two years previously. When 'D' found out that Giovanni Bonanno had never given back some money that belongs to other families, money raised through extortion, he informed the *capimandamento*. The matter causes a scandal among the Mafiosi. Antonino Cinà observes: 'Fuck, that bastard is a *carabiniere*, he took all that money for himself.' Antonino Rotolo: 'He's an idiot, the guy really is an idiot.' For a few days they mull over what is to be done. Then Rotolo suggests: 'I would like to do it through . . . through his brother-in-law, yes, because he seems to trust him.'

Killing a man of honour has never been simple within Cosa Nostra. You always have to respect the rules, have all the 'authorizations' you need. The authorizations from the *capimandamento* and from *rappresentanti* or their proxy if the *rappresentanti* are in jail. Antonino Rotolo opens and closes the consultation and reports: 'It has the OK from everybody.' Antonino Cinà replies: 'Perfect'. But the last word always goes to the commander in Resuttana. And the commander in Resuttana is 'D'. The 'bitter decision' has been taken, Giovanni Bonanno is already dead.

'Your Excellency has carte blanche, the authority of the state must be absolutely, I repeat, absolutely, re-established in Sicily. If the laws currently in force stand in the way, that will not be a problem, we will draw up new laws.' Signed Benito Mussolini.

That was on 22 October 1925, and with that telegram sent to Cesare Mori, who had just been appointed prefect of Palermo with extraordinary powers over the whole of the island, Il Duce declared 'total war' on the Mafia.

Democracy or dictatorship, Cosa Nostra has always adapted. Internally, too. There have been times when they had lots of capi*; there are others that have just had tyrants. An old Sicilian proverb says: 'When the wind blows become a reed.'*

'If there's democracy in Italy today, you've got me to thank'*

Luciano Leggio

He only gets out the Cuban cigar for show. He twirls it around in his fingers, chews it in front of the television cameras. With that fur collar on his black coat and that swaggering pose, he looks more like a gangster from 1930s Chicago than a Mafioso born among the sun-burnt fields of a feudal estate. The defendants in the Maxi-Trial don't even look at him. He's brought only his name to the feast. Every now and again he opens his mouth but he doesn't say anything. He's acting. In the bunker courtroom in Palermo, the old Luciano Leggio of Corleone is adding a bit of local Mafia colour. Until 15 April 1986, when he makes the mistake of opening his mouth.

He's furious, he yells from his cage: 'I don't want to go showing my ass off but given that Signor Buscetta is denying the hospitality I gave him in Catania, I have to talk to you about affairs of state. In the summer of 1970, he and Totò Greco came to see me for political reasons. They had a large-scale, megalomaniac plan to subvert the state. Some politicians were promising big things; they wanted to enrol two, three, ten thousand men, but eventually I refused to see them again. Your honour, Signor Buscetta has never said these things to you, has he?'

In the middle of the room, alone, facing the court, is Cosa Nostra's number-one *pentito*.

---

* Speaking at the Maxi-Trial, Palermo, 1986.

Luciano Leggio is purple in the face, he goes on shouting: 'They promised me freedom in return for my participation in a coup d'état. I wouldn't be bought. I've never wanted to take Italy into a dictatorship. If there's democracy in Italy today, you've got me to thank. And what have I had in return? One life sentence, one for twenty-two years and another for six. All without any proof whatsoever. Some people believe in God and some in the Devil. Socrates was sentenced to drink hemlock, I'm still paying the consequences of that refusal. The first sentence was, as it happens, in 1970, the last in 1974.'

The bunker in Palermo is stalked by the ghost of Prince Junio Valerio Borghese, the former commander of the infamous Fascist X MAS naval flotilla. It's the Corleone boss who brings him into the Maxi-Trial. For the Mafiosi it's like a betrayal, '*un atto di sbirritudine*'.* Like informing. Silence falls among the cages. Someone gets a message to Leggio: 'Smoke your cigar, but act like a prisoner.'

From that moment until the end of the trial, Corleone's former Scarlet Pimpernel, the head of the *Anonima Sequestri* kidnapping gang, the living myth of the Mafia, would not say another word.

In fact, the judge, Falcone, had become aware of the attempted coup almost two years previously, on 4 December 1984. It had been Buscetta himself who had told him what had happened in that far-off summer of 1970.

Prince Borghese, the head of the conspirators, already had 'the support of certain politicians', but also sought the help of the Mafia to attack police stations, disarm officers in their barracks and occupy the headquarters of RAI in Sicily. In exchange the coup participants guaranteed amnesty for all imprisoned Mafiosi.

Many bosses – Pippo Calderone, Giuseppe Di Cristina and Leggio himself – seemed to agree in principle. Only Totò Greco was

* Literally: 'act of coppitude' or 'policery'.

dubious. He went to Rome to meet the prince. He then came back to Sicily and told his friends that operation 'Tora Tora' – the coup's code name – was to go ahead. He wanted all Mafiosi to wear a green sheaf – *fascio* – on their arms by way of recognition. And they also wanted the complete list of Mafia affiliates, family by family.

In the end it was the whole of the Sicilian Mafia – not just Leggio – who chose democracy in 1970.

'The Mafia is a democratic organization'*

Leonardo Messina

In Sicily it's Cosa Nostra that *defends* democracy. After the war in the rest of Italy, and even in the rest of Europe, military or paramilitary organizations were set up 'with an anti-Communist function', all secret and all bound up with the security services, but on the island at the centre of the Mediterranean the natural bulwark against 'the red peril' is the Mafia. It's the Mafia bosses and *campieri* who guarantee – as early as the 1950s and in the scorching season of the occupation of the lands[†] – the military and cultural shield against subversive movements and the advance of the Italian Communist Party.

A criminal structure at the service of Western democracy, and itself a democratic system: that was the Cosa Nostra known to Leonardo Messina, the *capodecina* of the family of San Cataldo.

'By now the Mafia is a democratic organization. One of the most important democratic organizations: there are no secret ballots, voting is done with a raising of hands, in front of everybody. The epicentre of everything is the family, the *capo* is only its representative. It's always the family that decides, the *capo* is voted for by

* Questioning of the *pentito* Leonardo Messina, Parliamentary Anti-Mafia Commission, Rome, 4 December 1992.

† The occupation of Sicily by Allied Forces during the summer of 1943.

the grass roots, by the men of honour, who have the same power as the *capodecina*.'

Free votes. Posts held on a temporary basis, not in perpetuity. Direct control of business management, sharing of organization policies, regulations.

'The *capo* who does not advance the interests of the family that elected him is automatically removed from office at another meeting. If he has been careless he is removed and a new one is elected who, in his turn, has the duty of choosing the *capodecina*, that is, the *capo*'s right-hand man. If he has done seriously bad things he is killed, but if the crime is minor he is *posato** or put *fuori confidenza*.† The man who is *posato* doesn't know that he has been *posato*, while someone who is *fuori confidenza* receives a letter from his *capodecina*.'

But this is the Sicilian Mafia before the Corleonesi. Before Totò Riina's coup. With the conquest of Palermo and its families, the Corleone bosses twist the soul of Cosa Nostra.

Elections are abolished, the *capi* of each village no longer choose their delegate to nominate the *capimandamento*; those *mandamenti* are imperiously dissolved and reconstructed from one day to the next for a new redistribution across the territory. In the province of Palermo, twenty-four become five or six. They stretch from the centre of the city for thirty-five kilometres to the west, in the direction of Trapani, or eastwards towards the Madonie. At their peak Totò Riina places only his most trusted men. There are no longer any new alliances or formations in Cosa Nostra.

The new *Commissione* is a government without powers, drained of all authority. It no longer makes decisions, it no longer deliberates. And it only meets every now and again. Its members are always presented with events once they have already happened, and

* 'Put down'.

† 'Out of confidence'.

from now on there's only one party: the party of the Corleonesi. There's only one man in command: Totò Riina. By 1984, Cosa Nostra is a dictatorship.

'And then his hand went up'*

Gaspare Mutolo

Judge: 'So the *substitute* took part, he acted as deputy for the *capomandamento* within the *Commissione*?'

Gaspare Mutolo: 'Yes, sir, a *capomandamento* had the option of being substituted by a member of the same family, or delegating another *capomandamento*. People knew in advance what was going to be up for discussion, so they were able to vote. At the time there was still a bit of democracy, so they would say who had the authority for whatever and then his hand went up . . .'

Judge: 'I understand . . . And then, obviously, the person who substituted for the *capo* always provided information on what had been decided in the *Commissione*.'

Mutolo: 'Yes, sir, he always reported everything that had been said in the *Commissione* . . . I took part in so many discussions during that time, before the *Commissione* met we talked about things in groups, so we knew all the pros and cons and . . . and then we did a count.'

Judge: 'You said that if a man of honour is to be killed it requires the *Commissione* to decide in plenary session . . .'

---

* Quotations from the questioning of the *pentito* Gaspare Mutolo in documents from the trial of Giuseppe Agrigento + 51, Palermo, 12 July 1997.

Mutolo: 'There was a time when for those decisions you also needed four *capimandamento*, but afterwards – after the death of Angelo Graziano – they needed everybody, unless all the *capimandamento* already knew. Whether or not they took part in the *Commissione* was another matter, but they all had to know.'

Judge: 'And were the *capimandamento* informed before or after the decision was taken, I mean those *capimandamento* who weren't present for the debate?'

Mutolo: 'Always before. And they had a right of opposition. But a rule had been put about that the friends of Totò Riina were never to be touched because he defended them.'

'He's the dictator of everything and for everything'*

Giovanni Brusca

'So when I'm handed over to Totò Riina I'm told specifically: "From this moment onwards you will be at the disposal of Totò Riina without having to ask me what he asks you to do and not to do." That's what Father Bernardo said to me. So it's true that then, when I go and do the murder of Colonel Giuseppe Russo, I didn't go to my father, who was the *capomandamento* of San Giuseppe Jato, to explain to him: "You know, I've got to go and murder Colonel Russo." Salvatore Riina asked me to put myself at his disposal and I immediately made myself available. I presented my father with a *fait accompli*.

'After the Mafia war it was for reasons of secrecy, of prudence, of strategy, that they stopped doing the extended commissions as they had once done, everyone sitting around a table and deciding case by case. So I know from personal experience that I was told one thing, and someone else was told another thing . . . But actually sitting together around a table – I've never seen a *Commissione* do that. They'd changed the ways of doing things. The rules themselves hadn't changed, because Cosa Nostra lives on rules, but the more important the deed, the more restricted it was, so the systems changed.

* Files from the trial of Giuseppe Agrigento + 51, ruling of the Court of Assizes, Palermo, 12 July 1997.

'Say, for example, I go to kill Ignazio Salvo and I go to a *mandamento* that isn't mine – so under Cosa Nostra rules I shouldn't be going there – I go to the *mandamento* of Villabate, which is Bagheria, where Ignazio Salvo was killed . . . and I go to kill a man from another province and another *mandamento*, because Ignazio Salvo is part of the *mandamento* of Salemi . . . so before committing this murder I say to Salvatore Riina, "Can I do it or not?" Riina says to me, "Just go ahead and there won't be any problems." I do the murder and I'm not chased out of the milieu of Cosa Nostra, because I was protected by Salvatore Riina . . . and this was a fact, I think, that was now under everyone's eyes.

'When Maurizio Costanzo said on television that lots of men of honour had enjoyed the benefits of hospital arrests . . . I go to Salvatore Riina and I say to him, "Why don't we break this guy's balls?" So it's me, a *capomandamento*, who goes to Salvatore Riina, so he already knows that I've agreed to go ahead, that is, he already knows that I've agreed to carry out the massacres. And like me, all the other *capimandamento* went to Salvatore Riina and said, "Why don't we do this, why don't we do that?" That's how Salvatore Riina, without needing to hold a *Commissione*, knows people's moods. He knows who's with him and who isn't. Salvatore is the dictator of everything and for everything.

'In that time everything had to take place in a sealed compartment, it all had to be very constricted, we were at war, we had enemies. We couldn't just turn up at a meeting and say, "sorry, we're going to kill you" . . . In times of war everything was permitted . . . That is, in times of war it had been decreed that everyone who was against the winning group, against the Corleonese groups, was to be eliminated.'

There were fifteen deputies and fifteen senators in the first Parliamentary Commission into 'the Mafia phenomenon in Sicily'. It was set up on 20 December 1962 by law 1720 'to examine its genesis and characteristics, to propose the measures necessary and suppress its manifestations and eliminate its causes'. It was a reaction to a sense of Italian public opinion about events in Palermo, the Greco and La Barbera families killing each other in the streets of the city, shoot-outs in crowded areas, building-sites being blown up every night.

The work went on for thirteen years. Between 1968 and 1974, under President Francesco Cattanei, the Anti-Mafia Commission conducted 'deep-level investigations' into the communal administration of Palermo, into wholesale markets, and into Luciano Leggio.

'Your honour, if the Anti-Mafia exists . . .'

Luciano Leggio

For a long time nobody talked about it. The word was annoying, disturbing, irritating. 'Literature, it's all just literature of the worst kind; it's all inventions of Northern newspapers,' the most famous Sicilian criminal lawyers said scornfully. At the start of the year, the word vanished from the reports of the attorneys general.

The mayor of Palermo, Franco Spagnolo, who would later be succeeded by Vito Ciancimino, was unconvinced: 'The goal of the Anti-Mafia Commission is to discover that the Mafia doesn't exist.' Another mayor, Giuseppe Sinesio, first citizen of Porto Empedocle and under-secretary of state, candidly admitted, 'Here, in my village and the villages close to Agrigento, there's nothing but smuggling-related crime.' In Agrigento – this was in 1986 – no Mafia trial had been held in forty-two years. The last one dated back to the end of Fascism.

Mafia. What is it? 'To me it sounds like a brand of cheese,' replied Gerlando Alberti, known as *ù paccarré*, 'the imperturbable one', man of honour of the Danisinni family.

Mafia. What is it? 'As far as I know it's a brand of detergent,' replied His Eminence Cardinal Ernesto Ruffini, Archbishop of Palermo.

Mafia. What is it? 'A phenomenon dreamed up by the press to sell papers,' said Ninetta Bagarella, wife of the fugitive Salvatore Riina.

But one day the boss Luciano Leggio was invited to give a statement to the Parliamentary Anti-Mafia Commission. The president asked him, 'Signor Leggio, in your opinion, does the Mafia exist?'

And Leggio replied: 'Your honour, if the Anti-Mafia exists . . .'

Almost a quarter of a century went by. It's 1999. In a television studio, Michele Santoro is under the lights. He turns round to his guest and asks, 'Senator, does the Mafia exist?'

'I will reply with a phrase from Luciano Leggio: if the Anti-Mafia exists, then the Mafia exists too . . .'

The interviewee was Marcello Dell'Utri, a Sicilian and Forza Italia senator on trial in Palermo. There would be 200 hearings before the trial was over. On 11 December 2004 Marcello Dell'Utri would be condemned to nine years' imprisonment for collusion with the Mafia, though this is pending appeal.

Mafia and Anti-Mafia. Either it's never talked about at all or it's talked about too much. Outstanding crimes and invisible instigators. So many murders, no witnesses. Everything is Mafia or nothing is Mafia.

'Viva la Mafia, viva Ciancimino'

The construction workers of Palermo

He's been the mayor of Palermo for eleven days, a boss for thirty years.

'Viva la Mafia, viva Ciancimino,' cried the construction workers processing around the City Hall in 1984 when the former mayor Don Vito Ciancimino was interned in a little village in Abruzzo. 'You can't eat with Anti-Mafia', the demonstrators wrote in white-wash on the walls of Via Maqueda, as they demanded the return of the most sinister of the Christian Democrat bosses on the island.

The barber's son from Corleone came to the city without a cent. He went into politics and won his first contract: 'Transport of railway cars back to base on trolleys'. In 1953 he was elected to the provincial committee of the Christian Democrats; in 1954 he was made communal commissioner; in 1956 he was elected councillor to the villages and farms; in 1958 he hit the jackpot: councillor of Public Works with Mayor Salvo Lima.

Then, in a single night, 3,011 licences were released to just five contractors. The city turned its back on the sea, building went on everywhere. This was the 'sack' of Palermo.

'This man is dangerous,' read the headline on *L'Ora*, the campaigning Sicilian newspaper. He was already extremely wealthy in the early 1970s. Colonel Carlo Alberto dalla Chiesa, commander of the Legion of Carbinieri in Palermo, always had a dossier on Don Vito on his desk. The first Parliamentary Anti-Mafia Commission had a weighty file dedicated to him. The former mayor sued everyone, even the chief of police, Angelo Vicari.

He clung on in the Christian Democratic Party until 1983, when the national secretary Ciriaco De Mita imposed 'renewal' in Sicily. Everyone abandoned Don Vito – including Lima. He officially left the Christian Democrats, but remained in command. He controlled votes, factions, council decisions. He always received the local councillors in Via Sciuti: at his house. The *pentito* Tommaso Buscetta told Falcone, 'Ciancimino is in the hands of the Corleonesi.' One of his men is in the Urban Planning Department. He is blind. Engineers present billion-lire projects to the City Council in Braille.

Don Vito's first arrest comes in 1984. Then the obligatory residence. The second arrest is in 1989. Sentenced to thirteen years for Mafia association. In 1993 Vito Calogero Ciancimino is declared bankrupt.

After the murders in Capaci and Via D'Amelio he announces that he wants to 'talk'. He says things and he says nothing, he warns, he blackmails, he spreads poison. He plots and deals with two representatives of the Secret Services. His tip-off might also have played a part in the mysterious capture of Totò Riina.

He dies leaving a vast fortune that has never been fully accounted for. So far the investigators have found yachts, luxury flats, Ferraris. And current accounts. And companies. In Spain, in Romania, in Kazakhstan, in Russia.

Yet his youngest son, Massimo (a convicted money-launderer), recalls: 'The only thing my father passed on to me is correctness, which, in my view, is the key to everything. It is the key to life, not just to the world of business: keeping your promises and always being correct.'

'OK, call it Mafia, because that suits everybody'*

Vito Ciancimino

The former mayor of Palermo explains his view of the Mafia. When he died in 2002 a large portion of his fortune, an estimated 60 million euros, was still missing.

'What does it mean, opting out? I don't really even believe in "repenting", because repentance is a divine matter, not something men do for money. And besides, the murders were ordered by the guys at the top. Very high up in the state, not the Mafia.

'You have to see what the Mafia is. If it's identified with the crimes that have taken place, it's a problem of statistics, and of murders. As far as I'm concerned the Mafia is identified with arrogance, the Mafia is a mentality. It's an individual who acts arrogantly and forces someone else to do something that it isn't right, whether he be a politician, or a magistrate, or a Mafioso. And I'm not a person to accept arrogance from anyone, or to be arrogant myself.

'The Mafia is skilful. In 1961, when the city plan† got underway, I received threatening phonecalls, which I dismissed as unimportant. I'm not in the habit of being scared. Then I got a threatening

* Interview with the former mayor of Palermo Vito Ciancimino by Massimo Martinelli in *Il Messaggero*, 9 June 2000.

† After the Second World War there was a huge building boom in Palermo. By the 1960s this was almost entirely under Mafia control.

letter that I sent to the police – if I'd been a Mafioso I wouldn't have done that. To my knowledge there is no relationship between the Mafia and politics . . . I am certain that the Mafia doesn't coerce politicians. I should become a politician myself. In the five years in which I've been councillor, I haven't had pressure from anyone.

'The Mafia hasn't existed since 1958. It came to an end that year, with the murder of my fellow Corleonese citizen Dr Michele Navarra. Because that day, along with Dr Navarra, they killed another young doctor, whose wife was pregnant. So that day these so-called Mafiosi killed a poor wretch of an informer. From that moment everything was over. Because the Mafia, my father always told me this, had rules of justice and correctness that it respected and made sure others respected. Of course, the Mafia couldn't put anyone in jail, so when someone made a mistake they killed him. But just him.

'Today everything's changed. They're dealing in cocaine, they're in control of the building trade, they're demanding protection money – and that's Mafia? It's just ordinary criminality. OK, call it Mafia, because that suits everybody. The journalists, the politicians, it suits the judiciary. Because that way, if they're dealing with these matters, it's more prestigious. The truth is that the Anti-Mafia Commission should change its name and call itself the Anti-Crime Commission.

'For many years I was a witness and minor protagonist in a certain political context, but I'm at the disposal of this Commission if they're willing to listen to me. The Lima crime* can't be dismissed with simplistic hypotheses concerning the motive. I'm convinced that it's part of a bigger design, a design that might explain other things, lots of other things. Individual elements of the state have used this crime to engage in murders. Ones which are, in my view, connected by a single thread: Salvo Lima, Giovanni

* The 1992 murder of the politician Salvo Lima.

Falcone, Paolo Borsellino . . . They were ordered by political organizations. That's at the root of it all, because they had to block the election of Andreotti to the presidency of the Republic . . .

'In Italy 85 per cent of people evade tax, I'm not part of the 15 per cent. They've never found the rest of the money, and I'm not telling you where it is or they'll confiscate it.'

'He was more dangerous as a spiteful pensioner than as a prefect with special powers'*

Salvo Lima to Vito Ciancimino

'Even before the murder of Pio La Torre, in April 1982, the newspapers were still talking about the *carabinieri* general Carlo Alberto dalla Chiesa, the prefect of Palermo. The general's arrival in Sicily had been accompanied by controversies, not least in the press. Over matters of protocol he managed to make an enemy even of the mayor of Palermo, Nello Martellucci. In the end he found himself completely isolated.

'In the eyes of everyone – politicians, senior and junior magistrates, bankers – you could read the terror that General dalla Chiesa created . . . wanting to find the Mafia everywhere, while the Mafia isn't everywhere . . . finding bribes, while bribes are in fact everywhere. There was a genuine collective psychosis in Palermo. All this was going on, while in Rome . . . even the stones knew that in Rome they didn't want to give General dalla Chiesa special powers.

'The general was so isolated that in Sicily we were all expecting him to be forced to resign. [People were saying] they had heard from Spadolini that the general wouldn't have special powers because everyone was against him. When the prefect was killed, it was immediately said that it was the Mafia. After some time I met Salvo Lima; the tax-collector Nino Salvo was there as well. We

---

* Questioning of Vito Ciancimino on 17 March and 11 June 1993 from the files of trial no. 3538/94, 'brought against Andreotti Giulio'.

talked specifically about the general. I said, "But if he was finished on every level, and even the stones knew, why kill him?" Salvo Lima, his eyes red with hatred and losing his natural reserve, replied: "For some people in Rome he was more dangerous as a spiteful pensioner than as a prefect with special powers." Then Lima added, "It'll be us who get fucked over" – meaning Sicilians – "and who knows how long for." Next to him was Nino Salvo, who nodded in agreement. His face was contorted too.

'At first, we used to go and see Salvo Lima at his house for lunch every Sunday. But then my visits to Salvo Lima and my meetings and contacts with the Salvo cousins became more frequent. Now, I've never asked the Salvo cousins if they knew Giulio Andreotti or they didn't. For the simple reason that, by listening to what they said, I had ruled out the idea that the Salvo cousins knew Andreotti.

'Be that as it may, I once saw Giulio Andreotti with Nino Salvo . . . Nino Salvo was paying for lunch at the Hotel Zagarella and, when Giulio Andreotti came into the restaurant, he and Nino Salvo greeted one another like two old friends and started talking to each other. There was a vigorous handshake and then they started to have a conversation. I was sitting at the table next to Andreotti's. Nino Salvo flew from one table to another and exchanged words with more or less everybody. Of the regional presidents who died later, I remember that Salvo Lima was there, and the MP Rosario Nicoletti.'

The members of Cosa Nostra, according to the police survey of autumn 2007: 5,113 men of honour and 181 families. The stronghold is Palermo: 3,201 men of honour and 89 families. The largest numbers are in the district of Brancaccio: 203 members. The smallest families are those in the village of Santa Rosalia, with 3 men of honour, and the Vucciria with 2. The record for Mafia density in the province of Palermo is San Giuseppe Jato – the village of Giovanni Brusca and Balduccio Di Maggio – with 174 Mafiosi on police file. After Palermo, the highest number of men of honour is in the Trapani region: 982 distributed among 20 families. In the area around Agrigento, there are 41 families and 461 Mafiosi; in Caltanissetta, 17 and 272 Mafiosi. In eastern Sicily, Catania has 135 Mafiosi and 5 families; Enna, 40 Mafiosi and 6 families; Messina, 19 Mafiosi and 2 families. Finally Syracuse with 3 men of honour, all in one family. Of the nine Sicilian provinces, only Ragusa has no Cosa Nostra based in its territory.

Famiglie, decine, mandamenti, cupole. *Mafioso behaviour is passed on from generation to generation.*

'The Mafia . . . was love'

Francesco Di Cristina

The village lies in the middle of hollow-bellied hills, scarred by pigeons, criss-crossed by rusty railway-lines. Riesi is surrounded by sulphur mines, *pirrere* in Sicilian. It's almost halfway between Caltanissetta and the stormy sea of Falconaro, resting on harsh land that produces an ink-coloured wine. The village consists of peasants and sulphur-miners. And Mafiosi. The most important is Francesco Di Cristina, the one who managed to defeat the Tofalos and the Carlinos, a gang of bandits, highwaymen who terrorized the interior of Sicily. He re-established order and guaranteed public safety from the Salso Valley to the Besaro Valley. The local inhabitants saw him as a benefactor. After the war, he became the ruler of Riesi.

Time passes and Don Ciccio Di Cristina is almost seventy and very ill. He realizes that it is time to appoint a successor.

As happens every year in Riesi, on the second Sunday in September the plaster statue of the Madonna of the Chain leaves the Chiesa Matrice. The strongest men carry her on their shoulders, the statue wobbles its way along the streets of the village. The procession passes through the square for the first time, moves down towards the cemetery, comes back up, passes through the square for a second time and then suddenly stops below a balcony.

Old Francesco Di Cristina appears, unsteady on his feet. He turns round, his movements are slow, his voice a breath. 'Now you can come,' he commands. And now Giuseppe, one of his four sons, comes forward to stand beside him. He looks him in the eyes, hugs him, kisses him on the cheeks, witnessed by the crowd in the procession of the Madonna of the Chain, the village's patron saint. It's a coronation. Giuseppe Di Cristina, in 1960, becomes the new *capomafia* of Riesi.

He marries Antonina Di Legami, the prettiest girl in the village. He finds a job, as a bank-clerk at the Cassa di Risparmio. But when his name is listed in the archives where they keep the files marked 'M' for Mafia, he has to leave the bank. He is taken on by So.chimi. si, the Sicilian Chemical Society, one of many money-losing operations in the region. They call him '*il boss dal colletto bianco*' – literally, 'the white-collar boss'. He knows everyone, in the high plains of politics. One of his acquaintances is Aristide Gunnella, the 'king' of the republicans of Palermo who will a few years later be a minister of the Republic. Another is Graziano Verzotto, a Christian Democrat senator who will a few years later be a fugitive in Paris.

In the Sicilian Cosa Nostra, Giuseppe Di Cristina is *inteso* – he is listened to and respected. He has close emotional ties to Stefano Bontate, the son of Don Paolino of the Palermo suburb of Santa Maria del Gesù. He is like a brother to Pippo Calderone, the representative of Cosa Nostra in Catania, and also the head of the *Regionale*, the Commission of the nine provinces of the island. They are all men of honour of the old guard. They embody the pure Mafia tradition.

When Don Ciccio dies, the whole village turns out to bid him farewell. Giuseppe Di Cristina has thousands of funereal images of saints distributed. On one side is the image of his beloved father. On the other the statement: 'I will demonstrate with words and works that the Mafia was not criminality but respect for the law of honour, defence of all rights, nobility of mind: it was love.'

'He shoots like a god but has the brain of a chicken'*

Giuseppe Di Cristina

The meeting is in a cottage three kilometres from Riesi, on the road that climbs towards Mazzarino. The *carabinieri* captain Alfio Pettinato listens in the darkness, sitting on a tree-trunk. He is stunned. The man in front of him is revealing all the secrets of Cosa Nostra. He starts with an important murder: 'I know who killed Colonel Giuseppe Russo, I always held him in high esteem even though he pursued me tirelessly.' The man speaking is not just any old informer, he is Giuseppe Di Cristina, the head of the Riesi family, one of the most powerful Mafiosi in Sicily.

He tells Pettinato that he is frightened: 'You've got to stop them, you don't know them, but you've got to stop them, they're dangerous to me but above all they're dangerous to you.' Giuseppe Di Cristiana is agitated, he's like a hunted animal. His memories trip over each other, he comes out with one name after another.

'It was two wild beasts who killed the Colonel: Totò Riina and Bernardo Provenzano. They had already tried to whack him at a meeting in Palermo, but Tano Badalamenti and Saro Di Maggio said no. But they killed him anyway. They've already killed about eighty men – they're crazy, they've got it into their heads to declare war on the state.'

---

* Declarations made by the known Mafioso Di Cristina Giuseppe recorded in Judicial report no. 2734/116-1977 concerning the Palermo Police report against Riina Salvatore + 25 .

The Riesi boss doesn't feel like a *muffutu*, a spy. For a long time he's been trying in every way to convince the *Commissione* of the threat constituted by the Corleonesi. But the others pay him no heed, they pretend not to see; the Palermitani make fun of him, they think he's consumed with envy and paranoia.

Giuseppe Di Cristina couldn't find peace. He talked to Stefano Bontate. He talked to Salvatore Inzerillo. He talked to Tano Badalamenti, perhaps the wisest man in the whole of Cosa Nostra. And now he's talking to Captain Alfio Pettinato, the commander of the *carabinieri* unit in Gela.

He repeats, in the cottage: 'They're two bloodthirsty monsters. Salvatore Riina is called Shorty, the other one, Bernardo Provenzano, is known as the Tractor. Luciano Leggio says he shoots like a god but has the brain of a chicken . . .'

During that spring of 1978 Shorty and the Tractor are in hiding. Totò Riina has been for nine years, Bernardo Provenzano for fifteen. They're in hiding at home, in Corleone. But no one is looking for them. And no one imagines that the two of them are almost at the top of the Cosa Nostra pyramid. And that they're unleashing a big Mafia war.

Giuseppe Di Cristina also tells the captain about the men who are protecting them: 'You've got to follow Bernardo Brusca of San Giuseppe Jato, Giuseppe Giacomo Gambino of Resuttana, Nenè Geraci of Partinico, Mariano Agate of Mazara del Vallo . . .' Before leaving the cottage he warns: 'The Corleonesi want to kill Terranova, too.'

Cesare Terranova, judge and independent deputy of the elected chamber, is on the Italian Communist Party list and a member of the Parliamentary Anti-Mafia Commission. He is about to return to Palermo as an investigating magistrate. As soon as he gets back he is killed.

Giuseppe Di Cristina doesn't witness the killing he has foretold. He dies before that can happen, shot down on a street in

Palermo on 30 May 1978. Thirty days had passed since his meeting with the captain. His 'singsong' leads to a report signed by Major Antonino Subranni, the commander of the operations department of the *carabinieri* in Palermo. It's the first official document about the two Mafia 'parties' confronting one another in Cosa Nostra. It's the discovery of the Corleonesi.

'Where is this Mafia, these days?'*

Angela Russo, known as Nonna Eroina ('Granny Heroin')

She struggles up the hill, dragging her feet, bent-backed and aching. Arthritis, diabetes, cholesterol. She's small and slender, always dressed in black. She's nearly eighty years old. There are sixty-five accused, and she's the oldest of them. Since the trial began she hasn't seen her son Salvino. And she doesn't want to see him, either: 'He's crazy, completely crazy. He got meningitis when he was four, and the doctor told me he would always be sick in the head, that he'd never be quite right again. He's even enough of a skunk to send his own mother to jail.'

The woman is in the dock, accused of drug-smuggling. Salvino admits that his mother is a drug-smuggler. His mother is Angela Russo, 'Nonna Eroina' in the newspaper headlines.

She gets to her feet and addresses the judge: 'I've forgiven Salvino, but I don't know if God will ever be able to forgive him. They say he'll be out in a year, and he knows he's been condemned – he knows that if he gets out they'll kill him, they'll never forgive him . . . He hopes he will have the time to avenge his brother Mario, who was killed because of him. But what does he think he can do? First we had to think of Mario. Now when Salvino comes out he'll die.'

---

* Speaking to Marina Pino in the 1988 book *Le Signore della droga* ('*The Drug Ladies*').

Nonna Eroina's outpouring opens the trial against 'the organizers of drug-trafficking'. Some are from the family of Villagrazia, others from the family of La Noce. Four men and four women are all related to each other, all from the Coniglio clan: they are the sons and nephews and sons-in-law of Angela Russo. Nonna Eroina is defending herself. And amidst her self-defence she is also accusing herself: 'So according to them I travel the length and breadth of Italy, transporting parcels and packages on behalf of other people. So, after always issuing orders to others throughout my whole life, I would have performed that service to order. Things that only these judges who know nothing of life and the law could imagine.'

The phone-taps nab everybody. For two years the couriers have been transporting drugs from Sicily to Milan, from Naples to Sassari. They talk about 'golf sweaters' and 'Coca-Cola', about 'shirts', 'ducats', 'shit' and 'super-shit'. Then Salvino Coniglio, Angela's son, tells the rest. The sixty-five accused are done for: 350 years in jail.

In revenge the hitmen kill Mario, one of Nonna Eroina's sons. And then Salvatore Anzelmo, the one who drove Salvino around.

Nonna Eroina seems distraught with grief. But now she speaks every time she gets the chance.

She gives lessons in what it means to be a Mafioso: 'People go around saying Mafioso this, Mafioso that. Are they joking? It's reached the point where, if any little fool steals something or other, it immediately makes him "Mafioso". I didn't see any Mafiosi in that trial. Is that a serious way of talking about things? Where is this Mafia, these days? My father, Don Peppino, now he was a real man. The whole of Torrelunga and Brancaccio trembled with fear and respect for him, all the way to Bagheria.'

And: 'Certainly, yes, madam, I know what I'm talking about because the Mafia used to be there in Palermo in the old days, and so was the law. And that law didn't allow for the killing of innocent mothers' sons. The Mafia didn't kill anyone before they were absolutely sure of their ground, absolutely sure that this was what had to be done and that it was within the law. Of course, people who sinned were made to weep; if you made a mistake you paid for it.'

Angela Russo, aka Nonna Eroina, is sentenced to five years. Almost blind, she sits out her house arrest in an old working-class district on the outskirts of Palermo.

'The shame was too great'

Agata Di Filippo

The road passes through the middle of Lo Sperone, a cluster of houses, gates, terraces hidden by tarpaulins, aluminium verandas, satellite dishes. The sea is a hundred yards away, but you can't see it. The last vegetable gardens are below the mountain, which seems about to roll down, menacing and bare. The Di Filippi house is on Via Generale Albricci. The house of dishonour.

A family intrigue is the source of a major Palermo Mafia drama. Agata di Filippo is the sister of Emanuele and Pasquale, men of honour and *pentiti*. Agata is married to Antonino Marchese, who has a brother and a sister. His brother is Giuseppe Marchese, Totò Riina's driver. He too has turned state's evidence, in Pianosa. His sister is Vincenzina, the wife of Leoluca Bagarella, Uncle Totò's brother-in-law. These *bravi ragazzi* are dragging the Corleone bosses, the pure blood of the family, into disrepute.

On the night of 29 June 1995, Agata Di Filippo shuts herself away in a room. She opens a drawer beside the bed, takes out three packs of medicine and swallows everything she finds. Thirty-one pills.

'The shame was too great,' she whispers to her mother Marianna when she wakes up in hospital, after having her stomach pumped.

The mother comforts her daughter only for a few minutes; she's in a hurry to get away, she wants to tell the whole world what her feelings are. She calls the Roman desk of *Ansa*. She leaves only one message, simple and direct: 'My daughter Agata nearly died because of my two wretched sons. From today those bastards are no longer my sons; it's as if I'd never had them.' She throws down the receiver and calls the local journalists to her house. To repudiate 'publicly' Emanuele and Pasquale, her two boys, 'my former sons'. A *pupiata*, a staged 'puppet-show' in front of the whole of Palermo.

'He will reproach us, he will reproach us!' is the constant cry of Agata, as she discovers over the following days that she has another *pentito* in the family. His name is Giovanni Drago, he is her brother-in-law's brother-in-law. In a whisper she manages to say, 'I, my father and my mother dissociate ourselves completely from the decision taken by my two wretched brothers.' It's a women's tragedy, at Lo Sperone di Palermo.

Three blocks further on there are two other wives in a state of torment. 'It would have been much better if they had been killed,' Giusy Spadaro and Angela Marino wail; the first is married to Pasquale Di Filippo, the other to Emanuele. They both live in a high-rise the colour of sandpaper that looks like a monument to Mafia construction. It looks out over the sewer that is the estuary of the Oreto River. They run down the stairs and hurl themselves into the street. They too, Giusy and Angela, have to 'communicate' to the whole of Palermo that they are renouncing their husbands.

Their children sit in silence on a low wall. 'Our children are orphans; we've told them their fathers are dead, dead for ever,' says Giusy, the daughter of Don Masino, the king of the Kalsa, the great cigarette-smuggler who became the big heroin-trafficker.

There's only one woman left in Lo Sperone who doesn't cry, doesn't shriek, doesn't speak. That's Vincenzina. Vincenzina Marchese, who is no longer alive. Her husband, Leoluca Bagarella, has buried her in a secret place.

'We're on the outskirts of Mafiopolis'*

Giuseppe Impastato, known as Peppino

'At around 12.30 a.m. on 9 May 1978, a person provisionally identified as one Giuseppe Impastato arrived aboard his own Fiat 850 at the 30+180km spot† on the Trapani–Palermo railway to place an explosive device there, which detonated, blowing him to pieces . . .'

The police carbon copy closes the case at 9.00 on that same morning of 9 May 1978, the day when the body of Aldo Moro‡ is found in the red Renault on Via Caetani. A rigged investigation from the outset. A botched assassination attempt. Guiseppe 'Peppino' Impastato, thirty years old, son of a man of honour of the family of Gaetano Badalamenti, a far-left activist, journalist on a free radio channel in Cinisi, was *suicidato*§ by Cosa Nostra. It was an inevitable death. For the 'order' that reigned in a little village in Sicily in the late 1970s.

The bomb-disposal expert, Salvatore Longhitano, ascertains

---

* The record of the Impastato murder and quotations from his radio show are taken from the files of the Sicilian Documentation Centre, which fought for years to prove that Impastato was killed by the Mafia.

† A point on the Trapani-Messina railway line on the outskirts of Palermo, 30km outside Trapani, with 180km to go before Messina.

‡ A former Christian Democrat prime minister, kidnapped by the left-wing Red Brigades and killed after fifty-five days in captivity.

§ Murdered so as to look like a suicide.

'that the explosion was probably caused by quarry explosives'. Yet over the days following the young man's death, the *carabinieri* didn't search a single quarry in the hills around Cinisi. Only Peppino's house was turned upside down.

The village gravedigger, Giuseppe Liborio Briguglio, gives the investigators a rock that he has found in a cottage near the railway line. It is stained with blood. In the first inspection record there is no trace of it.

On 30 May the *carabinieri* present their report to the Public Prosecutor's Office in Palermo. They write: 'Even if we were to presume that a crime had been committed, we would have to rule out the idea that Giuseppe Impastato was killed by the Mafia.'

There's a link between some civil servants within the state apparatus and former heads of Cosa Nostra. 'Information' is swapped, favours are done. This is the Sicily inherited from the landing of the Americans.

Gaetano Badalementi is a friend of his father Luigi, one of the most important Mafiosi on the island. He has stalls full of cattle and strongboxes full of money. Peppino calls him 'Tano Seduto' ('Sitting Tano'). From the microphones of Radio Aut he mocks him, ridicules him in front of everybody. His broadcast is called *Onda Pazza* ('Crazy Waves'): 'We're on the outskirts of Mafiopolis. The buildings commission has met. On the agenda is the approval of Project Z 11. The great *capo* Tano Seduto will be circling the square like a sparrowhawk.'

Drugs. Punta Raisi airport lies behind Cinisi, his territory. A Boeing sets off every week. For the Palermitani it's *Il Padrino,* the Godfather: the direct flight from Palermo to New York.

For many months Luigi Impastato was given a talking-to; it was suggested that he keep an eye on that no-good, disrespectful son of his. But Peppino is a rebel: 'Tano Seduto . . . Tano Seduto . . .'

Luigi threw him out of the house, then left Cinisi for New Orleans. He died in a traffic accident in September 1977.

After ten years the inquest into the 'assassination' became an inquest into 'murder by persons unknown', but no charges were brought. Another ten years passed before the magistrates reopened investigations, at the request of Peppino's mother Felicia and his old friends. In February 1996 the public prosecutor Caselli takes the bundle of papers out of the archives. On 20 March 1997 Badalamenti is formally accused of having ordered the crime. The trial for the killing of Peppino Impastato begins on 10 March 1999. On 11 April 2002 Gaetano Badalamenti is sentenced to life imprisonment for the murder of the boy from Cinisi. It is the following century before justice is done.

'He got himself killed because he couldn't bear all this'

Felicia Bartolotta Impastato

'Yes, I talked to him. I told him, "Giuseppe, look, I'm against the Mafia too. Can't you see that your father's the same? Be careful, son." My husband understood that I agreed with my son. They threatened my husband and my husband threatened me, me directly. Otherwise he was calmer, because he could see his son's honesty, he could see that some people were speaking highly of him. But when the Mafia got involved . . . when the elections began, he said, "Tell your son not to go talking about the Mafia."

'He told his father straight to his face. He said, "They disgust me, they appal me, I can't bear them." And he said to me, "I can't bear them, no. All the injustice, they're abusive, they take advantage of everybody, they're in charge at the Council" . . . He couldn't bear them, absolutely not. He got himself killed because he couldn't bear all this. Yes, because the more they stood up to him, the more determined he got. You know, when you slap a child and he gets angry . . . If his father had handled it better and told the Mafiosi, "Mind your own business, I'll sort out my son myself," things would never have got to this point. With my son they were able to get on with the business of killing him undisturbed, because his father threw him out . . .

'I understood why he'd left straight away. But I didn't know he was in America. I said to him, "Where are you going?" . . . He said, 'I'm going because I can't stay in Cinisi. Then I'll come back, when they change their minds, otherwise I won't come, I'll sell all these things . . ." He said, "I can't stay in this house any longer. The shame of it!" But what shame? It's not as if your sons have stolen from you, it's not as if they've killed, it's not as if they've taken up with loose women. So where's the shame? He says, "I can't stay here, I've got to go." But he didn't tell us where he was going, he didn't say that, though the Mafiosi and his brother knew . . . I imagined there'd been a meeting, because his brother took him to see the Mafiosi. My niece Maria had seen him: "Peppino Sputafuoco took him to see Don Vito." So it was the Mafiosi . . .

'Talking about Badalamenti, my husband . . . said he was a valued young man. Once he said to me, "You know in the end Badalamenti said he'd got rid of *lu criaturi.** When they held the trial of the 114." I said, "He got rid of him?" My sister-in-law was there, the American, and she asked him, "So where's he going?" "To Cinisi." "What business has he got in Cinisi? He has apartments in Palermo, what's he going to do here?" As soon as they told me that Badalamenti was coming back here, for me it was as if . . . everything collapsed on top of me. I said, "This is where the troubles start." Because my son really couldn't bear to look at Badalamenti. He was the boss of Cinisi, so they wanted his decision. Because if anything was ever done without him, he went and ripped their heads off. So it all needed orders from above. Simple as that. My son was an irritation to him . . . They have meetings. He says, "This guy needs killing, this one doesn't. This stuff needs stealing." That's their way of thinking . . .

'That was really right at the end, because Giuseppe made a flyer that said Badalamenti was "an expert in white shotgun" . . . They called him in: "Look what he's done." That was it. *Ù malu mangiare.*† How I got through it I don't know. It was hell.'

---

* 'The kid'.

† Literally 'bad food'.

THE STATE

THE COMMISSIONE, 1992

Capo: Salvatore Riina
Capimandamento:
Francesco Madonia (Resuttana-San Lorenzo family), in prison
Francesco Di Trapani, his free deputy
Bernardo Brusca (San Giuseppe Jato family), in prison
Giovanni Brusca, his free deputy
Antonino Rotolo (Pagliarelli family)
Salvatore Buscemi (Boccadifalco family)
Pietro Aglieri (Santa Maria del Gesù family)
Giuseppe Giacomo Gambino (Partanna Mondello family), in prison
Mariano Troia, his free deputy
Giuseppe Calò (Porta Nuova family), in prison
Salvatore Cancemi, his free deputy
Giuseppe Lucchese (Brancaccio family), in prison
Giuseppe Graviano, his free deputy
Salvatore Montalto (Villabate family), in prison
Giuseppe Montalto, his free deputy
Nenè Geraci, 'the young one' (Partinico family)
Procopio Di Maggio (Cinisi family), in prison
Vito Palazzolo, his free deputy
Francesco Intile (Caccamo family)
Giuseppe Bono (Bolognetta family)

Some go with it, some don't go with it, some die.

Pietro Scaglione, chief public prosecutor of Palermo. The Corleonesi shot him on 5 May 1971. Scaglione is the first magistrate to be killed in Italy after the war.

Cesare Terranova, examining magistrate in Palermo. Totò Riina issued the order for his killing on 25 September 1979.

Gaetano Costa, chief public prosecutor of Palermo. The Inzerillo family of Passo di Rigano killed him on 6 August 1980.

Gian Giacomo Montalto, deputy public prosecutor of Trapani. Alone in investigating Cosa Nostra in the province of Trapani. He is shot down on 25 January 1983.

Rocco Chinnici, examining magistrate in Palermo. Blown up by a car bomb on 29 July 1983. The Corleonesi again.

Alberto Giacomelli, sectional president of the Court of Appeal in Palermo. Finds the killers of a carabinieri *captain guilty, and Totò Riina in turn finds him guilty. He dies on 25 September 1988.*

Rosario Livatino, deputy public prosecutor in Agrigento. The Mafia in Palma di Montechiaro orders his murder on 21 September 1990.

Giovanni Falcone and Francesca Morvillo, 23 May 1992.

Paolo Borsellino, 19 July 1992.

'They fired sixty-three shots into my back, but I'm sure it was by mistake'*

Stefano Giaconia

Not so much a Court of Assizes as a *cour des miracles*. Defendants are leaving prison in droves, all acquitted. Not a single guilty verdict for the accusations of homicide, only a few soft sentences for criminal association. It's the run-up to Christmas 1968 – 22 December – and the trial of the Palermitan Mafia ends with toasts and celebrations of the sentence. They're held in Catanzaro, in Calabria, on the grounds of 'legitimate suspicion':† too much local influence, too much fear, are driving the debate outside of Sicily. Everyone calls it 'the Trial of the 114', while in the official files it refers to 117 names: La Barbera Angelo + 116.

In the dock are the Bontate, Chiaracane, Mazara and Nicoletti families, the Salamones and the Gnoffos, the Manzellas, the Di Peris, the Torrettas. There's also Tommaso Buscetta. They're on trial for the murders of the early 1970s, the car bombs going off in streets and gardens, Palermo's first big Mafia war.

The capital of the island is both a big building site and a battlefield. Cranes turning in the sky, and assassinations. Reinforced concrete, ambushes, art nouveau villas blown up with dynamite, building licences signed in the middle of the night. And shootings.

---

* Record from the questioning of the Mafioso Stefano Giaconia at the trial of La Barbera Angelo + 116, 19 December 1967.

† *Legitima suspicione*: the idea that a local court will not be able to provide a fair hearing.

The most spectacular of these, in the middle of the crowd, is the one at the Impero fish shop on Via Empedocle Restivo, among the high-rises of the new city. It's 19 April 1963 when three hitmen, having got out of a cream-coloured Fiat 600, discharged their machine-guns and shotguns at about twenty men. Some of them are inside the fish shop, others in the doorway checking out the sea-bass and bream. They all flee. So does Stefano Giaconia, the owner of the Impero fish shop and a Mafioso. He's a friend of Angelo La Barbera. He is struck by sixty-three bullets. He survives. He's one of the defendants in Catanzaro.

His hearing begins at 10.20 on Tuesday 19 December 1967, almost exactly a year before the acquittal verdict.

President: 'Why did you never apply for a licence for the revolver they found on you?'

Stefano Giaconia: 'I am thinking about it. I'll put in an application for the licence.'

President: 'How many bullets hit you?'

Giaconia: 'More than sixty, I'd have said sixty-three . . .'

President: 'Shotgun? Buckshot?'

Giaconia: 'I don't know.'

President: 'How many do you still have in your head?'

Giaconia: 'Two or three left in my skull.'

President: 'Listen, Giaconia, you must have had some suspicions about a shooting like that . . .'

Giaconia: 'I don't know any of those 114. It's true that they fired sixty-three shots into my back, but I'm sure it was by mistake.'

President: 'So who were the shots aimed at?'

Giaconia: 'There were lots of people . . .'

President: 'Were you afraid of being attacked?'

Giaconia: 'I never have fears of that kind.'

President: 'Have you ever bought an apartment from Angelo La Barbera?'

Giaconia: 'I want to be precise, Mr President: I personally haven't.'

President: 'Do you know Salvatore La Barbera?'

Giaconia: 'He might have been one of my customers at the fish shop.'

President: 'Why did you tell the examining magistrate you'd never met Antonino Sorci?'

Giaconia: 'I can't imagine. I took more than sixty shots. Perhaps I was betrayed by my state of health.'

'I've talked to the judge . . . That's the adjustment of a trial'*

Tommaso Buscetta

'What really bothers Cosa Nostra is not being able to keep the promises it made to the people who went to prison. The man of honour always goes to a secure unit. It's always been like that, at all times. He knows his family will be fine, that they'll never go hungry, and he knows that they'll do their very best to make sure that he gets out. There will never be a man of honour – excuse me – there had never been one until now – who has anything to fear on that score. He doesn't fear justice, because he feels very strong. Collaboration with non-Mafia people – we're always talking about Mafia, just Mafia, Mafia, Mafia – but there are other people who collaborate with them who aren't Mafiosi, and who are collaborating with them at a very high level.

'I have personally never bribed a judge, but trials have been adjusted in Palermo. Always. But if I was asked to give the names of those judges, I'd say I didn't know even if I did. As I've said already, *ù carbuni si nun tinci mascarìa.*† No, I can't talk about these things now. I'd be going to a place that's absolutely unthinkable. If it's hard enough establishing a relationship between two Mafiosi, imagine doing the same with a judge. Would

* Questioning of Tommaso Buscetta, Parliamentary Anti-Mafia Commission, Rome, 17 November 1992.

† 'If coal doesn't burn your hand, it stains it'.

I be crazy enough to set off down that path? For God's sake!

'What does "adjusting a trial" mean? It means: I've talked to the judge, I've talked to the public prosecutor's office, I've talked to the chief of police, I've talked to the witness, I've talked to the jury. That's the adjustment of a trial.

'The honourable Salvo Lima wasn't the only one people turned to to have trials adjusted, there were the other politicians too. And politicians who weren't elected in Sicily. Cosa Nostra gets involved with all trials concerning the men of honour, and at every level, not just the Court of Cassation.* Trials aren't only adjusted in Palermo or in Sicily, it happens outside, too. Especially in Calabria and around Naples. Obviously.

'There were even adjustments at the Maxi-Trial . . . but of course . . . they weren't just trivia . . . The Catanzaro trial ended up with nothing. They all went home. Even in the trial of the 114, which is something I know a thing or two about . . .'

* The court of last resort.

'No one says: I want money. Things just happen like that . . .'*

Antonino Calderone

The judiciary in Sicily according to Antonino Calderone, man of honour of the Catania family.

Juries: 'If there's a jury trial, you get hold of the list of where they are. If they come from a little village and maybe one of them is a schoolmistress, then that's pretty easy. You just need the *look* to put the wind up her. I remember one time there was this murder, a man had been gunned down in the province of Enna. We had a word with the jury and the trial was adjusted.'

Lawyers: 'You ask the lawyer: what's this judge like? And the lawyer tells you who might know him. We had this guy who earned his whole living by adjusting trials. As a boy he wanted to be a lawyer, but after a point he couldn't do it. All the low-lifes in Catania came to him, because he knew everything about the judges' lives, who they were related to, where you could get hold of them, all that . . . he went to see the president of the court, the associate judge. You can always find something.'

Public prosecutors: 'One of them helped us a lot, a state prosecutor in Catania. They'd proposed obligatory residence for me; they maintained that I'd enriched myself illegally. I didn't know him, but one of our lawyers told me he would have a word. He withdrew

---

* Questioning of Antonino Calderone, Parliamentary Anti-Mafia Commission, Rome, 11 November 1992.

the charges. After a few months, the judge told me he needed a favour. Near Catenanuova the Costanzo company was building the Catania–Palermo motorway, which abutted a property belonging to his wife. He asked us to deviate the road slightly to avoid doing him any damage. Of course the road was deviated, and the lane leading up to his land was sorted out as well . . .'

Stipendiary magistrates: 'I remember once in the Court of Appeal a friend of mine arranging a meeting with him. I asked him a favour for one of our affiliates and he did it. In return he wanted to have the marble floor cleaned at his house. It was stained. That was all he asked. He told me his wife had this problem, I told him a friend of mine did that kind of work. No one says: I want money. Things just happen like that . . .'

Judges and public prosecutors again: 'Two or three magistrates lived in a building, where they weren't paying rent. One of them – he's dead now – was the public prosecutor at a murder trial of a friend of ours. People were afraid of him. Our friend was acquitted, but it was feared that the public prosecutor would appeal. So I once went to his house to talk to him and he said, "Don't worry, the mice can eat it now." He had let the deadlines lapse, he had filed the case away. They gave those judges receipted invoices, which indicated that they'd paid. In reality no money ever went out.'

Clerks of court: 'After the assassination of General dalla Chiesa, none of us was arrested, because we already knew about the arrest warrants. There was a man called Zuccaro, who isn't a man of honour but who was close to us, who said he knew a judge's secretary who typed everything out. Then, when she went to buy eggs or chicken, they talked about when the judge was going to issue the warrants. Once he'd signed one against a cousin of mine. Even the fortune-teller knew it. This fortune-teller was the sister of the lover of a public prosecutor in Catania. He brought his work home and she read it. Then she told her sister. My wife went to that fortune-teller as well. And she made sure that things went well for me.'

'The jury was contacted for an "adjustment"'*

Francesco Marino Mannoia

'Paradoxically, then, we must conclude that this court's belief in guilt would have been less problematic, if not in fact certain, had the amount of evidence been smaller . . .'

These were the closing words of the closing statement in one of the most controversial sentences passed by the Sicilian magistracy over the past fifty years. It was the morning of 31 March 1983 and the first section of the Court of Assizes in Palermo acquitted, on the grounds of 'too much evidence', Giuseppe Madonia, Vincenzo Puccio and Armando Bonanno, the hitmen of three Palermitan families who, on the night of 4 May three years previously, had allegedly killed an officer of the *carabinieri*. Captain Emanuele Basile, commander of the Monreale unit.

The three killers emerge from a dark alleyway; the town is celebrating the feast of the Most Holy Crucifix: fireworks in the square, the procession of the *confrati*,† all dressed in white, through the streets of Monreale. The captain is walking towards his barracks, carrying his daughter, Barbara, who is four years old. His wife Silvana follows him at a distance of several metres. They fire. The captain staggers, Barbara slips to the ground in her father's blood.

---

* Record of the questioning of Francesco Marino Mannoia by deputy prosecutor Giovanni Falcone, November 1989.

† Literally: brothers. The members of a confraternity.

An hour later Giuseppe Madonia, Vincenzo Puccio and Armando Bonanno are arrested, seven kilometres from Monreale. Four witnesses identify them: 'They're the murderers.'

Yet the sentencing takes seventeen years. It is later claimed that the Cosa Nostra bosses *approach* judges and legal doctors, they *talk* to deputy prosecutors and examining magistrates, they terrorize juries. The first trial gets bogged down in an expert report ordered into a pair of stained trousers. For the plain-speaking Palermitans it is *la prova del fango*, 'the trial of mud'.

Then the trial ends with a noisy acquittal by the Court of Assizes, presided over by Salvatore Curti Giardini: 'too much evidence' against the hitmen. The day after the verdict they're sentenced to obligatory residence in Sardinia; a few hours later they're already in hiding. They are sentenced twice in the Court of Appeal. And twice the sentence is quashed by the Court of Cassation.

The three accused are always innocent, always fugitives. Between one committal to the Court of Cassation and the next, on the morning of 8 June 1988 the trial reaches another Court of Assizes. This is the fifth hearing of the captain's hitmen; the judge's name is Antonino Saetta. The trial is over after two weeks: the killers are sentenced to life imprisonment. And Judge Saetta is sentenced to death.

The *pentito* Frencesco Marino Mannoia recalls: 'The jury was contacted for an "adjustment", Vincenzo Puccio told me; we were in the same cell at the time. He told me there was a good chance of an acquittal . . . But when they were convicted, Puccio told me it was all down to the judge, the jury told us that Judge Saetta had imposed his own point of view.'

The grounds for judgement are deposited in the clerk of court's office on the morning of 16 September 1988. A week later, Judge Antonino Saetta is assassinated on the main road between Caltanissetta and Agrigento.

It will take another nine trials and another eight years for

Giuseppe Madonia, Vincenzo Puccio and Armando Bonanno to be sentenced at last. This is 'adjusted justice' in Sicily in the hands of Cosa Nostra.

'No door is ever closed'*

Leonardo Messina

The men of honour are all innocent. There's a market in Mafia trials between the 1960s and 1970s. Police investigations moulder away in the prosecutors' filing cabinets, preliminary proceedings seldom lead to a committal for trial, inquiries are postponed. And the hearings that do take place always end up with the same verdict: insufficient evidence.

The Mafiosi approach, discuss, adjust, invalidate the trials. They always get out of jail early. Verdicts are never definitive where men of honour are concerned. In Palermo and Trapani, in Caltanissetta and Agrigento, justice is in the hands of Cosa Nostra. There are hordes of deft advocates who defend them passionately; some are even advisers to the family. They buy and sell temporary freedoms, they negotiate house arrests, they bribe medical investigators. 'When decisions are made in chambers, the lawyers go in and out, no door is ever closed and there are always five or six lawyers. There's the *avvocato di corridoio,* who has to look on even if you haven't appointed him. And there's the *avvocato di controllo,* who tells you straight away if you made a mistake under questioning,' says Leonard Messina, a *pentito* from San Cataldo.

The *avvocati di corridoio* are the trusted lawyers of the state; the

---

* Questioning of Leonardo Messina, Parliamentary Anti-Mafia Commission, Rome, 4 December 1992.

avvocati di controllo are those of Cosa Nostra. Men of honour always want the certainty that they'll be acquitted sooner or later, whatever happens. Impunity is the supreme privilege of Cosa Nostra. Until the second half of the 1980s the Mafiosi are always out, always free. Leonardo Messina again: 'Every time a new magistrate arrives, an entrepreneur steps forward and sets about finding him a house, a garden, whatever he needs and wants. Some go with it, some don't. Some die, some stay alive and choose a middle way.'

The first move is to 'talk to' the magistrate. 'The politician or the Mafioso, the representative, goes straight to him . . . In a setting like ours, when the politician introduces himself, the important party is the Mafioso, not the politician. And then there's freemasonry, which is a meeting-point for everyone. It wasn't by chance that Michele Sindona came to hide in my village, San Cataldo, when he was on the run.'

That was how things were in Sicily until the start of the 1980s, until the first real investigations into Cosa Nostra. The sentence that acknowledges the 'existence' of the Mafia won't come until much later, however: on 30 January 1992. It's the ratification, the last word on the 'unique, pyramidal and apex-type criminal organization'. The verdict of the Court of Cassation on the Palermo Maxi-Trial. The final judgement of the preliminary inquiry made by Giovanni Falcone.

Spioni, muffuti, infamoni, tragediatori, confidenti di questura, cantanti, carabinieri a cavallo, ammalati di sbirritudine, indegni, scatascini, vomitini, lenti di panza. What they call pentiti* *in Palermo and Sicily.*

* Literally: 'spies', 'informers', 'mouldy ones', 'tragedians', 'police station confidants', 'singers', '*carabinieri* on horseback', 'coppitude sufferers', 'wretches', 'the lowest of the low', 'pukes', 'lazybones'.

'I hold the Noce family in my heart'*

Leonardo Vitale, known as Leuccio

Palermo's lunatic-in-chief is a melancholy boy. Extremely religious, obsessed by the memory of that white horse that his uncle Titta made him kill with a shot from his rifle in the countryside. Every night he dreams of the horse with its belly up and its legs covered in blood, and himself standing drenched in sweat in the middle of the olive trees, and he really wants to throw up but he can't, he can't show weakness. Uncle Titta wanted to know if Leuccio was brave, if one day he might become like himself: a man of honour. At the age of sixteen he shot the white horse, at seventeen he shot Vincenzo Mannino. At sunset, in the gloom of Via Tasca Lanza.

Then they take him to a cottage at the Uscibene farm, where lots of men are waiting for him around a table. There's Salvatore Inzerillo, there's Ciro Cuccia, there are Giuseppe Bologna and Domenico Calafiura. There's Uncle Titta, too. They prick his finger with a bitter-orange thorn and kiss him 'on the lips, no tongues'.

Leonardo Leuccio Vitale has been a Mafioso for three years. Just three years and he's already insane.

'This evening I plan to unburden my conscience of the things that have been tormenting me for a long time,' he tells Bruno Contrada, the head of the mobile unit. He gives himself up

* Record of spontaneous declarations delivered by the *pentito* Leonardo Vitale to the mobile unit of Palermo, 30 March 1973.

spontaneously to the police, climbs the stairs of the former monastery that houses the offices of the detectives and slips into the smoke-filled room at the end of the corridor. He starts talking.

Murders. Extortion. Kidnapping. At dawn the following day, the head of the mobile unit is holding in his hand the file for the whole of Palermo's Mafia. Thirteen sheets of paper full of names. At the end of his statement Leuccio remembers: 'I also know Riina from Corleone. I saw him at the meeting that was held at the Campfranco farm, organized by Raffaele Spina, Pippo Calò and Vincenzo Anselmo to decide which of the two families – Altarello or Noce – was to take the kickback from the Pilo company which was doing some work on the borders of the two villages in that zone . . . I thought it would be fairer to give something to our family from Altarello as well, but Riina said, "I hold the Noce family in my heart."'

In that spring of 1973 Totò Riina has been in hiding for four years. At this point everyone still thinks he's just a *viddano*, one of those 'peasants' who have unleashed an extremely bloody war in their village. Someone from Corleone, who matters only there.

Leuccio's confession comes unexpectedly: Totò Riina is already in command in Palermo, too. When he decides, the others lower their eyes and don't open their mouths.

Leonardo Vitale's statement is passed on to the public prosecutor. Someone puts it in a drawer. It stays there for months. Then a judge signs forty-eight arrest warrants. They are the names from when Leuccio spilled the beans.

His face ends up on the front page. They call him 'the neighbourhood Valachi', a *pentito* like Joe Valachi, who had made Brooklyn tremble in 1962. The Mafia lawyers say that the boy from Altarello di Baida 'is sick in the head'; reliable psychiatrists confirm his schizophrenia. Leuccia is locked up in the psychiatric prison of Barcellona Pozzo di Gotto. Straitjacket, ECT, drugs. He is treated like that for seven years. He is freed in 1984.

'Life played a trick on me, in the form of the illness that has poured in on me since childhood,' he writes in his diary. Every morning he goes and kneels in the little church of San Martino delle Scale. He prays that day too, on 2 December 1984. The hitmen come from Corleone. Everybody thinks Leuccio's mad. Everybody but one. Totò Riina.

They walk arm in arm . . . and they tell lies, the *pen-ti-ti*'*

Totò Riina

'Yes, I know Gaspare Mutolo; we were in jail together. He was a *ladruncolante* by day, he stole from all over the place. We were cell-mates, I'm not sure whether in '66 . . . we went outside, a walk, then I think the mother of that Mutolo if I'm not misremembering was in the asylum at the time, so she was a poor mad thing, and he was a poor devil too . . . Mutolo is the kind of person who, every time they arrest him, they catch him red-handed doing drugs. He's always doing drugs. *He's* a fantastic pharmacist, a fantastic grocer, that Gaspare Mutolo.

'If you see, Mr President, what someone says, what everybody says, it's a kind of photocopy of everyone else, Mr President. It's easy for the *pentiti* to accuse Salvatore Riina because that way they get more houses, more money, more villas, more *affluence.* And then Riina is in charge, and then Riina did this. I want to tell you, Mr President: they walk arm in arm, they hold hands and they tell lies, the *pen-ti-ti.*

'The *pentiti* are too dangerous a weapon; they do what they want. I'm the lightning conductor for those people. They dump all this on one person because it means people are more likely to

---

* Testimony of Salvatore Riina in the trials for 'indirect' and 'political crimes' in Palermo, bunker court of Rebibbia, Rome, 1 and 4 March 1993.

believe them. You know, Mr President, what I mean to Italy today? I'm the Tortora of Naples. You remember the Tortora trial? Those *pentiti* who did drugs with Tortora, who associated with Tortora and all those things, then in the end they broke Tortora's heart and he was acquitted because there was no proof, he wasn't associated with anyone. That's why they're all accusing me; they talk about Riina and hold up their report cards.

'I don't know anyone. These guys have to say where we're sitting, they have to bring evidence, they don't have to say Bontate told me, Badalamenti told me, this one told me and that one told me: evidence, Mr President. And if you're talking about the Cupole or the Scupole,* I couldn't have been alone, there must have been lots of us.

'Forgive me, Mr President, if I call them *pentiti*. I call them this in my dialect because I only got to the second year of elementary school and I'm a poor illiterate . . .

'In the old days there were anonymous letters, but now they come by the basketload and they're not valid any more: these *pen-ti-ti* have made them up. What are they doing? Letters weren't signed once upon a time, but they sign their names and it's "all my love", they take wages. You have to look and go into the depths – what are these *pentiti*? The other day I was reading a book – I think it was by Cardinal *Martino*.† I think he said, "God, where are we going?" . . . But, Mr President, with these *pentiti*, where is Italy going?'

---

* A nonsense word, the equivalent of saying, 'Mafia, Schmafia'.

† Cardinal Carlo Maria Martini, Archbishop of Milan, 1980–2002.

'There's times when I remember and times when I don't remember'*

Stefano Calzetta

Nightmares choke him, now he isn't even afraid of dying. It's one hot summer night in 1986 that he decides to lose his memory. To forget everything. What he entrusted to police superintendent Ninni Cassarà and what he told Judge Falcone. He feels like a 'dead man walking', Stefano Calzetta, a Corso dei Mille thug who tried to act the *malacarne*† and then repented. He's one of the big accusers at the Palermo Maxi-Trial. The day comes for him to give evidence.

The bunker is an arena; all his old friends are inside the cages. Carmelo Zanca, the Tinnirellos, Salvatore Rotolo, the Vernengos, the Marcheses. Everyone coming and going from the 'Room of Death' behind the marina of Sant'Erasmo, the stable where they used to melt the *cristiani*. First they tortured them and interrogated them to find out what they knew, then they made them disappear in vats of acid. Stefano was always there too, in Sant'Erasmo.

The questioning begins.

Public prosecutor: 'Do you confirm what was said in the preliminary investigations, that Salvatore Rotolo always smiled, even when he was committing a murder?'

---

* Testimony of Stefano Calzetta at the Maxi-Trial in Palermo, 4 July 1986.

† Literally 'bad meat'. A criminal.

Stefano Calzetta: 'I don't remember.'
State Barrister: 'Do you, Calzetta, know Pietro Zanca?'
Calzetta: 'I have a headache today, I don't remember.'
President: 'Will you remember if someone knows you or not?'
Calzetta: 'There's times when I remember and times when I don't remember. I fell and bumped my head.'
President: 'Do you remember when you bumped your head?'
Calzetta: 'Who remembers . . .'
President: 'Had you bumped your head by yesterday?'
Calzetta: 'I don't remember, I've got a headache.'
President: 'So you feel ill?'
Calzetta: 'I don't remember.'
President: 'Do you remember what your name is?'
Calzetta: 'Mr President, who am I?'

A week later Stefano Calzetta reappears in the bunker and changes his mind again. He speaks. He reveals the horrors of the family of Corso dei Mille, he provides the motives for forty murders, he names the killers. At the end of the hearing, the public prosecutors ask that he be sentenced to five years and six months in jail, but the Court of Assizes acquits him. In the appeal process, in 1989, Stefano loses his memory once more.

He is finished as a Mafioso and finished as a *pentito*. His family abandon him. Stefano is left on his own. He has no wife, no brothers, no job. He has nothing. His new home is a bit of pavement among the old palm trees of Piazza della Vittoria, outside the front door of the Palermo mobile unit. 'This is the only place I feel safe,' he says to passers-by.

Leftover food in a plastic bag, a bottle of water, an old blanket. Stefano lives on alms. He's a tramp. Stefano's worth nothing now, either to the state or to the Mafia. They put him in a hospice on Via dei Biscottari, but he escapes after a few days. He goes back among the palm trees, close to 'his' policemen. He always repeats the same phrase: 'You know why they call it Cosa Nostra? Because it doesn't belong to anyone else.'

'A handful of rogues'

Salvatore Cocuzza

'The idea of *dissociazione** was that it was a way of not being called *infame*. Collaboration, in Palermo, is seen as something negative, even by normal people. You don't have to be a man of honour to say that anyone who collaborates is an *infame*. With dissociation you can talk about what you've done and not upset anybody. In this case the pill was sweetened, so that people could even justify themselves. Because, in Sicily, what you can't give up is the consideration that other people have for you.

'You're an important person and that's what you live on. You'll have someone who's nobody outside of the street he lives in, but in that street, in that neighbourhood, he's someone who issues commands, who is respected and who makes himself respected. So, a person of that kind finds it difficult to decide to make that leap. Then there are prejudices and ignorance: if I collaborate, they'll take away my property, my wealth, my affluence; my family abandons me. Maybe this person doesn't want to have to leave Sicily. I think there are lots of feelings you have inside you, but you can't rationally explain them, because I realize that someone who collaborates today hasn't resolved his problems, perhaps his son or grandson will . . . So instead, an important person in the street says, "Don't believe it, they're *infami* . . . they're *una manata di indegni*† . . ."

* Dissociation.

† A handful of rogues.

'By now I don't recognize myself in Cosa Nostra, because it's not what it used to be. I only worked that out after I got out of jail, after the massacres. But I was proceeding by inertia, because you're there, you have no other choice, you're a fugitive, you have no support, you have nothing to live on . . . so I start to understand why all these collaborations took place . . . with dissociation I actually thought that fifty or sixty people would get out. But they didn't work out that this was the moment. If dissociation had a meaning in 1996, what does it mean now? The state won't make peace with people who have lost; that is, the state will try to do this when it wants to win, but not after it's won.

'As a *dissociato* I accused myself of everything that I've done; with collaboration I haven't added anything or taken anything away. When I dissociated myself I wasn't accused of everything, just one murder, but I wasn't even responsible; in fact they took it away from me because I had nothing to do with it.

'I told them all about what I've done in my life when I dissociated myself. I thought: this way I can make a notable contribution and then if a hundred people dissociate themselves, by degrees you end up with the truth. Because, if we've done a murder, and you dissociate yourself and so do I, we'll both say the same thing – and so we resolve this murder, this crime.

'At the public prosecutor's office in Palermo they told me the things I should say: we respect dissociation, if you want to dissociate yourself you dissociate yourself, but there's no law. I wasn't interested in the law, but I was interested in being judged for what I've done, in balancing my books with the judiciary. I talked to my family about it, if they'd been opposed I wouldn't have done it. Since neither I nor my wife are of the Cosa Nostra generation, there aren't such deep roots. It's a recent thing . . .'

'Cosa Nostra is over, Totuccio. You can talk.'

Tommaso Buscetta

Palermo doesn't care much about the dead. It's a city of gravestones, bunches of flowers, little altars at every crossroads. A hundred murders in 1981. A hundred murders in 1983. 'They shoot at each other,' many Palermitans say in their resigned singsong voice. Every time there's a corpse on the ground everybody runs to take a look; they take their children by the hand, lift them up, put them on their shoulders: '*Talìa, talìa* . . .', look, look. The sickly smell of blood stagnant in the air, the flies, the startled expression on the faces of the victims. '*Talìa, talìa* . . .'

But it's not true to say that they just shoot 'at each other'. In Palermo they've already killed the head of the mobile unit, Boris Giuliano, and the chief prosecutor, Gaetano Costa, General Carlo Alberto dalla Chiesa and the examining magistrate Rocco Chinnici, Judge Cesare Terranova, *carabinieri* captains Emanuele Basile and Mario D'Aleo, the agent Calogero Zucchetto, the regional secretary of the Italian Communist Party, Pio La Torre, the forensic doctor Paolo Giaccone, the regional president, Piersanti Mattarella, the provincial secretary of the Christian Democrat Party, Michele Reina, and the legal correspondent of the *Giornale di Sicilia*, Mario Francese.

Palermo is opulent. 'It's not rich, it's extravagantly rich,' the journalist Camilla Cederna writes in an article about Sicily. 'It's the Italian city where they sell the most jewels . . . everything that's branded, expensive, exclusive . . . what's surprising are the elegant shops on Via Ruggiero Settimo with their windows lined with pigskin, furnished with multicoloured woods and crystals . . . the owner is an ex-shop assistant, but we know that when the money circulates there are usually no witnesses.'

Palermo's hostile. There are two or three magistrates who dart down the streets of the cities in armoured cars. Sirens, noises. There are 'indignant citizens' who send letters to the local rag, which is happy to publish them. One of these is Patrizia S.: 'Every day, even on Saturdays and Sundays, in the morning, in the very early afternoon and the evening (with no cut-off times!) I am literally assailed by continuous and deafening car sirens escorting various judges . . .' Signora Patrizia is a neighbour of Judge Falcone.

So Palermo is in shock when, on 29 September 1984, late on the day of the feast of St Michael, patron saint of the police, its bosses aren't at liberty any more: 366 arrest warrants are signed by the head of the investigation, Antonino Caponnetto. It's the century's biggest anti-Mafia bust.

From July, Tommaso Buscetta speaks. He reveals the mystery of Cosa Nostra to Falcone. 'He's an *infame,*' yells half of Palermo.

Buscetta is hidden, protected by the police officers of Gianni De Gennaro and Antonio Manganelli's Criminalpol. On one of the days that follow the St Michael's Day blitz, they also take Totuccio Contorno to the secret place where Don Masino is being hidden. He's a man of honour of the family of Santa Maria del Gesù, with strong ties to its boss, Stefano Bontate.

As his code name he has chosen Coriolano della Floresta, a member of a secretive sect in the novel *Beati Paoli* by Luigi Natoli. In a report by police superintendent Ninni Cassarà he is identified as 'First Light'. He is already informing the police about forays by the Corleonesi. But he is still undecided about whether to take the big step. Tommaso Buscetta goes to see him, kneels in front of him and kisses his hand. Don Masino rests it on his shoulder and gives him the blessing: 'Cosa Nostra is over, Totuccio. You can talk.'

'Why should they keep quiet?'

Giuseppe Madonia, known as Piddu

There are five of them when the Palermo Maxi-Trial begins in 1986. Ten years later, in 1996, there are 423. Small and big, sincere and lying, desperate or calculating *pentiti* and not *pentiti* at all. In the legal jargon they are dubbed 'collaborators with justice'. In Sicily they are despised.

In the neighbourhoods of Palermo they coin expressions and insults that recall the protagonists of the events described in the trials. '*Cornuto e* Buscetta' they say, instead of '*cornuto e sbirro*'.* They play on double meanings. 'We don't serve any '*contorno*' here.† The use of the terms reveals ancient fears and worries. The truth is that the *pentiti* are shaking Cosa Nostra to the core.

The first is Tommaso Buscetta. Then come Totuccio Contorno, Vincenzo Sinagra, aka Tempesta, and Stefano Calzetta. There is also Vincenzo Marsalo, the son of the old *capo* of the Vicari family. In 1988 he 'repents' – and it is a very painful human repentance – and Antonino Calderone, brother of Pippo, the head of the *Commissione regionale* until the day the Corleonesi hitmen kill him. In 1989 Francesco Marino Mannoia is the first of the Corleonesi to talk to Falcone.

---

* 'Asshole Buscetta' rather than 'asshole cop'.

† 'Contorno' is both a proper name and the word for a side dish of vegetables.

After the mass-murders they arrive in droves. Gaspare Mutolo, Leonardo Messina, Balduccio Di Maggio, Francesco Di Carlo, Salvatore Cancemi, Gioacchino La Barbera, Mario Santo Di Matteo, Pino Marchese. And: Angelo Siino, Calogero Ganci, Francesco Paolo Anzelmo, Vincenzo Sinacori, Gioacchino Pennino. Down to Giovanni Brusca, the one who holds the remote control in Capaci. At the first trial against Senator Giulio Andreotti, thirty-eight of them testify.

'Buscetta and all the others, the more they talk the more they get paid, why should they keep quiet?' the representative of the family of Caltanissetta, Piddu Madonia, shouts from the cave of the bunker in Catania. All hell has broken loose in Cosa Nostra. Even the men of honour in Leoluca Bagarella's 'group of fire' are turning state's evidence. The first was Pietro Romeo, then Salvatore Grigoli, the murderer of Don Pino Puglisi. It looks like the beginning of the end for Cosa Nostra. The last 'important' one is Antonino Giuffrè, Bernardo Provenzano's right-hand man. There are many of them, a great many. Perhaps too many.

'Managing' them is complicated. The Palermo state prosecutor's office addresses the big associations; the one in Caltanissetta is responsible for massacres. There are 'collaborators' who supply investigative material on which to base trials in one district while at the same time taking it apart in the other, confusing the magistrates and setting them against one another. Others, still at liberty, start shooting again. They repent their repentance and go in search of their old enemies. Others start talking 'politics'. They end up as mincemeat.

Very special treatment is reserved for Salvatore 'Totò' Cancemi, a member of the *Comissione*. At dawn one day in July 1993 he turns up voluntarily at a *carabinieri* barracks, saying, 'I'm a fugitive, I want to repent.' His new life as a 'collaborator' is spent almost entirely in an old barracks, mysteriously shadowed by an old special unit marshal. It doesn't take the people of Palermo long to find a custom-made name for the ex-Mafioso from La Cupola: Totò Caserma – Totò Barracks.

It's an octagonal fortress, concealed by an iron fence that surrounds a surface area of almost 10,000 square metres. Inside are the officers of the clerks of court, the rooms for the lawyers, a bar, the rooms for the chambers of the judges and juries. An underground walkway links the 'sections' of the Ucciardone to the gigantic bunker, the obligatory passageway along which, every morning, the imprisoned defendants are transferred to the thirty cages arranged in a semi-circle around the hall. All the windows are bullet-proofed. At the top, suspended like the tiers of a stadium, there are the galleries for the public and the press. Spherical television cameras hang from the ceiling, electronic eyes connected to thin metal wires. Outside the big armoured doors stand the security guards. Every document and every ID is microfilmed, even the smallest objects go through the metal detector. It's a technological Colosseum. The predominant colour is green.

At the sixth hearing of the Maxi-Trial a Sicilian travel agency organizes a special tour of Palermo. The gold of the Royal Palace, the Byzantine mosaics of the Palatine Chapel, the monastery of Monreale Cathedral and then the 'stopover' at the bunker. The first tourists announced at the court come from Carpi in the province of Modena.

'I wish you all eternal peace'*

Michele Greco

It's a beautiful November in Palermo. The sun is hot; a violent light pierces the chinks in the steel and concrete courtroom where the Maxi-Trial is being held. Two thousand uniformed men guard the bunker, 250 just to keep an eye on the inside of it, 500 to protect the '*collaboratori di giustizia*'† and their families, the public prosecutors, the witnesses. The mobile units of the police and the battalions of *carabinieri* are stationed between the port and the district of Sampolo, from the fruit and vegetable market to the shipyards. The main entrance to the hall is in Via Remo Sandron, next to the old gasometer. The windows of some of the houses have been walled up. Many people who live on the street have insured their flats against damage from explosion and attack.

Almost two years have passed since that first morning, the rain and wind of 10 February 1986. Six hundred and thirty-eight days, 349 hearings, 1,330 hours of debate, 637 hours of pleadings and 50 hours of final addresses. There are 475 defendants.

In the twenty-one months of the trial so far, there has been a turnover of three governments. Craxi, Craxi again and then Fanfani.

---

* Record of spontaneous declarations made by Michele Greco, Maxi-Trial, Palermo, 14 December 1987.

† Collaborators with the law, *pentiti*.

Palermo is dirtier than before, mountains of rubbish disfigure the beautiful streets that cross Via Ruggiero Settimo, the 'drawing room' of the city. The sea of Mondello is hidden even in winter. There are no spaces on the white beach, now closed off by the metal net of a lido.

Palermo is uneasy, holding its breath as it awaits the verdict on its bosses. The first. The only one. Never before have Mafiosi been put on trial just for being Mafiosi.

Everything is ready for the big conclave, the long council chamber awaiting the president of the Court of Assizes, Alfonso Giordano, the assistant judge Pietro Grasso, the six ordinary jurymen and the other two deputies.

Memories about life in the bunker fill the thoughts of the defendants locked up in their cages. The American-style 'face-to-face' confrontations between the big *capi* and the big *pentiti*, blackouts real and fake, fear, shouting, grief. They are all waiting for the patriarchs and the *picciotti* of the Palermo suburbs, clutching the bars of their cages, arranged in a semicircle before the judges' bench. The big green hall, now the symbol of the liberation of the other Palermo, looks like a zoo. The lawyers are bent over their papers as they count up the years – 4,756 – and the life sentences – twenty-eight – that have just been requested by public prosecutors Giuseppe Ayala and Domenico Signorino. And forty-five requests for acquittal on grounds of lack of evidence, four requests for amnesty, six requests for the trial to be terminated on the grounds of the 'death of the defendant'.

The court is about to withdraw to the council chamber; these are the closing minutes of the first Cosa Nostra Maxi-Trial. All of a sudden a hoarse, far-away voice comes from the cages. It comes from cell number 22. It's Michele Greco speaking. The Mafioso that they call 'the Pope'. He wants to say goodbye to the court.

He gets to his feet, his hands following the rhythm of this voice. 'I wish you all eternal peace, Mr President. These aren't my words but the words of Our Lord,' he says, keeping his eyes lowered. And he adds: 'You must excuse me, Mr President, but peace and serenity are the fundamental bases for judgement: may this peace go with you for the rest of your life.'

It is a sinister farewell. It is 11.15 on 11 November 1987 and the judges of the first Court of Assizes disappear behind an armoured door.

'Tell me where I'm supposed to have "Mafiaed"!'

Michele Greco

He looks like a little country squire. He has pleasant manners, very Sicilian. He invites counts and princes and generals to his magnificent estate, La Favarella. Once he even had His Eminence Cardinal Ernesto Ruffini at one of his banquets. Everyone goes up there, to the village of Croceverde Giardina, at the meeting of two roads that descend steeply from the mountain of Gibilrossa and end up actually touching his farm. He is admired in Palermo, revered, in fact. While the others have already been in hiding for ten years, he still has a firearms licence and a passport. Until 1982, Michele Greco, 'the Pope of the Mafia', has a clean record.

The bosses of the nine Sicilian provinces always meet up at La Favarella for a *mangiata* and a *parlata**. Rosario Riccobono of the Colli plain, Giuseppe Di Cristina from Riesi, Gaetano Badalamenti from Cinisi, Vincenzo Rimi from Alcamo. They meet al fresco at Don Michele's, where they have to debate their issues, decide whether to kill someone or approach someone else.

'He's the head of the *Commissione*, but he's a puppet of the Corleonesi,' Buscetta confesses to Falcone. He's the great traitor, the one who stabs his Palermo friends in the back and hands Sicily over to Totò Riina.'

A policeman who hasn't even turned thirty, Calogero Zucchetto,

---

* An 'eat' and a chat.

ventures towards Croceverde Giardina on his own, and they kill him a week later. The head of the Catturandi squad, Beppe Montana, is looking for fugitives around La Favarella and they kill him too. And then they also kill Ninni Cassarà, the head of the crime management unit, who signs the report entitled Michele Greco + 161, the first piece of evidence in the Maxi-Trial. Don Michele is now a wanted man.

He's hiding in a cottage. He's on his own, just him and a mule in the hills of Caccamo. One day someone gives him away. The Judas who hands him over to the *carabinieri* for 200 million lire is dead by nightfall.

Don Michele is in chains. He is accused of blowing up the examining magistrate Rocco Chinnici, of having 'ratified', in the *Commissione*, the murder of a hundred men, of having refined hundredweights of base morphine.

'Violence is beneath my dignity,' he tells his first questioner in the Court of Assizes. 'Tell me where I'm supposed to have "Mafiaed"!' he shouts at Maxi Ter, the third Maxi-Trial: 122 defendants, one of many trials carried out by Falcone's examining magistrates. The hearing concludes with a surprising verdict in which everyone is pardoned. The 'Pope of the Mafia' is delighted. Of the judge who acquits him says, 'He's got a pair of balls on him like my mule in Caccamo.' But he stays in jail. Other accusations rain down on him.

He despairs: 'They're all accusing me just because my name's at the top of the bill.' He lets off steam: 'If instead of being called Michele Greco, if I was called Michele Roccappinnuza, I wouldn't be here in the Ucciardone.' He torments himself: 'The devil's friends will never let me see the sun again.' One morning Falcone interrogates him and he refuses to answer. He only whispers: 'You're the Maradona of the law: when you get the ball no one can get it off you.'

He's buried away in a wing of the Ucciardone while a film, *The Saga of the Grimaldis,* is being shown in Palermo's cinemas. It's the story of an old godfather of the 'good Mafia', horrified by the violence of the bosses of the 'bad Mafia'. The one that deals in drugs. The director's pseudonym is Giuseppe Castellana, registered as Giuseppe Greco. He's Michele's son.

'[Socrates is] somebody I admire because he never wrote anything'

Luciano Leggio

'I only ever read the third page of the papers. Stories and the odd review. The rest is all fake. Or else it's an apologia for someone. And I've never in my whole life come across a trustworthy journalist who does his duty with honesty and integrity. The day I meet one I'll throw a party. And I don't believe in *segreto istruttorio*.* I've never believed in it, because in the end it isn't all that secret. After all, I started hating tailors ever since I heard someone say: the judge keeps himself buttoned up . . . all in all, I hate tailors because they don't know how to button up those judges' robes. They always seem to leave those buttonholes open. I don't know, but they open up . . . My myth was created by the police, the police with the support of the journalists.

'In almost all great men I've found a remarkable incoherence between their life and their works. I'm at peace with my conscience. I hope that, if God exists, we have to look for him inside ourselves and live simply, to seek a balance between the material and the spiritual side that exists within all of us. To experience each moment in an integral form, never denying the evil that exists in each of us or exalting the good that is in each of us. I've read Socrates, and he's somebody I admire because he never wrote anything. I've read the classics. And history, philosophy, pedagogy. I've

* Secrecy concerning a preliminary investigation.

read Dickens, Dostoevsky, Croce. I studied sociology for two years. But I was disappointed. It gives the diagnosis for social ills but not the cure.

'If by Mafia and Mafioso you mean everything that Tomasso Buscetta and all the other *pentiti* have said, then I have nothing to do with it. I have no secrets; mine are out there in the cold light of day . . . I've rubbed up against the law . . . but Mafia? Mafioso? I don't know what the Mafia is. As to the term Mafioso, if you understand it according to Pitré's definition of it as something beautiful and magnificent – a pretty girl in Palermo used to be called *mafiosa*, just as *mafioso* used to refer to a fine horse – and yet, even though I don't consider myself superior, I would say that in this sense, in the sense of someone who is good, if they think of me as a *Mafioso*, then it does me credit even if I acknowledge that I don't have those great qualities.

'I don't belong to any clan or any group and never have done. I don't like and I have never liked teams. Even in sport I prefer individual disciplines: cycling, athletics, boxing. Drugs? I don't even know what drugs are, I only know about them from what I've read in the papers. I am and have always been a big farmer. And when I say big, I mean really big. I know every branch of the sector: from olives to vines, from kitchen gardens to animal-breeding. And not theoretically, but practically. I'm a born farmer. And as a farmer I follow the environmental situation with apprehension. I'm in favour of clean energy as against the idiocy of nuclear, which will take us to ecological disaster sooner or later. To death.'

'It wasn't us'*

Giovanni Bontate

It's dark in San Lorenzo, buildings crammed up against one another on a plain where there once stood yellow villas of volcanic stone, surrounded by lemon trees. Claudio is eleven. He's off to buy bread before going back home. He walks quickly along the pavement; someone stops behind him. He's on a motorbike, a Kawasaki. The man calls him by name and tells him, 'Come here.' The child is confused, he doesn't understand. The man is holding a 7.65 calibre automatic pistol. *Bam.* A shot to the forehead. And so it is that Claudio Domino dies in Palermo, at about nine o'clock on 7 October 1986.

There's an order not to shoot in the city; the Mafia trial is going on in the bunker. The murder breaks a silence that has lasted for months. Since February, when the Maxi-Trial began. It's the murder of a child. It puts the fear of God into everyone. Even the Mafiosi. Why did they kill him? 'Because he saw something he shouldn't have,' the bewildered authorities explain. But it doesn't add up.

There isn't so much as a fly stirring in Palermo, and in San Lorenzo they're racking their brains over Claudio. Who was it? A drug addict? A small-time crook? A solitary mugger, one of those

* Record of statements made by the Mafioso Giovanni Bontate at the Maxi-Trial, Palermo, 7 October 1986.

desperate characters from the 'Zen' – the Zona Espansione Nord, the ghetto of ghettos in Palermo – since hungry folk come down into the suburbs from there every now and again, to get hold of some money?

The little victim's father is stunned, overwhelmed with grief. His name is Antonio, he used to work for the phone company, and then, with his wife Graziella's savings, he opened a card shop in San Lorenzo. He's questioned during the night. The police discover that Antonio has a cleaning company, La Splendente, the company that won the contract to clean the bunker. That's one lead. The bosses in the Maxi-Trial are placed under investigation.

The morning after Claudio's death the hearing in the Court of Assizes starts a few minutes late. One defendant asks President Alfonso Giordano for permission to speak. It's Giovanni Bontate. He has an announcement to make.

'Mr President, we have children too . . . we have nothing to do with this murder, it wasn't us, it's a crime that offends us, and we're even more offended by attempts in the press to hold the men on trial in this hall responsible . . .'

It's the first time that a Sicilian Mafioso has uttered that word: we. We means *we Mafiosi*. It's a proclamation of the living existence of the organization, of Cosa Nostra. A public, official confession. In the name of all those accused in the Maxi-Trial. It's an unprecedented declaration for the men of honour. And, what's more, not made by just any old man of honour, but by the lawyer Giovanni Bontate, brother of Stefano, the prince of Villagraia, the most charismatic of the Palermo bosses before the arrival of the Corleonesi.

A month after Claudio Domino's murder, Salvatore Graffagnino, a meat-roaster, disappears in Palermo. White shotgun. The Mafiosi had discovered that it was he who killed Claudio. The motive: he's Claudio's mother's lover and Claudio saw them together. A wretched business.

A year later, Giovanni Bontate is under house arrest in his

beautiful villa. It's the morning, and the lawyer and his wife Francesca are drinking coffee together. The hitmen slip into the garden, enter the kitchen and open fire. They kill both of them.

Francesco Marino Mannoia, the first *pentito* of the Corleonesi to speak after the deaths in Palermo, said, 'He was punished partly because of what he said in the bunker. Giovanni broke the rules.'

'It was a political trial; we had to pay the price'*

Gaspare Mutolo

The big Palermo trial is over. After twenty-two months since the first hearing, it's time for the verdict: eighteen sentenced to life imprisonment, a total of 2,665 years in jail. It's the evening of 16 December 1987; the men of honour shut in their cages see the president of the Court of Assizes, Alfonso Giordano, coming into the bunker, and hold their breath: 'Salvatore Riina, life imprisonment. Bernardo Provenzano, life imprisonment. Francesco Madonia, life imprisonment. Salvatore Montalto, life imprisonment. Michele Greco, life imprisonment. Giovanbattista Pullarà, life imprisonment. Antonino, Giuseppe and Filippo Marchese, life imprisonment. Benedetto Santapaola, life imprisonment. Giuseppe Lucchese, life imprisonment. Giuseppe Calò, 23 years. Giuseppe Bono, 23 years. Bernardo Brusca, 23 years. Mariano Agate, 22 years. Salvatore Greco, 18 years. Antonino Rotolo, 18 years. Gaspare Mutolo, 10 years. Vincenzo Puccio, 10 years. Giuseppe Giacomo Gambino, 8 years. Giacomo Riina, 7 years and 6 months. Giuseppe Leggio, 7 years. Leoluca Bagarella, 6 years . . .'

For the first time in Italy, the Sicilian Mafia has been defeated in a court of law. Everyone. From soldiers to the *capi*. It's a historic outcome: Judge Falcone's preliminary investigations are supported

* Record of the questioning of Gaspare Mutolo in the records of court case no. 3538/94, 'brought against Andreotti Giulio'.

in the hearing. Many of the defendants are accused only of Mafia association, 'only' because they are men of honour. It's an enormous change, a reversal of the order of what happened twenty years earlier in the hearings in Catanzaro and Bari, the big Mafia trials held outside of Sicily for reasons of *legitima suspicione*.

'That was what should have happened in the Court of Assizes. We knew it was a political trial; we had to pay the price. The verdict was a massacre, but no one felt too bad about it in the end. We were sure the appeal would go better. . .' says Gaspare Mutolo.

'When the Maxi-Trial began, it was felt by all of us men of honour that the progress and outcome of the case would be the ones that the government of Rome wanted. The government had to demonstrate that it had dealt a hard blow to Cosa Nostra and given satisfaction to national public opinion and the whole world, indignant about the crimes that had been committed in Palermo. The message received in Palermo was to be patient, because it was politically necessary . . . These assurances were based on political and legal sources.'

On 10 December 1990, in the Court of Appeal, the number of life sentences drops to twelve, the years of imprisonment fall to 1,576. The statements of reasons by the second-level judges partly dismisses 'the uniqueness of the command of Cosa Nostra' as revealed by Buscetta and Falcone. In essence, the *Commissione* is not held responsible for all the outstanding crimes.

Mutolo still recalls: 'The verdict of the Court of Appeal was a good one because in a way it demolished the theory of the *Commissione*. Of course there couldn't be any problems with the Court of Cassation . . . Riina told us to "stay calm" . . . so then we understood how they expected the Court to treat us, and that reassured us.'

'As far as I'm concerned Judge Carnevale is as righteous as Pope John'*†

Pieruccio Senapa

The front gate to the Ucciardone is open, the Mafiosi are coming out. The first to cross the room of the roll office is Salvatore Rotolo, a hitman from Corso dei Mille. He's known as Anatredda, the little duck. He's astonished to breathe in the air of freedom. He's been inside for eight years, since being arrested for the murder of Paolo Giaccone, the pathologist. There's a small crowd of relatives outside the jail. They're waiting. Anatredda lets the bag that he's clutching in his hand slip to the ground and walks towards an old woman. He hugs her. She's his mother. Then he too waits outside the Ucciardone. He waits for his inseparable friend Pieruccio.

A few minutes pass and finally Pieruccia Senapa comes out too, having been sentenced for four murders. He's extremely elegant, in a blue jacket. He gets into a car, greets a colleague, then turns towards the journalists who are following him and says, 'As far as I'm concerned Judge Carnevale is as righteous as Pope John.'

In that cold afternoon of 18 February 1991, forty-three Mafiosi are freed, one after the other. It's a chilling list: the 'pope', Michele Greco; the drug-trafficker of the suburb of Arenella, Stefano Fidanzati; the head of the Mazara del Vallo family, Mariano Agate; the hitman of Caculli, Mario Prestifilippo.

---

* Interview with Pieruccio Senapa by the author, February 1991.

† Pope John XXIII was described as 'righteous among nations'.

They are free by law, the law of the president of the first penal section of the Court of Cassation, Judge Corrado Carnevale. Many Mafiosi sentenced in the Maxi-Trial, between the first level and the Appeal, have already served their terms on remand. Defence and prosecution clash on the interpretation of a rule of law, the dispute revolves around a legal quibble. The bosses' lawyers maintain that, for the defendants on remand, the days dedicated to hearings and the deliberations of the verdict count, while the state prosecutors reply that there's an article in the Code of Penal Procedure – Article 297 – that automatically freezes those dates. The controversy ends up in the Court of Cassation. Judge Carnevale agrees with the defence.

The president of the Parliamentary Anti-Mafia Commission, Luciano Violante, writes to Minister of Grace and Justice, Claudio Martelli: 'Are you aware of the most serious errors in the first penal section of the Court of Cassation, which makes this powerful magistrate inviolable?'

Giorgio Bocca appeals to the head of state, Francesco Cossiga: 'Dear President, what are the Italians supposed to believe? That Carlo Alberto dalla Chiesa was killed like that only because he had got up the nose of a Mafioso called Santapaola . . . while all they've seen is those magistrates in the Court of Cassation who see the *Cupola* as a fairy-story?'

The bosses return to freedom. Giovanni Falcone has just left Palermo. After ten years leading the prosecution in the bunker, and another two as a deputy prosecutor, the Sicilian magistrate is appointed Director-General of Penal Affairs in the Ministry of Grace and Justice. The Mafia raise their glasses to the departing Falcone. And to the forty-three members of the organization leaving jail with a snigger. Seventy-two hours. That's how long their freedom lasts. The hitmen of the Corso deil Mille and the *capi* of the families are rearrested three days later and locked up again in the Ucciardone. It's a *coup de théâtre.*

Amidst great secrecy, Minister Martelli had signed a decree to have them put back inside. A provision that leaves everyone in Palermo stunned. For the bosses, it's the 'government's arrest warrant'.

‘Things are getting more and more *trubbole*’*

Giuseppe Gambino, aka Joe

Judge Giovanni Falcone is alone, both in Palermo and in Rome. In Palermo his colleagues hate him, fear him, wage war on him. The Sicilian tribunal is full of spies and moles and people writing poison-pen letters. On the front pages of the newspapers it's ‘the Palace of poison’. In Rome, the Governing Council of the Judiciary appoints Antonino Caponnetto as interrogating magistrate, the same Caponnetto who replaced Rocco Chinnici and officially set up the anti-Mafia pool. It isn't Falcone. It's the end of spring 1988. And it also seems like the end of the big investigations into Cosa Nostra.

The chief prosecutor of Marsala, Paolo Borsellino, issues a bill of indictment against anyone who wants to stop it all, Falcone threatens dismissals, President Francesco Cossiga intervenes. The climate is feverish: the head of the mobile unit goes, his deputy goes, the police superintendent of Palermo goes. At the Palazzo dei Marescialli, dozens of magistrates give evidence. There are months of arguments and suspicion. There is also a lot of fear. At the end of the summer the ‘Palermo case’ is filed away by the Governing Council of the Judiciary. But not by the men of honour.

---

* Intercepted phonecall between Giuseppe Joe Gambino and person unknown, in files from the drug-trafficking trial (Iron Tower), ruling by the court of Palermo, 30 January 1991.

The Mafiosi carefully follow the tangled tales of police and judges. They are aware of the growing hostility surrounding Giovanni Falcone; they pray that he will become more and more institutionally isolated, and hope the new code will come into effect very soon.

Giuseppe Joe Gambino, of the powerful Sicilian-American Gambino family, and one of his associates, an anonymous drug-trafficker, discuss the subject on the phone. Joe receives the call at Caffè Giardino, John Gotti's headquarters in Brooklyn.

Anyonymous: 'How's things?'

Joe: 'You're back from Palermo?'

Anonymous: 'Yeah, the other day.'

Joe: 'And how are, how are things over there in Sicily?'

Anonymous: 'Things are getting more and more *trubbole*, more troublesome . . .'

Joe: 'And this guy – Falcone – what's he done? Has he resigned?'

Anonymous: 'No, things have levelled out over there, and he's withdrawn his resignation. He's back where he was before, doing what he was doing before.'

Joe: 'Shit!'

Anonymous: 'And now they've put through – or they're putting through – a new law, now they can't do trials liked they did before. Now the law demands that a person's been seen doing or is caught doing . . . the way they're doing it now isn't enough any more . . . now they can't arrest people when they feel like it, they have to find proof first, they have to indict you first and then arrest you . . .'

Joe 'Oh, so it's like it is here in America?'

Anonymous: 'No, it's better, it's quite a lot better. Now those bastard judges, cops and officers will only be able to dream of arresting people like they're doing now . . .'

Joe: 'Oh, the cops *intra ù culu sa pigghiaru* . . .* which is why that other guy's come back – Falcone – so he can't do anything more? Then they're fine too, our men over there . . . fine, fine . . . *intra ù culu sa pigghiaru.*'

Anonymous: 'Yes, *intra ù culu sa pigghiaru.*'

* Have let themselves be fucked in the ass.

Palermo, 14 metres above sea level, latitude 38°, longitude 13°, 665,434 inhabitants, is the fifth city in Italy – after Rome, Milan, Naples and Turin – and the thirty-first in Europe. The city's patron saint is Rosalia. Its story changes the day they kill Salvo Lima.

'The Anti-Mafia shouldn't play the Mafia's game'

Salvo Lima

The journalist asks: 'So, Mr Lima, whenever there's a new illustrious corpse in Palermo, people always talk about you.'

Salvo Lima was a deputy in the European Parliament, twice mayor of Palermo: from 1959 to 1963 and then again from 1965 until 1968. He's said to be 'very close' to Mafia circles, some Cosa Nostra *pentiti* say that he himself is 'the same thing': a man of honour. Francesco Marino Mannoia makes it known that he belongs to the family of Matteo Citarda, on Viale Lazio.

He is the hardest Sicilian of all to interview. Most of his known thought is summed up in a single sentence: 'Palermo is beautiful, let's make it more beautiful.' He's also the most powerful man in Sicily. He never talks to the national press; he's always impossible to contact. When he has something to say he says it only to the local papers. As he is doing now, on 11 September 1980.

Salvo Lima replies: 'It's the usual disgrace. I have nothing to do with the Mafia and I want to clear that up once and for all.'

Journalist: 'So it's all made up?'

Lima: 'Obviously.'

Journalist: 'What's your view about everything that's happened recently in Palermo?'

Lima: 'As a Sicilian it causes me great pain; as a politician I'm very critical of the state, which still hasn't really understood the real extent of the phenomenon.'

The European Christian Democrat Group is meeting in Taormina, and Salvo Lima, 'a die-hard supporter of Andreotti . . . is doing the honours, explaining to his colleagues the problems of that region of the deep South . . . and apparently he made a terrific impression . . .'

He grants his other interview on 28 June 1987. The Social Democratic Party in Sicily is divided. Salvo Lima: 'All that is needed is for people when they get up in the morning to decide who are the good guys and who are bad guys, the Anti-Mafia shouldn't play the Mafia's game, I'm definitely in favour of a complete clarification of the past, present and future.'

On 23 March 1988 he is touched by accusations from the *pentito* Antonino Calderone over his links with Nino and Ignazio Salvo, the men in charge of tax-collecting on the island, who financed the Andreotti tendency in the Sicilian Christian Democratic Party. Lima also concedes to the Palermo press: 'They're always linking me to the Salvo cousins. That acquaintanceship, like huge numbers of others, is confused with a non-existent political alliance . . . I can only say that I've never been involved with either passing or approving laws concerning tax-collecting by the Salvos.' And he adds: 'Too often, just from the criminalization of a disagreement, people resort to easy sensationalism, to the construction of more hateful and gratuitous suspicions.'

On 12 March 1992 the Corleonesi kill him in one of the lanes in Mondello. It's revenge 'for not guaranteeing a good outcome of the Maxi-Trial'. They shoot him in the back, as they do with Cosa Nostra traitors.

'They're coming back'*

Salvo Lima

'On 12 March 1992, at 9.45, an emergency call came in to the local police station, saying that a murder had been committed on Via delle Palme in Mondello, Palermo's spa area.

'A "flying squad" team arriving on the scene noticed on the ground the corpse of a person immediately identified as the Honourable Salvo Lima, as well as the presence of two other people, Professor Alfredo Li Vecchi and Dr Leonardo Leggio. They declared that they had been with Mr Lima at the moment of the attack, in the Opel Vectra automobile, registration number PA A4466, owned by Professor Li Vecchi.

'Once the alarm had been raised, the magistrates of the Public Prosecutor's Office arrived at that Tribunal along with officers of the police and the *carabinieri*. After the initial checks had been made, the corpse was transported to the Pathology Institute of Palermo University for post-mortem, witnesses were examined, all the routine evidence was collected, searches were made in the victim's home and offices in Palermo, in Rome and at the seat of the European Parliament in Strasbourg.

'Professor Li Vecchi declared that that morning, as often

---

* From 'Details and course of investigation of the custodial sentence against Salvatore Riina and others for the murder of Salvo Lima', 11 October 1992.

happened in the pre-election period, he had picked up the Honourable Mr Lima from his villa in Mondello to accompany him to various meetings; that day they were supposed to go to the Palace Hotel in Mondello to prepare for Mr Andreotti's imminent visit to Palermo. After a few minutes, Dr Leonardo Leggio arrived, and together they had climbed into Li Vecchi's Opel Vectra to go to the Palace Hotel.

'Immediately afterwards they had left and had travelled a short distance when a large-cylinder motorcycle had drawn up beside them with two people on it. One of him had fired various firearms, forcing Professor Li Vecchi – who was driving – to halt his car. At the same time, Lima had shouted, "They're coming back," and all three occupants had run from the car, trying to escape and heading instinctively in the opposite direction from the one in which the car had been travelling.

'Professor Li Vecchi and Dr Leggio had sought shelter behind a rubbish bin, and immediately noticed that Mr Lima was lying on the ground, open-mouthed and lifeless. The two witnesses were not able to give a better description either of the motorcycle or of the two killers riding it, both of whom were wearing full-face helmets. They were certain that they had not noticed anything unusual or suspicious, either that morning or on the previous days.

'It was established at the post-mortem that Lima's death had been caused by a bullet from a revolver to the back of the head, from right to left, from a distance of around 60 cm or slightly more.

'In the Honourable Mr Lima's house and offices various documentation was recovered concerning the Honourable Mr Lima's long political career, but nothing emerged that might be useful to investigations into the cause of the crime.

'In relation to Mr Lima's murder, some anonymous calls were also received by the police. One of these, which came in at 10.15 on 12 March, claimed that those responsible for the crime were in Partinico. Another – at 15.42 on the same day – stated that "The list doesn't stop at Lima" . . .'

'Judge Carnevale was also somebody who felt . . . the tug on the reins'*

Salvatore Cancemi, known as Totò Caserma

'It was Cosa Nostra who killed the Honourable Salvo Lima, and it was Totò Riina who made the decision because Lima hadn't kept his promise. Above all, Lima hadn't acted as our guarantor at the Maxi-Trial. I myself heard Totò Riina complaining about those promises that hadn't been kept . . .

'For a long time Totò Riina had reassured us all. He told us all that the Maxi-Trial would go well, because it would all be cancelled out by the Court of Cassation. But then, when the trial went badly, Totò Riina claimed it had happened because of an intervention by Judge Falcone. He didn't explain what Falcone had done. Salvatore Biondino, Raffaele Ganci and Michelangelo La Barbera also told us about that intervention by Judge Falcone.

'When Totò Riina said the Maxi-Trial would go well in the Court of Cassation, one of the reasons was that there was this idea in Cosa Nostra that Dr Carnevale was a judge that you could "get to"; that Judge Carnevale was also somebody who felt the *retinata*, by which I mean he feels the tug on the reins. As regards the way we thought of getting to President Carnevale, Riina and Ganci and La Barbera claimed that he could be reached through the interests of the Honourable Salvo Lima and the Honourable Giulio Andreotti.

---

* Quotations from documents deposited by the public prosecutor of Palermo in court case no. 3538/94, 'brought against Andreotti Giulio'.

'I was informed before Lima's murder – we were at a meeting called by Totò Riina in Girolamo Guddo's villa. Raffaele Ganci and Salvatore Biondino were there too. Totò Riina told us "This thing can't go on," and that Lima's "horns need breaking". What he actually said was: "We have to kill that bastard Lima." Raffaele Ganci told me that, after the first-level verdict in the Maxi-Trial, Totò Riina set about obtaining a more favourable verdict in the second level. According to what he told Ganci, Totò Riina had received a promise that all the life sentences would be quashed.

'In fact, the second level did quash the life sentences of some men of honour like Bernardo Provenzano and Giuseppe Lucchese, but not Totò Riina. Raffaele Ganci said of this idea: "Lifting Totò Riina's life sentence would have been like the end of the world" . . .'

'Then, when in January 1992 the Court of Cassation confirmed the sentences, Totò Riina went mad . . . the murder of the Honourable Mr Lima was the first consequence. Then, Riina, with his eye on a revision of the trial, started trying to discredit the *pentiti* in every way possible. He was convinced that he would bring about a revision of the Maxi-Trial. After his arrest, his strategy of discrediting the *pentiti* was continued by Bernardo Provenzano.

'It was Raffale Ganci, again, who confided in me that Provenzano was interested in having the laws about *pentiti* annulled or modified. Bernardo Provenzano always had relationships with the political world that were even stronger than those of Totò Riina . . . Provenzano slipped in everywhere.'

The court acquits the life senator Giulio Andreotti. The court acquits Judge Carnevale. Andreotti, who had denied ever knowing Salvatore Riina, leaves the scene in 2004, after an eleven-year trial. He had been charged with the crime of simple criminal association, charges of the crime of Mafia-type criminal association being dropped previously for lack of evidence. Judge Corrado Carnevale, accused of external involvement in Mafia-type association, after a first-level acquittal and a sentence to six years' imprisonment on appeal, is definitively acquittted of all charges at the end of 2002 and he has since been reinstated as a Judge in the Court of Cassation.

‘ Totò Riina . . . greeted all three men with a kiss’*

Baldassare Di Maggio, aka Balducccio

‘Totò Riina arrived for our appointment in a van and got into my Golf, telling me we had to go and see Ignazio Salvo. When we reached the gate of the garage of the building where Ignazio Salvo lived, we found Paolo Rabito, who opened the gate for us and then told us to park the car in the garage. Totò Riina, Rabito and I took the lift up to Salvo’s house. He brought us in and made us walk all the way down a corridor. There was a room on the right, and he ushered us into it. In the room were Giulio Andreotti and the Honourable Salvo Lima. Both got up and greeted us.

‘I shook hands with Andreotti and Salvo Lima and kissed Ignazio Salvo, who had already greeted us before. Totò Riina, on the other hand, greeted all three men with a kiss: Andreotti, Lima and Salvo. I left immediately afterwards, along with Paolo Rabito, and went into a different room. We left them alone. The room where we saw Giulio Andreotti was really a drawing room, with at least two windows, a partly carpeted wooden floor . . . as we walked in you could see a big library on the left, and then there was a sofa with its back to a desk, and a big armchair . . .

‘I waited there for about three hours, three and a half. Then

* Quotations from files deposited by the public prosecutor of Palermo in trial no. 3538/94, ‘brought against Andreotti Giulio’. Andreotti claimed this meeting never took place.

Ignazio Salvo came to get me and I went back into the drawing room, I greeted the people who were still present, that is, Senator Andreotti and the Honourable Lima, shaking their hands. And off I went with Totò Riina. Ignazio Salvo walked us to the lift, and Paolo Rabito came down with us again to open the gate.

'On the way back Totò Riina didn't say a word about the content of the discussion he had had in the house. We talked about other things. I remember he asked me for information about his *compare*,* Bernardo Brusca. And then about my family.

'I think – though this is just my deduction based on an earlier meeting with Ignazio Salvo that took place about a fortnight earlier – that the subject of the meeting was the Maxi-Trial. I remember that Ignazio Salvo was under house arrest. I can't say exactly what phase the Maxi-Trial was in, but I think it was quite early, but going quite well for the defendants.

'I'm absolutely sure I recognized Senator Giulio Andreotti and also the Honourable Salvo Lima, who I'd seen many times on television. I'd never seen them in person. Nor did I see them again. And after that meeting I never even saw Ignazio Salvo again.

'I don't know how the two MPs got to the Salvos' house. I didn't notice any official cars in the street, or any bodyguards. I didn't see anybody else in Ignazio Salvo's house. After the meeting I've been talking about Totò Riina advised me that the matter should be absolutely secret, and he made the gesture of someone locking a door, to say that this was a subject I wasn't to mention to anybody, not even Bernardo Brusca . . .

'Totò Riina told me several times in person that it isn't possible for a politician, of whatever level, to become a man of honour. Nor is it possible for a man of honour to go on doing politics . . . Cosa Nostra despises politicians, who aren't considered serious enough to be part of our organization.

---

* 'Comrade'.

'So I interpreted the kiss between Andreotti and Riina as a sign of respect, "so that things go in the right direction" . . . My impression, but it's just an impression, is that the three men knew each other already.'

'They could use at least one man like him on every street in every city in Italy'*

Tommaso Buscetta

The Rimi family are to Alcamo what Gaetano Badalamenti is to Cinisi, Paolino Bontate to the district of Santa Maria del Gesù, Michele Greco to Croceverde. They are venerated men of honour, masters over other people's lives and deaths. They are everything.

Vincenzo Rimi is the patriarch. Filippo is his firstborn, Natale his other son. They are related to the Badalamenti family; Filippo is a brother-in-law of Don Tano. Vincenzo and Filippo are in jail, sentenced to life for the murder of Salvatore Lupo Leale. But even so, the Rimis are still issuing commands. The only one still at liberty is Natale; he works in the treasurer's office of the town council of Alcamo, a small town between Palermo and Trapani.

In 1970, all of a sudden, Natale is transferred 'officially'. In forty-eight hours, from being an obscure clerk in Alcamo council, he is a functionary at the conservancy for the region of Laio. It's a scandal. The name of the Rimis, unknown until then outside of Sicily, ends up on the front pages of the big Italian newspapers. The state prosecutor of Rome has thirty reels of magnetic tape with recordings of the voices of Filippo Rimi and some members of parliament, lawyers, drug-traffickers and important ministers. The

---

* Questioning of Tommaso Buscetta on 11 September 1992 by the state prosecutors of Palermo, files in case no. 3538/94, 'brought against Andreotti Giulio'.

Anti-Mafia Commission acquires files on the prisoners Vincenzo and Filippo Rimi. They are all 'notifications' that had been sent to Minister of Justice Oronzo Reale for a transfer from one jail to another, recommendations from 'personalities', most of them unknown.

'Rimi's wish to be transferred to Ragusa was made very publicly.'

'Pressure for the Rimis to stay together in Perugia.'

'Repeated, intense pressure for Filippo Rimi to be transferred, even temporarily, from Noto to Ragusa . . .'

The Rimis had connections in Palermo. And also in Rome.

This is how Tommaso Buscetta remembers the Rimis of Alcamo: 'One day, when I was in Brazil with Gaetano Badalamenti – in 1982 or in 1983 – he told me he had personally met Giulio Andreotti, a meeting arranged by Andreotti concerning a trial involving his brother-in-law, Filippo Rimi. At first he had been condemned to life imprisonment, but in the end the Court of Cassation ruled in his favour.'

Buscetta adds: 'Gaetano Badalamenti, a member of the Rimi family, one of the Salvo cousins of Salemi, I don't remember which one, whether it was Nino or Ignazio, claims he went to Andreotti's office. Tano told me Andreotti had personally congratulated him, telling him that they could use at least one man like him on every street in every city in Italy.'

It's 11 September 1992 when Tommaso Buscetta, eight years after his first statements to Judge Falcone and four months after the Capaci massacre, talks again to the Palermo state prosecutors. He decides to say what he didn't say in 1984. He talks about relations between the Mafia and politics, he talks about Salvo Lima, about deputies and senators who are friends with men of honour. It's the Rimi family of Alcamo that begins the twenty-second chapter – the 'adjusted trials' – of the memorandum lodged by the public prosecutor of Palermo in criminal proceedings 'brought against Giulio Andreotti, born in Rome on 14.1.1919, for the crime in violation of Article 416-bis CP (of 29 September 1982) . . .'

Simple criminal association and Mafia-type criminal association.

'Once upon a time I called him Masino; now I'd say: Signor Buscetta'*

Gaetano Badalamenti

'It was 1989 and I was at the New York state attorney's building. I'd just finished an interrogation, Antonio Manganelli was asking the questions, he's now the police superintendent of Naples, and Gianni De Gennaro from the police. I greet him, I start walking along a corridor, and all of a sudden from an open door there comes this voice, Buscetta's voice: "Hey, Tanino, how are things?" So I say to him: "Oh, you almighty great wretch, did you think I'd start crying if you treated me like this?" and he says: "No, not at all, that was never what I had in mind, I know you." And I say: "End of story." Once upon a time I called him Masino; now I'd say: Signor Buscetta.

'Signor Buscetta is a weak man – he wasn't once – and if, as he says, he was once a Mafioso, then he's biting the hand that fed him. But he's not doing this off his own bat, someone's prompting him . . . I know this is the age of the *pentiti* . . . You see, in Sicily we've got a word, *'ngusciare*, for when children cry, cry till they faint. Well, that story about the kiss between Riina and Andreotti makes me *'ngusciare*. It's really too much. The people are childish; in fact they're babyish. And I don't get it: why would he kiss Riina and then have the Mafiosi arrested?

---

* Interview with the Mafioso Gaetano Badalamenti by Stefano Zurlo, *Il Giornale*, 18 October 1999.

'If I behave myself, I might be out in seven years. But will I manage that, at the age of eighty-three? I'd like to go back to Cinisi, where my wife lives, and reunite the whole family, my two sons. But they're on the run . . . I subscribe to the *Giornale di Sicilia*; in the evening I watch American TV. Here in Fayrton a lot of Italian Americans have asked to serve out their time in Italy. They think the police pay you a visit, put the armband on you and leave again. When in fact the Communists . . . To give them their dues, the Communists do have balls . . .

'I saw Buscetta twice. That time in New York and then at the Pizza Connection trial, in which he was sentenced to sixty-one and a half years in the first instance, forty-five as head of the association, fifteen as an associate, one and a half for contempt of court. Luckily, on appeal, the sentence was reduced. I didn't see Buscetta again, but there are some questions I'd really like to ask him. But they haven't taken me to Italy . . . In 1993 or 1994 I was in jail in Memphis, Tennessee. I'm having a shower, the warder tells me I've got a visitor. The captain comes in, the assistant governor, but what happens? Here are three people who speak Italian: they're three public prosecutors from Rome. They ask me, "Do you know Tommaso Buscetta?" "Yes, but what are you doing here? Have you come to question me without consulting my lawyer?" "We didn't know you had one." "I've got two in America and one in Italy." "Mr Buscetta's accusing you of the Pecorelli murder . . ." "Pecorella?" "No, Pecorelli, the journalist from Rome." "And what have I got to do with the journalist from Rome? That's it, I'm not answering your questions, but if you put me up against Buscetta, whenever you want to, I'll show you how much of a liar Buscetta is."

'In a human sense, I hope Andreotti gets off. But if they sentenced him I'd go and see him on my own two feet. He calls Gaetano Badalamenti the Mafioso, the boss, the head of the *Commissione*, so I'd go and say: you see, you must be a boss as well . . . He should be a bit more cautious in his judgements, given that he's been a statesman. And instead he does the same as all the other people who turned me into a colossus. I've never met him and I'd never meet a guy like that . . .'

The history of Cosa Nostra is divided in two: before 1992 and after 1992. 1992 marks the start of an era. 12 March: murder of Salvo Lima; 23 May: massacre in Capaci; 19 July: murder of Mariano D'Amelio in the street; 17 September: killing of Ignazio Salvo. 'Now they're giving us all a good hiding,' the men of honour locked up in special jails had been saying since the start of the year. The Maxi-Trial went badly; the bosses were all sentenced to life. Totò Riina and the other capi *told the people of Cosa Nostra that the Court of Cassation sentence would unleash an unprecedented attack. Against the state. And against two old friends who were unable or unwilling to 'keep their promises'.*

But that Supreme Court verdict isn't the only motive; it's not just the Maxi-Trial. There are hidden hands at work, too. In 1992, in Sicily, a 'great game' has begun.

'The meat's arrived'*

Domenico Ganci

There's only one city in the whole of Italy where the butcher's shops are called not *macellerie* but *carnezzerie*: Palermo. Its most famous *carnezzieri* are the Ganci family, Raffaele and his sons, Domenico and Calogero. They live in the working-class district of La Noce, they own 140 flats, some land around Trapani, some construction companies, delicatessens, big clothes shops and four *carnezzerie*. In the spring of 1992 the Gancis are estimated to be worth around fifty-eight billion lire. Raffaele Ganci is the man of honour who hid Totò Riina on the day the Corleonese came down to Palermo as fugitives in the late 1970s. The Gancis blindly obeyed Uncle Totò. In the spring of 1992 they received an order: 'Keep an eye on all of Judge Falcone's movements.'

The armoured car belonging to the magistrate who has been director general of Penal Affairs in the Ministry of Grace and Justice for over a year, is parked in a courtyard behind Via Notarbartolo. The Gancis have one of their *carnezzerie* on the corner of the street. Domenico Ganci is constantly following that armoured car, on foot or on a moped. When Giuseppe Costanza, chauffeur to the Palace of Justice, arrives in the courtyard on the afternoon of 23 May, Domenico tails him. The chauffeur starts the Fiat Croma and

---

* Quotations from files in the ruling on the Capaci massacre, Court of Assizes, Caltanissetta, 26 September 1997.

slips into the chaotic traffic of the ring-road. Everybody works out that Giovanni Falcone is about to land at Punta Raisi airport. The half-ton of explosives has already been hidden underneath the motorway, not far from the Capaci turn-off.

'The meat has arrived,' Domenico Ganci tells Giovanbattista Ferrante. It's Ferrante who calls Giovanni Brusca, who is waiting on the hill beside the motorway, holding a remote control. Then Ferrante also calls Gioacchino La Barbera, who is in Punta Raisi to check when the judge gets into the armoured car. La Barbera pulls up beside it to check its speed, and calls Giovanni Brusca again.

At 17 hours 56 minutes and 48 seconds the seismographs of the Ettore Majorana Institute in Erice record a telluric shock eight kilometres west of Palermo. An earthquake. There's a smoking crater in the motorway.

The victims are Giovanni Falcone, Francesca Morvillo, Antonio Montinaro's bodyguards Rocco Di Cillo and Vito Schifani. This is the Capaci massacre. Three months after Lima's murder. Fifty-six days before the murder of prosecutor Borsellino. It's a declaration of war by the Corleonesi on the Italian state. With the Capaci massacre, the election of Giulio Anderotti as president of the Republic goes up in smoke.

On the evening of 23 May 1992 Totò Riina raises a glass of champagne to the death of his biggest enemy. Five years later, all the main Cosa Nostra members are sentenced to life. Salvatore Riina. Nitto Santapaola. Giuseppe Madonia. Bernardo Provenzano. Pietro Aglieri. Bernardo Brusca. Pippo Calò. Filippo Graviano. Giuseppe Graviano. Carlo Greco. Michelangelo La Barbera. Giuseppe Montalto. Matteo Motisi. Benedetto Spera. Leoluca Bagarella. Giovanni Battaglia. Salvatore Biondino. Giuseppe Giacomo Gambino. Salvatore Biondo. Domenico Ganci. Raffaele Ganci. Pietro Rampulla. Antonino Troia. Giovanni Brusca turned *pentito*. Twenty-six years' imprisonment. Other *pentiti* are Giovanbattista Ferrante, Gioacchino La Barbera, Mario Santo Di Matteo and Calogero Ganci. Antonino Gioè died, by his own hand.

'I didn't even get to hear the bang'*

Gioacchino La Barbera

'I got the call on my phone, announcing the arrival of the judge's car, I couldn't say exactly who it was who called me, the conversation didn't last long and I didn't recognize the voice . . . Falcone's car was followed, as agreed, to the point where we had a mathematical certainty that it would turn into the road leading to Punta Raisi airport. I was in the cottage along with Antonino Gioè, Giovanni Brusca, Salvatore Biondino, Antonino Troia, Giovanni Battaglia and Giovanbattista Ferrante. Pietro Rampulla wasn't there because he'd decided to go away that Saturday, but he'd been with us until the previous evening.

'As soon the call came in . . . the conversation was as we had established . . . in the sense that I was given the name of a person and I replied that it was a wrong number . . . As soon as the call came in Ferrante went towards the airport to confirm that the judge's car had actually arrived or was about to arrive at Punta Raisi airport; Gioè, along with Troia, went to place the receiver in the manhole, also setting the switch and then with Brusca and Battaglia they climbed up the hill, on the mountain side, where the remote control would be activated; I, in a green-coloured Delta four-wheel drive, went along a road parallel to the motorway and

---

* Record of the questioning of the *pentito* Gioacchino La Barbera in the Capaci Massacre trial, 2 December 1993.

I stopped there and waited to see Judge Falcone's cortege passing by. From where I'd stopped I had a perfect view of the motorway, I could identify the car with the naked eye. I knew that Judge Falcone's armoured car was a white-coloured Fiat Croma.

'When I spotted the vehicle, I set off, followed the procession of cars and immediately phoned the man on the mountain. Antonino Gioè answered the phone. The conversation went on for a long time . . . we talked about various things without touching even slightly on what we were doing, for fear that our call might have been intercepted. I was going at the same speed as the cars in the procession, around about eighty kilometres an hour, much less than the speed we had calculated when we'd been doing our practice run. That detail was picked up by Gioè, because, knowing my position and knowing that I would lose sight of the car by the Johnny Walker bar, by using the duration of the call he was able to calculate how long it would take for Falcone's car to reach the point of the explosion.

'Having reached the Johnny Walker bar, I interrupted my telephone communication with Antonino Gioè. I entered the motorway heading in the direction of Partinico and drove away. I didn't even get to hear the bang . . .'

'*Minchia,*[*] the way the young men walk around in Palermo . . .'[†]

Antonino Gioè and Gioacchino La Barbera

Ten months earlier, the two men had been in Capaci to kill Giovanni Falcone. Now they're hiding in Palermo, in an apartment on Via Ughetti, and they're being bugged. They're afraid of ending up in jail. Meanwhile they're dealing. Meanwhile they're talking.

Antonino: 'Do you think he's got the stuff?'
Gioacchino: 'Cocaine.'
Antonino: 'What are we supposed to do with cocaine, we haven't got any . . .'
Gioacchino: 'I'm leaving tomorrow evening and in case you need him, Michelino's coming up wth Totò.'
Antonino: 'If there's anything to be loaded on, you come up in the Nissan; we'll load it on and go back down again.'
Gioacchino: 'We're putting it in the car up there?'
Antonino: 'Both of them, and a hired car as an outrider . . . OK? . . . What does Roberto want? Doesn't he know what we want? We want the "black stuff" . . . we have to do the deal with the same things that we can sell, don't we?'

---

* Literally: 'penis'. A general swearword.

† Overheard conversation recorded in the files in the trial of Giuseppe Agrigento + 17, Capaci Massacre, 10 October 1993 and 2 November 1993.

Gioacchino: 'That's right, we've got to take . . .'

Antonino: 'Forty, forty-five is fine. Ten kilos to a block . . .'

Gioacchino: '*Minchia*, the way the young men walk around in Palermo. Shocking . . . bodyguards. But they really are bastards. You know what they do? As soon as somebody stops for some sort of traffic jam, two of them come down with machine-guns and start watching like arseholes . . . They'll turn up one morning, here in Politeama . . . *Minchia*, he says a Croma went by, and after a bit two police patrols checked us over . . . they're in constant direct contact. *Minchia*, the way they walk . . .'

Antonino: 'They, they know something. Whereabouts are they, in the province of Trapani?'

Gioacchino: 'The two guards?'

Antonino: 'The two guards who did the beating . . . those guys in the hoods, the guys from Pianosa who beat people up . . . there's a guard from Trapani who came from Pianosa and talked about all those things . . . who are the guys who did the beating? Four are from the province of Trapani, about three from Sciacca, one from Palermo . . .'

Gioacchino: '*Minchia*, so all those names aren't ready yet?'

Antonino: 'We'll have to see . . . The guys from the province of Trapani have been intercepted already. Now they're trying to find out where the guys from Sciacca are, the doors, the house, everything . . . Santa Ninfa. *Minchia*, as soon as he gets there they say they have to take him alive and he mustn't be found again. They have to find him hacked to pieces with a billhook . . .'

Gioacchino: 'Of course, that makes sense.'

Antonino: 'There must be somebody else.'

Gioacchino: 'Could be. Santinu once reminded me . . .'

Antonino: 'Eh . . .'

Gioacchino: 'Basically . . . You remember a garage nearby where you waited up *ddocu a Capaci unni ci fici l'attentatuni,** there was this office . . .'

Antonino: 'Eh . . .'

Gioacchino: 'There's Nicola, Mariano Graviglia, Uncle Troia . . . *minchia*, the names match up! Look at this, but . . . Who was this guy? Mariano's office was near the pizzeria in Capaci . . .'

---

* Up 'at Capaci where we carried out that big attack on him'.

'I represent the end of everything'*

Antonino Gioè

'Tonight I'm finding the peace and serenity I lost about seventeen years ago. Having lost those two things, I became a monster and I remained one until I picked up my pen to write down these few lines, which I hope might serve to save innocent people and unjustly subjugated people who will find themselves involved in legal proceedings solely as a result of my monstrosity . . .

'In this, my first moment of lucidity, I am trying to remember all the nonsense I said either on Via Ughetti or on the phone. My brother Gaspare is a person who has never shared my lifestyle, but unfortunately, being my brother, he had to put up with me without ever staining his own character. My brother Mario has always been more critical about me than anyone, but unfortunately after I was arrested he had to intervene because he was forced to try and recover some of his reputation from my filthy affairs. My brother Pino and my sister Anna have always got ont with their lives without ever approaching me for any kind of favour . . . My brother-in-law Pietro and my sister Giulia became my victims to some extent because I rented a flat from them . . . My wife was a victim of my monstrosity only in terms of our marital life. Rome Salvatore, known as the Tuscan, was a victim of mine because, even

* Quotations from files in the trial of Giuseppe Agrigento + 17, Capaci Massacre, 10 October 1993 and 2 November 1993.

though he was anxious, I forced him to give me a photocopy of his driver's licence . . .

'Once on Via Ughetti I talked about Ugo Martello and Gino as if I knew them well and saw them often. The reality is very different and I haven't heard anything of Gino for many years. As regards Ugo, if my memory serves, apart from having known him in jail, I saw him only once when he got out, but only by chance, and that was just a moment to swap greetings and promise each other that we would have lunch together some time . . . Often I have stated that I am the owner of who knows how much wealth; in reality I have nothing but debts. If my wife has something it's only her mother's pension, and I think that is provable . . . At this extreme moment in my life I swear that I am writing nothing but the truth.

'Among the many things I said in the flat and elsewhere there must have been a lot of nonsense, and if you saw me regularly you would realize that at this precise moment in time I don't remember any other people that I have besmirched with my chatter and shamefulness. I represent the end of everything and I think that, from tomorrow or at least very soon, the *pentiti* will be able to return to their houses certainly with much more honour than I, who have none.

'Before I go I want to ask forgiveness of my mother and God because their love is unbounded; the whole rest of the world will never be able to forgive me. The future of the world belongs to normal human beings and true *pentiti*. The latter if they are truly honest can do nothing other than to confirm what I have written about the people I have listed.'

'These people are the lowest in the world since the days of Nero'

Tommaso Buscetta

Their village is San Giuseppe Jato, thirty-one kilometres from Palermo and eighteen from Corleone. Ten thousand inhabitants, ninety-five of them Bruscas. The ones who seem more Corleonesi than the Corleonesi have land around I Dammusi: vines and sharp rocks with a main road that still comes down through the fields to Monreale. The head of the Brusca clan is Emanuele, a powerful man of honour who knows the mysteries of the first Italian state massacre, Portella della Ginestra, on 1 May 1947. Eleven dead and thirty-seven injured, the peasants slaughtered on a windswept plain on May Day. A few hours before the massacre Emanuele Brusca is at the farm of Kaggio, where the desperadoes of Salvatore Giuliano's gang meet the Mafiosi of Cosa Nostra and together decide to burn down Portella.

After Emanuele comes his son Bernardo, a peasant turned landowner. By the late 1980s he is one of the Cosa Nostra leaders, along with Salvatore Riina. He is the one most loyal to uncle Totò. If in Palermo the Corleonesi can count on the Madonia family of Resuttana and the Gancis of La Noce, in the province they have Bernardo Brusca.

After Bernardo comes his son Giovanni. In Sicily almost everyone has an *inciuria*, a nickname inherited from his father or grandfather, from a physical defect or his way of speaking or moving. Giovanni Brusca is called *ù verru,* the boar. He is the one who, on the hill at Capaci, presses a button and blows up Falcone. 'These people are the lowest in the world since the days of Nero,' says Tommaso Buscetta, when, in 1984, he comes back from Brazil and starts talking. More than ten years later Giovanni Brusca will also turn state's evidence. First he tries to derail investigations, then he confesses. Between one and two hundred murders. Including that of little Giuseppe Di Matteo, the son of Santino Mezzanasca, dissolved in acid. 'Even today I can't remember all the names, one by one, of the people I killed,' says *ù verru*.

'The truth is that the law is not the same for everyone'*

Antonina Brusca

'I'm proud of my children and my husband Bernardo. I brought up my children well and in a God-fearing way. People talk rubbish. About Giovanni they talk nothing but rubbish. That business about the remote control and Di Matteo's son . . . You know what the truth is? The truth is that the law is not the same for everyone. All the privileges go to the *pentiti*, only to them. But God alone knows what things are really like. I raised my children with religion. They are all baptized and, like me, they went to Catholic Action. I'm also a charitable lady, a Vincentian volunteer . . . I'm a human person. Should I be ashamed? Should my son be ashamed? And of what? But if the Holy Spirit shines in our minds, and shines in the judges' minds, he will not be found guilty.

'But I would have liked Enzo, the younger one, to give himself up. My husband is of that opinion too. But with 41-bis, how do you go about giving yourself up? And they've just given Bernardo life, and I know he won't come out. Vito Ganci met the lawyer yesterday at the Ucciardone. He told me that when he knew they'd arrested Giovanni and Enzo he threw up his arms as if to say, "May God's will be done." But I say: Giovanni could well "repent". But he won't because he's not a coward.

* Quotations taken from interviews with Antonina Brusca (the wife of the Mafioso Bernardo Brusca) in *Tg2*, 24 May 1996 and in *La Repubblica*, 22 and 24 May 1996.

'I don't know what's going to happen now. I pray every day . . . everybody's always talking about him . . . So it will be the fault of the Communist judges throwing the cell keys away. And besides, now they've started exploiting the *picciriddi** at school. They tell me my Giovanni is a brute. And they raise a great scandal if a child has a fight with another child of some wretched *pentito*. And now, for the anniversary of Falcone's "accident", there's all this hoopla, all this publicity. But the dead should be remembered in silence.

'The *pentiti* have said that my son was on that hill above the motorway to press the remote control. By way of evidence they collected the cigarette stubs to do a DNA test, but my son Giovanni has never smoked. Enzo did, though; in fact I came here this morning because I wanted to bring him two packs of cigarettes and a piece of bread. First the police told me I could give them to him, then they attacked me, they chased me away horribly, calling me terrible names. They told me that twenty of those hooded men, those jackals, had hurled themselves at Giovanni. The children were terrified and the poor *picciriddi* got a temperature. Are those things humane? They say my son killed the son of Santino Mezzanasca, but it's not true . . . They make their statements in instalments like in a TV soap.

'I found out about the arrest of Enzo and Giovanni from the TV. At three o'clock on Tuesday morning my sons' partners, Sara and Piera, came here, to Feotto, with the two children. But before I saw them I had to wait outside police headquarters from six till ten in the morning. Locked in my car. Outside, policewomen were shouting at me that my son is a brute and a murderer, but they were the ones who were acting like wolves. I know they raised their glasses to Giovanni and Enzo in the station, and made fun of them. I saw Giovanni with his face swollen and Enzo had a huge bruise on his belly. I don't know if they beat them up, though Giovanni

---

* 'Little ones', children.

told me it happened. I'm just saying that they found them guilty with no evidence. And it's a good job, yes, it's a good job that they still have respect for the Bruscas in San Giuseppe Jato . . .'

The Bruscas are Totò Riina's *canazzi da catena*;* he releases them when he needs them and then puts them back on the chain. They are always at his command, his servants, sticking blindly by the side that seems fiercest in the Mafia war. The *pentito* Tommaso Buscetta is very well acquainted with Bernardo, who is only a few years older than him: 'He stinks, and he goes on stinking even if you put a litre of Cologne on him.'

On 4 April 2000 Tommaso Buscetta dies in the United States. On 8 December Bernardo Brusca also dies, in a hospital in Palermo. His son Giovanni is in jail. As a 'collaborator with justice' he has a 'free pass' every forty-five days to meet his wife Cristiana and their two children. The Mafia 'tradition' of the Bruscas of San Giuseppe Jato ends for ever with him. But the Mafia is far from dead.

There's nothing wrong with being a Mafioso. This is the opinion of 61 per cent of the inhabitants of the village of the Palermitan that fathered the Bruscas. More than half of the population, according to a survey carried out by Servizi Italia for the Archdiocese of Monreale, makes no secret of the fact that they have no qualms about the Mafiosi. The investigation was based on a sample of 1,200 people, fifteen years upwards, with a questionnaire of thirty-four questions by the Catholic University in Milan and Palermo University.

---

* 'Chain dogs'.

'In Palermo . . . the people are very polite about paying'*

Gaspare Mutolo

The shop windows gleam with gold, the doors of the jewellers' shops are always open. There are thirty-one of them, small, crammed in between the doors of tumble-down houses, deconsecrated churches, abandoned shops. An alleyway slides down towards the sea and the port of La Cala; on the other side are the Vucciria markets. At the end of Via Giovanni Meli it's forbidden to steal, it's forbidden to rob, it's forbidden to commit a crime. The jewellers are never afraid. They've paid their *pizzo*.†

After the goldsmiths, the street widens into a big square, with a magnificent fig-tree in the middle. There's a newspaper kiosk, a barber's, two shops, one selling electrical goods and the other spare car parts. The newsagent pays. The barber pays. Both shopkeepers pay. Discesa dei Maccheronai, Via dei Coltellieri, Piazza Fonderia. The more slippery the *balate*, the smooth stones that pave the alleyways, the closer you are to the market. Garish colours, smells of spices, the cries of the vendors. They all pay here, too, at the Vucciria.

Ice-cream-makers, roast-meat stands, sausage-makers, sellers of octopus and olives, bar-owners, tobacconists, *carnezzieri*, the

---

* Questioning of Gaspare Mutolo, Parliamentary Anti-Mafia Commission, Rome, 9 February 1993.

† 'Protection money'.

men selling *pani ca meusa** in the street, others with *panelle,* chick-pea fritters fried in boiling oil. The old prostitutes pay, the ones from the brothels hidden between the Basilica of San Domenico and the ruins from the Second World War.

The names, all their names, are in some ledger somewhere. Every now and again the police confiscate one. The name and the shop, the people going in and out, the whole district.

'Extortion is a great success in Palermo because the people are very polite about paying,' says Gaspare Mutolo. 'They have this mentality that means they act calmly. When I hear that some businessman or shopkeeper isn't paying, I lose it . . . Because sometimes they also have advantages. First, because a friendship arises between the guy who collects the payment and the shop-keepers; and because their safety is guaranteed. If a theft occurs, the guys from the Mafia milieu will see to it that everything stolen is returned. Or if someone commits a fraud, there's a whole gang ready to force them to give the money back.'

A reciprocal convenience. A tax that's far better than any kind of insurance.

'So it's not as if there are only losers, it's more a matter of give and take. Once this relationship come into being, logically, when a lady or a man comes to me and says, "Hey, my son has to get married and needs a job," I take an interest and give him a job. There's no problem: you talk to the owner and you say, "Find a job for one, two, three or however many it is." He might need a fort-night, or a month, to fire someone else or to create a job, but there's always a way.'

The smaller shops and the street sellers pay between 500 and 1,000 Euros a month. The jewellers and the bigger shops up to 3,000 Euros. When the activity begins, there's always *una tantum*†

* *Pane con milza,* spleen sandwiches.

† A supplement.

which is non-negotiable. You can pay it in instalments, but it all has to be settled by Christmas or Easter. You are only let off your *mesata* in one case: family mourning.

The time a shopkeeper feels true terror, however, is the first time he opens a shop and no one shows up. He starts getting worried, asks questions. He asks everyone, all his neighbours. '*Con chi posso mettermi a posto?*' Who can I fix myself up with?

Fixing yourself up. That's how *pizzo* works in Palermo.

'That's how I fixed things up'*

Davide De Marchi

'Via San Basilio. Bastiano Marino's wholesale cassettes and CDs pays up. Pub and restaurant inside the gate pay up. Carrieri button-makers pay up. Spinnato bakery pays up . . .

'Via Napoli. They all pay up without any exception, and Via Borzì's the same, and they can't refuse.

'Via Venezia. The newsagent, the restaurant, the frozen-fish-seller, the plumbers, the supermarket next to Bar Lucchese, the blacksmith, the garage, the Di Pari *carnezziere*, the Ferro di Cavallo poulterers, B—. belonging to the Lo Presti family and their [jewellery] recycler don't pay . . .

'Via Roma. They all pay, from the station to the first traffic lights. The only one that doesn't is the Bar Ciarli, which is seen as the police bar, and I've never been on friendly terms with the people who work in there.

'Rione Capo. The Puccio bakery pays, the Volturno pharmacy, Ganci chairs. The tobacconist on Via Volturno doesn't pay because we see it as being close to the *carabinieri*. The big lingerie shop on the corner of Via Volturno and the Teatro Massimo pays, the wig-maker's at the crossroads, the house of ill-repute of a certain Giulia on Via Volturno . . .

---

* Record of comments made by the former Mafia 'collector' Davide De Marchi at the ruling in the trial of Tommaso Lo Presti + 5, case no. 5847/03, court of Palermo.

'Via Bandiera. All the clothes and shoe shops pay. All the bridal shops apart from the shop belonging to Marino, who is the brother-in-law of the Lo Prestis . . .

'Vucciria. All the fruiterers pay, regardless. And then: Bonaccorso bakery, Garella bakery, Voglia di Pane, the Velardi bakery on Corso Vittorio Emanuele. All the fishmongers, regardless. All the sausage-makers apart from C—. Saccone's shoe shop pays, Signora Pina's poulterers, Valenti poulterers pays, Silvio's tobacconists pays, Vitale brothers' tobacconists pays, the clothes shops in the Vucciria pay, the Bar Bocceria pays, the Bar Corona doesn't pay – it belongs to Giuseppe Corona who's in jail for murder. The kiosk bar of S— doesn't pay because they're trusted people. Bar Le Cicale pays. Bar Caterina pays. The I Grilli pub on Via Bambinai pays. The roast-meat stall on Piazza Valverde pays.

'All the jewellers on Piazza San Domenico all the way to the end of Via Meli pay. All without exception. Apart from F—, recycler of stolen gold, who lends big sums of money and cashes big cheques. The ironmongers and the people at Sarpa Maurizio pay. The Simoncini Brothers' two second-hand car shops pay. Buccheri's scrapworks doesn't because he has two sons-in-law: one is a marshal in the *carabinieri* and one's a policeman. The tobacconist's on Piazza Cala pays. The only delicatessen on Corso Vittorio Emanuele pays. The musical instrument shop pays. The out-of-town delicatessen opposite the entrance to the Vucciria pays. The motor-bike shop pays. Franco 'ù Vastiddaru's *pane ca meusa* stall pays. The V— brothers' bar doesn't pay because they're involved in international drug-smuggling. They have particular connections with Holland. That was how I fixed things up.'

‘Even Garibaldi paid the *pizzo* to land at Marsala’*

Antonino Patti

He confesses to thirty-eight murders. Some of the men he killed he doesn’t even know their names; as for others, he doesn’t know why they had to die. He’s a hitman, and he is talking one evening to Massimo Russo, deputy state prosecutor of Palermo investigating Cosa Nostra in the province of Trapani. Antonino Patti is a man of honour of the Marsala family. He’s just finished listing all his ambushes and strangulations. All that’s missing from his statement is the signature and the date. It’s autumn 1997. The hitman makes a gesture with his hand; there’s something he wants to add. Something that happened 137 years earlier, on 11 May 1860.

Patti starts talking: ‘I found this out during a meeting with some old men of honour. They told me that Cosa Nostra has existed since 1800. Those old men of honour at that meeting were taking about a fact, the fact that even Garibaldi paid the *pizzo* to land at Marsala. He had to pay a certain sum to get across the city and another to get as far as Salemi.’

Deputy State Prosecutor Massimo Russo records this. A year later, Antonino Patti’s ‘revelations’ are filed at the prosecutor’s office. They are public, and highly contested.

The first to comment on them is Bettino Craxi, a great admirer

* Questioning of the *pentito* Antonino Patti by magistrate Massimo Russo, Court of Assizes, Trapani, 14 October 1998.

of Peppino Garibaldi and a collector of his relics. Interviewed by Tg2 in his refuge in Hammamet in Tunisia, the former president of the Council of Ministers replies sarcastically: 'This is a truth that I don't know; let's leave it to Signor Patti's great-grandparents.' The academic world also replies to the *pentito*. Massimo Ganci, professor of modern history and president of the Sicilian Modern History Society, states roundly: 'This is total nonsense, the Bourbon ships opened fire on the *Piemonte* and the *Lombardo* that day, and Giuseppe Garibaldi and his men, only after they had sunk the *Lombardo* and been protected by the English, managed to disembark and head inland, where they encountered genuine resistance at Calatafimi.'

Antonino Patti is judged to be 'trustworthy' by four Courts of Assizes as far as the thirty-eight murders were concerned. As to the rest, no believes him.

But, Garibaldi aside, did the practice of extortion exist in late nineteenth-century Sicily, which had just become a part of Italy?

On 31 August 1874, the interior minister, Giuseppe Cantelli, called a meeting with the prefects of the western provinces of the island 'for reasons of public order'. The chief of police of Girgenti – Agrigento – Luigi Berti, read out his statement: 'The title of Mafioso is acquired by carrying forbidden weapons, by remaining silent about any crimes, and by any form of sponging.' The next to speak was Giuseppe Cotta Ramusino, the former prefect of Naples who had just moved to the island and been appointed as the government representative in Trapani: 'Because the principal *Camorrista* who trained the Camorra was in jail, it was from in there that he collected the *pizzo*, the protection money from each new arrival, which varied case by case, according to the condition and the financial abilities of the unfortunates in question . . . This cancer has not yet come to an end, but if the Camorra arises out of the Mafia, the two should still not be confused.'

It's the first time that the word *pizzo* appears in an official document.

'With a litre of petrol, boom . . . you can set the whole world alight'*

Ruggero Anello

Ruggero Anello: 'You light a cigarette and you throw it.

Man: 'I throw it.'

Anello: 'You throw it in the middle. If you throw it over the box of matches it's better, in the middle of the petrol is better . . . I'll wait for you, you go down from this crossroads here . . . you get there . . . we pick you up and we go.'

Man: 'You see a car passing . . . after the car passes you run away and I throw the match . . . boom . . . I've got it, Captain Ruggero . . .'

Anello: 'Do you want to see how it's done?'

Man: 'I've got it . . . but I just have to put the match there . . .'

Anello: 'No, you see the cigarette, you light it in your mouth, you take it, you drop it, you throw the petrol . . . like that . . . and then you throw it. As soon as it gets there it takes and it goes up . . . or else you put it like this. It's better in the middle because then it takes on either side.'

Man: 'But first I've got to wait till it goes up, one bottle each . . . we're burning . . . which car is it?'

Anello: 'With a litre of petrol, boom . . . you can set the whole world alight.'

---

* Bugged conversation recorded in a report from Monreale police headquarters to the state prosecutor's office of Palermo, 3 December 1997.

Man: 'No one's going to stop us . . .'

Anello: 'No, they won't stop us.'

Man: 'There'll be fire tonight.'

Anello: 'Have you never done it this way?'

Man: 'Yes, I've done it, let me do it . . .'

Anello: 'Careful, if people get out of the car, you see?'

Man: 'Of course, I run off.'

Anello: 'I'll drop you at the lights and pick you up down there, I'll go and wait on the other side. You be careful, there might be cops around.'

Man: 'Just so you know that, at worst, after more than ten minutes, say, you know where you can find me, near the lights, there's a bar there . . .'

Anello: 'At worst, you shut up and I shut up. I'll go up to where the things are. You understand, as soon as it goes up, you hide yourself among the other cars.'

Man: 'Yes, I'll be quick about it . . .'

(*The man gets out of the car but he comes back a few minutes later.*)

Man: 'Ruggero, we're going . . . Ruggero, the guys in the Alfa 33 were cops . . .'

Anello: 'Uh . . .'

Man: 'They were parked, I was driving around, they were parked there . . . *Minchia*, I get out and they're driving around me.'

Anello: 'A Punto arrived when you . . .'

Man: 'Yes, the Punto arrived, the guys in the Punto and the ones in the Alfa 33. I went and filled up the car, I drove around and I did it again and I took out the stopper and I put it back in and set off again. As soon as I came back I saw that Punto again. I saw it, *minchia*, and I sat up straight and I came back to where we were parked. I put the petrol near the tree.'

Anello: 'Is it visible?'

Man: 'No, you can't see it because it's half-hidden so that we can come back another time . . . damn it all to hell . . . Ruggero, it was really close . . . it was really close.'

Anello: 'Let's go home, let's go home and sleep and after that we'll do it.'

Man: 'Yes, I know. You could see they looked like cops, sons of bitches. We'd practically done it.'

‘We’re putting on the glue’*

Aurelio Neri

There hasn’t been a Mafia crime in Palermo for thirteen months. That hasn’t happened since the unification of Italy. It’s late 1998 and there’s no sign of Cosa Nostra. Its *capo*, Bernardo Provenzano, seems to be a ghost. He has been in hiding for thirty-five years. The local papers publish the announcement that the city has been chosen by the United Nations as a symbolic city for the convention on translational crime in 2000, Christmas decorations are up in all the shops. From Piazza Politeama to the Quattro Canti, there are illuminations everywhere. The racket’s over. Without so much as the bang of a firecracker.

‘If this isn’t fixed, we’re putting on the glue,’ a voice hisses on the phone. The silence of Palermo is that glue: Cosa Nostra’s new weapon of choice. The man on the phone is called Aurelio Neri; he’s a man of honour from La Noce.

Every morning the shopkeepers raise their shutters, but they can’t get in, the key won’t go into the padlock. They try again and the key breaks. It’s a signal that they’ve got to get things fixed, that they have to pay up. It’s glue that seals the keyhole. Better than revolvers. Better than a bottle of petrol, which shatters into a million pieces when it lands and makes too much noise.

---

* Record of the questioning of Aurelio Neri by state prosecutor Maurizio De Lucia, 6 July 1996.

In Palermo it's the age of soft, 'calm' extortions. Intangibly cruel, never angry. The extortion is all for Cosa Nostra. More drug-trafficking, more contracts, more money. It's through demands for protection money that Cosa Nostra manifests its existence. Even when the organization's coffers are overflowing, Cosa Nostra never stops extorting. It's in a fatal embrace with its victims. It's like the air you need to breathe.

At the end of 1998, seventy-nine shop-owners between Via Bandiera and Via Maqueda sign a 'statement of solidarity' in favour of Giovanni Corallo: 'We the undersigned hereby express our support for Mr Corallo, who, for many years, has practised commercial activity in an exemplary fashion, in accordance with the rules of fair competition and maintaining good relations with his colleagues.' Giovanni Corallo, already found guilty with a definitive verdict of Mafia association, is suspected of putting the squeeze on those very same shopkeepers.

In that silent Palermo on the eve of a new millenium, 90 per cent of shopkeepers pay up. It's a default reaction. They pay up without a word. But not all of them, as they did in the past. If a shopkeeper happens to have a brother or brother-in-law who's a policeman or a customs officer, the collectors leave him alone. Better one *mesata* less than having the cops on your back. And if someone else refuses, Cosa Nostra don't do anything straight away. They don't break his legs or set fire to his shop. But he has to keep his mouth shut; he can't become an 'example' for the others. A refusal is part of the risk of the business. In Palermo now you can say no. It's a new policy from old Bernardo Provenzano. After the noise of the massacres the Mafia needs a bit of peace and quiet. It hides, it infiltrates, it blends in. It fixes things with glue.

'Because those guys eat everything'

Intercepted conversation between two Trapani businessmen

M: 'We ended up in the middle and got squeezed, *minchia,* like a sausage . . . we're hurtling out of the sky, if there was a parachute then we could attach ourselves to it, but since there isn't a parachute, we'll drop like a stone.'

D: 'It'll be difficult, but it seems difficult because there isn't one, it's a complete mess on all sides, you've worked out what the problem is . . .'

M: 'And yet . . . here we are . . . My complaint was just this: that I don't want to talk to 300 people, not just for Marsala . . . but for everyone, for Mazara, for Petrosino, for Trapani* . . .'

D: 'Of course . . .'

M: 'Now you're telling me, you of all people are telling me it doesn't work and it's like this, I realize that it isn't working because nothing works nowadays. Here from one moment to the next we're on the other side because you have to get it into your head that they're arresting us all . . . because none of us is squeaky-clean . . . to give them something to eat, meaning us . . .'

D: 'And I know . . .'

M: 'Because we aren't clean, because we have to support those gentlemen, so we are . . . the risk that by selling yourself to

* Thought to be the names of Mafiosi the businessman has to pay.

those gentlemen . . . Anything can happen, if you ignore them and because, either way, they'll kill you, or they'll do something to you or they'll set fire to you, they'll do something, and you'll find yourself between the hammer and the anvil . . .'

D: 'What did you do in Strasatti? Did you sort things out or not?'

M: 'What am I supposed to sort out . . .!? It's a complete mess on all sides . . . to sort things out I have to pay, and by paying for everything you sort things out, but not at those rates . . . I, where my personal affairs are concerned, I no longer know what I'm supposed to take, what road I'm supposed to travel on, and I'm under enormous pressure and I'm in great difficulties, the thing that I've got, the fear that nags away at me, do you know what it is? It's those children that are growing up and I don't know whether I'll be able to keep them. Because if I have to support those guys I won't be able to support my family . . . Because those guys eat everything . . . I haven't got tons of cash, so I don't know where to go and get it, even by cheque . . . where are you going to get your money from? . . .'

D: 'You've got to make out invoices . . .'

M: 'And who makes out invoices these days?. . . the tax men will turn up tomorrow and have your balls . . . where are you going to find invoices today? So it's more difficult to get your money out, and unfortunately they don't understand that . . .'

D: 'Of course, of course . . .'

M: 'Until you're talking about ten million . . . but when you start talking about certain numbers, *minchia* . . .'

D: 'Ten, fifteen million . . . you can even get hold of twenty, thirty million . . .'

They're all rigged from the start. An inquiry by the Palermo prosecutor's office discovers in the spring of 2003 that in Sicily 96 per cent of public contracts of around five million Euros are assigned with rebates between 0 and 1 per cent. Figures that speak for themselves: all businessmen agree. The 'crime notes' are published in the 'Official Gazette' of the Sicilian region. For the same kind of contracts, the national average of rebates varies between 16 and 22 per cent.

'We're hostages of these gentlemen'*

Filippo Salamone

It's a big story in *Il Giornale di Sicilia*: seven columns on the front page: 'After thirty-six years, the Cassina company cedes its contract to Lesca.' It's the end of the summer of 1974, and the Palermo newspaper informs the citizens that, from the following month, the streets and sewers are entrusted to a new company. The business, the most lucrative in Palermo, had always been the privilege of Count Arturo Cassina. He was a man from Como who had come to Sicily between the wars; his court included bishops and generals, barristers and ministers. So who was usurping the Cassinas after all this time? A few weeks after the announcement, it was discovered that the man behind Lesca was Count Arturo himself. The story of the Cassinas is the story of all the big contracts in Palermo. Vast wealth, the shadow of Salvo Lima, a web of complicity. The first Parliamentary Anti-Mafia Commission dedicates an entire chapter to the streets and sewers of Palermo: 'The Cassinas and the system of Mafia power'. In 1972, the Corleonesi kidnap one of the count's sons to affront Stefano Bontate and Gaetano Badalamenti. At the beginning of the 1980s a judicial storm comes crashing down on the empire. One scandal after another. One judicial inquiry after another. Yet in the end the Cassinas are acquitted of all charges.

---

* Interview with Filippo Salamone by Attilio Bolzoni, *La Repubblica*, 23 September 1997.

When the Cassinas' power was nearly on the wane, on the other side of the island the star of the Cavalieris was shining. There were three of them: Carmelo Costanzo, Mario Rendo and Gaetano Graci. They built everything and everywhere. Dykes. Motorways. Airports. They were the masters of Catania. In Italy they came to fame when General Carlo Alberto dalla Chiesa, on 19 August 1982 – two weeks before his death – confessed to Giorgio Bocca in his famous interview: 'With the agreement of the Palermo Mafia, the biggest Catanese construction companies are working in Palermo today.' It was incendiary. In *I Siciliani* the journalist Pippo Fava – who would be killed a few years later too – called them 'the Horsemen of the Apocalypse'. The climate was incandescent; the Catanian authorities defended their Horsemen, but there were investigations, arrests, and *pentiti* hurling accusations at them. The police suggested obligatory residence for them, on the grounds that they were 'a threat to society', but a judge ruled that Costanzo, Graci and Rendo were 'victims and not accomplices of the Mafia'. After ten years of hearings in various tribunals, the Horsemen disappeared from the Sicilian stage.

In the late 1980s in Sicily, the era of Filippo Salomone was about to begin. He was from Agrigento, and his company was a giant in the field of construction. With close ties to the minister Calogero Mannino and the president of the region, Rino Nicolosi, 're Salamone' (King Solomon) was most importantly the cousin of Salvatore Totino Sciangula, the influential councillor for public works in the government of Palermo. He, Salamone, was the new prince of contracts on the island. He negotiated with Corleonesi ambassadors like Angelo Siino. He talked to the politicians. He forced the big northern business conglomerates to sign pacts with the companies close to Cosa Nostra. But after the massacres of 1992, even the kingdom of Filippo Salomone fell. Sicilia's 'Tangentopoli'* broke out.

* 'Bribe City', the kick-back scandal of the early 1990s in Italy.

Hundreds of arrests. Salamone spilled the beans, tried to defend himself: 'We're hostages of these gentlemen.' But he didn't get away with it. The final sentence – the definitive one – was passed in the spring of 2008. Six years by the Court of Cassation for external participation in Mafia association.

'Work in peace'*

Antonino Calderone

The knights of Catania according to Antonino Calderone.

'The Knights of Labour† of Catania have never been victims of the Mafia, at least not while I've been here. Of course, there was a difference between a Rendo on the one hand and a Costanzo on the other. But in the end they all also enjoyed the reputation of being linked to us. Now they say they don't know us. When he was confronted by me, Gino Costanzo actually denied having been a witness at my wedding and my brother's. He didn't remember!

'Having the Mafia on your own side – for businessmen like the Costanzo brothers and others like them – meant being able to work in peace and make lots of money without the risk of seeing your vehicles vandalized, without strikes stopping your work halfway through, without requests for bribes that even the lowest Mafioso feels he has the right to demand of anyone who wants to make an investment on his territory. That was the task that my uncle Luigi and my brother Pippo had performed for the Costanzos. When Pippo's company went bankrupt, he became the factotum for the Costanzo company. He went and inspected all the building sites, he came to Rome. He looked after everything. He had put his friendships within the Sicilian region at the disposal of the company . . .

---

* Talking to Pino Arlacchi in *Gli uomini del disonore* (*'Men of Dishonour'*)

† Senior industrial managers.

For example, they said to him, "We've got to do a site in Caltanisetta. What side of the city should we put it on?" And Pippo went there, he looked for the land to rent and reached agreements with the *capofamiglia* of the area so that the site and the machines would be protected . . .

'When the Costanzo company put in a bid for 20–30 billion, that bid turned into three or four years of work for the pieceworkers . . . The company's policy was to make an offer to each of the petitioners, and then to favour the Mafiosi by telling them the prices offered by the others. The Mafiosi offered a slightly lower figure, and in that way they won the subcontracts. How much money Pippo and Costanzo saved! And how many arguments Pippo resolved . . .

'There was always that competition between Rendo and Costanzo. Costanzo was made a Knight of Labour in the industry . . . there weren't enough places and Rendo had to be downgraded and made a Knight of Labour in agriculture. Kids' stuff. They divided up the work, but Rendo always did the lion's share in that. I don't know why; he always had something more than the others; he was probably more cunning. Most importantly, the meetings had to be held at his house, and everyone had to go and kiss his hand. Carmelo Costanzo only had one way of defending himself: every now and again, according to him, when he didn't agree with something, he would come out with the line "My brother's friends aren't very happy." The friends were me and my brother. We put bombs in the building sites.

'If you ask me, Rendo got much more involved with politics, and in that he got no support from the Mafia . . . They reached agreements between themselves, Costanzo, Graci and Rendo . . . and with the northern businessmen. When they came to Sicily, they added 10–15 per cent for the Mafia to their outgoings, because they were worried their building sites would be blown up.

'In around 1980, Nitto Santapaola, talking about Carmelo

Costanzo, said that he was always complaining, whatever happened to him. In particular, Totò Riina had got him a huge job on a building in Palermo, for which Riina asked for 100 million. Costanzo complained because he thought it was too much.'

'The eye of respect'*

Angelo Siino, known as Bronson

'The Mafia was etched on the face of my people, it was in the dust of my village, San Giuseppe Jato. My uncle Salvatore Celeste, one of the most important *capi* of Cosa Nostra, was the only Mafioso in my family. The bandit Salvatore Giuliano was part of his *cosca*. I met him as a child; when I was five I dreamed of being like him . . . Some years later, the men in his gang were my most trusted subordinates . . .

'Even the most powerful bosses feared me – my connection with the old people in Cosa Nostra was my strength. I liked challenging fate by doing business with unscrupulous men and driving along the mule-tracks of Sicily. I had a lot of passions: racing-cars, boar-hunting, a good cigar. I was as much at my ease in cottages in the country as I was in the most luxurious drawing rooms. Today I'm a "collaborator of justice", accusing murderers, pointing the finger at people who are above suspicion . . . my weapon is truth. I don't have anything now. All I have left is my wife and my son.

'I started car-racing when I was eighteen. I raced until I was forty-seven, when I was arrested. Well, I no longer did actual races, but Club Porsche, Club Ferrari races . . . I started with a

---

* Interview with Angelo Siino, *Sette*, 20 January 2000; interview with Angelo Siino by Gianni Barbacetto, *Diario*, 26 May 1999.

Cinquecento and ended up with Ferraris. I won a few rallies. In those days I was called Bronson, I looked a lot like the actor . . .

'I knew Stefano Bontate when he was about twenty. I was his driver too; Bontate was scared of planes, so he wanted to do some long journeys by car. He told me he felt safe with me.

'I knew Giuseppe Piddu Madonia of Caltanissetta, Nitto Santapaola of Catania, his brother Turi . . . Once I turned up at a farm near Catania and there was a terrible stench: a smell of sheep, a terrible smell. I was welcomed as always with hugs and kisses, but I saw a whole sheep boiling away in a cauldron. Nitto was nice, *grazioso*, but Turi was *grossier*.* With the tip of a knife he took the sheep's eye and passed it to me. It was the *eye of respect*, which I thought was invented, but it was real . . . I swallowed the eye whole, I still remember it with horror . . .

'I was a friend to Giovanni Brusca. I really wanted to shape him into my spitting image. I went with him to the best clothes shops in Palermo, to the barber, I cleaned him up . . . He became my shadow, I introduced him as my cousin.

'I'd also introduced him as my cousin to the businessman Filippo Salamone. But his associate, Giovanni Micciché, knew his true identity . . . Filippo Salamone felt like the king of the jungle, we were like two cocks in the chicken-coop. Salamone was more influential in the fields of politics and finance. He was the real manager of public works in Sicily. Cosa Nostra ordered for him to be killed if he didn't comply with certain rules. That's why I took the trouble to save his life a few times.

'In the 1970s, Vito Ciancimino took care of things when speculation was at its height. He looked after his own interests, letting the crumbs fall into the Mafia basket. Then the industry of public works exploded; it was almost entirely in the hands of politicians and businessmen. Until someone in Cosa Nostra said, "Are we

* 'Coarse'.

going to look on while these politicians get fat?" . . . And they understood they had the right person for zero cost: Angelo Siino. I was the skeleton key, I was Cosa Nostra's way into the nerve centre.'

'The politicians went mad: because a kind of protection money was being imposed on their bribes'*

Angelo Siino, known as Bronson

'I became Cosa Nostra's minister of public works by chance, you might say . . . Cosa Nostra has always been involved in pretty much every kind of business; protection money is collected in every area of activity in Sicily. But I'd have to say that the blame for Cosa Nostra's involvement in the contract sector lies with the politicians. The politicians, by misusing public funds, forced the Mafia to say: what, are we stupid or something? They stuff their faces while we stand and watch? That's when Cosa Nostra gets heavily involved in the game. It's the mid-1980s . . . with me, the Mafia doesn't just become entrepreneurial, it imposes its personalities and its regular companies on the politicians. The politicians went mad: because a kind of protection money was being imposed on their bribes. For the politicians, poor things, it was like having *pizzo* sandwiches . . .

'The Siino system is the oldest in the world . . . I tried to distribute contracts according to the size of the company, I tried to encourage a certain *regionalism*, a certain *localism* . . . always with the tacit or direct agreement of Cosa Nostra. No company escaped that system. Not one, whether regional or national. The northern companies working in Sicily got where they are *through politics*, and

---

* Interview with Angelo Siino by Gianni Barbacetto, *Diario*, 26 May 1999.

Cosa Nostra had been factored into that. Everyone knew that: aside from politics, you always had to remember that there was Cosa Nostra.

'My relationship with Lima began almost by chance. I went to see him to recommend a relative of mine, and Lima started saying he didn't even have the money to pay his bills. So I collected a few lire from the businessmen to make a present to Lima. He was very affected by that, and asked me if I felt like managing the "situation" for him. Lima was a panther, a person who moved like a big cat. He said to me, "Careful, if they realize it's me behind you, we'll last from Christmas to Boxing Day."

'There was the so-called "provincial agreement" that applied to the province of Palermo, which allowed for 4.5 per cent of the contracts to be distributed as follows: 2 per cent to Cosa Nostra, 2 per cent to the politicians, 0.5 per cent to the holding companies . . . which weren't so much holding companies as a way of forcing you to eat humble pie . . . Then the local families also had 2–3 per cent at their disposal, which came in the form of work transferred to local companies. Consequently, in fact, the Mafia earned the most.

'Then, in 1988, on the orders of Totò Riina, *il tavolino** was born. A meeting was held in the offices of the Palermo Concrete company, and the new system for checking public contracts in Sicily was decided upon. It was established that I would only deal with the works made by the province of Palermo, and would no longer deal with contracts above 5 billion, which Filippo Salamone would handle, and which would also have to correspond to a percentage of 0.80 on all work awarded to or managed by the Salamone group at the top of Cosa Nostra, meaning Totò Riina. I was also given the thankless task of accrediting the companies working on that territory with contracts from that zone.

---

* The 'little table', where Mafiosi, businessmen and politicians sit down together to discuss things.

'I referred this situation to Salvo Lima, who refused to recognize the agreement, saying that the province was his territory and he would accept no limitations on the sums involved.'

‘Angelo Siino could end up like Ciancimino if he gets involved in things like that’*

Toto Riina to Baldassare Di Maggio, aka Balduccio

Baldassare Di Maggio: ‘The story is this: towards the end of 1986, after the arrest of Bernardo Brusca, Angelo Siino came to me. I’d known him since 1980, because we raced cars together and he once lent me an Opel Ascona 2000 to race in the Conca D’Oro, and then we knew each other as fellow villagers and relatives because he’s a relative of my sister-in-law. So Angelo Siino comes to me and says, “There are jobs in the province being scattered around the place, people are making offers of 25, 30 per cent. If we get hold of those jobs, because I know some politicians who give me the lists of bids, we can organize the bids with a lower rebate and try to earn something ourselves.” I say, “Look, I’ll have to have a word and I’ll let you know.” He says, “Fine.” In fact, what I did, I went and talked about the situation to Totò Riina and Riina says, “But Angelo Siino could end up like Ciancimino if he gets involved in things like that.”’

Prosecutor: ‘What did he mean by that? What did Riina mean when he said “could end up like Ciancimino”?’

Di Maggio: ‘Since Ciancimino had had the law onto him with regard to contracts and things to do with the municipality of

* Questioning of the *pentito* Baldassare Di Maggio in the trial ‘Mafia and contracts’, Palermo, 14 September 2003.

Palermo, the province of Palermo . . . that's what Totò Riina, would have meant.'

Prosecutor: 'So he was exposing himself to the possibility of investigations, which could have been risky?'

Di Maggio: 'Yes. then Totò Riina says, "If he accepts the responsibility . . . then he can go ahead." So I said to Angelo Siino: "OK, if you want to risk ending up in jail." He says, "I have no problems with jail." He said it in a boastful way. I don't know why he said it.'

Prosecutor: '"I have no problems with jail" . . . did he explain why he "had no problems"?'

Di Maggio: 'No, he didn't explain why he had no problems with jail, but he was just giving himself a . . . a boastful air, let's say. He wanted to demonstrate that he was a hard man. And then after I gave him my reply he says, "Fine, I can go ahead." Three or four months later, he sent me the first lists of jobs. I meet Totò Riina and I say to him, "What am I supposed to do with these lists, who am I supposed to give them to?" Uncle Totò says, "The ones that belong to the Palermo family, pass those on to Raffaele Ganci; the ones that belong to Corleone, pass them on to my nephew Giovanni Grizzafi and your guys, in your zone, just wait a bit . . ."'

*'Ù pigghiaru,'** *hisses the old man in the seniors' club in Corleone. The other men playing cards freeze in their armchairs, startled, staring at the damp, mouldy walls. No one dares to say anything.*

It's just past eight o'clock in the morning. It's Friday. Special Branch police are waiting for Totò Riina among the buildings on Via Leonardo da Vinci. They spot him from a distance and capture him. The capo dei capi *of Cosa Nostra is on the ground, with his face in the dust and the barrel of an automatic pistol pointed at his temple. Palermo, 15 January 1993.*

---

* 'They've got him.'

'Somebody might turn cop'*

Totò Riina

Devil's Island isn't part of Sicily. It's further to the north, in the middle of the sea, a place where the men of honour never imagined they would find themselves. It's the night of 19 July 1992; the column of smoke is still high in the sky among the houses of Palermo, and the tip of Montepellegrino, the carcasses of prosecutor Paolo Borsellino's armoured cars are eviscerated, burnt out. Italy is at war.

The first to pass through the iron gates of the Ucciardone on that moonlit night is a Sardinian lieutenant. He runs up the stairs, through the first gate and then the second, and slips into the darkness of Section Seven. Behind him are all the soldiers of his parachute unit. It's a prison raid. At about three in the morning they take forty-seven men of honour, and another eighty-one at dawn. They pile them into Chinook helicopters waiting at Boccadifalco military airport, discharge them first in Pianosa and then at Asinara – Devil's Island.

Special prison, special wing, special regime. 41-bis: Cosa Nostra's worst nightmare.

Faceless, hooded warders. Lightless windows, barred with grilles 'so that they can't see the landscape'. The inmate is in

* Quotations recorded in the files of the Capaci massacre trial, Court of Assizes, Caltanissetta, 26 September 1997.

constant, total isolation. An hour's meeting at the most with wife and children, but separated from them by an armoured window. No access to the library, the courtyards or any of the 'common areas'. No phonecalls. No television. No hardback books in the cells. No cooking. No access to the shop. No music cassettes. A 'walk' is permitted only in 'concrete tanks' – narrow walkways, sewers, nightmare strolls.

From the lords of the Ucciardone to inmates sequestered in a kind of hell. The Madonias of Resuttana, the Grecos of Ciaculli and the others from Croceverde Giardina, the Vernengos of Ponte Ammiraglio, the Zancas of Corso dei Mille, the Tinnirellos, the Milanos, the Galatolos of L'Acquasanta.

'Somebody might turn cop,' Totò Riina fumes with rage as he talks to Salvatore Cancemi, the *capomandamento* of Porta Nuova.

It's almost the end of the summer of the Sicilian massacres. The *capo dei capi* of the Corleonesi meets his brother-in-law Leoluca Bagarella in a house in Palermo, below the Conigliera. Cancemi's there too.

'Uncle Totò was worried about that prison of suffering,' Cancemi says. 'He was worried that someone would give in, that someone might turn *pentito*. He always used an expression, he said it over and over again: *Mi rubo i denti,** meaning that at all costs he had to do something about 41-bis. All the slaughter he did afterwards was always subordinate to these things – to getting rid of tough jail sentences, to getting rid of the laws on *pentiti* . . .'

In Pianosa and Asinara are what the men of honour call *le squadrette,* the little squads. Select units of prison police officers – GOM: *Gruppo operative mobile,* mobile operational group. The *squadrette* move every night. The bosses' lawyers claim there are beatings, clubbings, slaps and kicks. The men of honour have never known the shame of this jail; prison for them has always been a 'holiday'.

---

* Literally: 'I'm fighting over my teeth'.

There's a helicopter in the courtyard at Pianosa. Another helicopter waits above a bay in Asinara. The tanks are always full of petrol, the pilot always ready to take off. These are orders from Rome; that's how Gianni de Gennaro, the director of the DIA* wants it. A helicopter is always waiting for a repenting man of honour.

'Somebody might turn cop,' Totò Riina goes on repeating. In autumn and winter 1992, the Mafiosi turn *pentito* en masse.

---

* *Direzione investigativa antimafia* – Anti-Mafia Investigation Department.

‘Totò Riina wanted to kill their children to the twentieth degree of kinship’

Salvatore Cancemi

‘We are dead men walking. With the decision we took we condemned ourselves; there could be gunfire behind us at any moment. And someone’s dead. I’m aware of all this, in fact I’m very aware of it, that I’ve condemned myself to death. Cosa Nostra doesn’t forgive, this is a bill that’s never out of date. Once someone turns cop, he has to die. Even if he’s an old man and he’s already dying in his bed. Even if he’s 100 years old, they’ll shoot him. That’s Cosa Nostra.

‘I used to see the typical *pentito* in a very negative light; he was a traitor, a liar. Many times, when I was talking to my lawyer, I would say, “He’s telling a bunch of lies, it’s treachery.” And in fact he was telling the truth. There are certain situations that only the *pentiti* can know. So a whole generation of Mafia family is going to be destroyed. For example the Gancis will never again have the same prestige that they did before: they have a *pentito* in the house, their son Calogero. In fact they’ve got three *pentiti*. There’s also the nephew Antonio Galliano and the cousin Francesco Paolo Anzelmo.

‘Totò Riina has a *pentito* in the family as well – Giuseppe Marchese. And in fact Riina ordered his brother-in-law Leoluca Bagarella to kill his wife Vincenzina. That’s what I think happened, even if Bagarella dressed it up as a suicide. And Giuseppe Marchese, Totò Riina made him take a life sentence . . . In my case, though, there will never be another Cancemi in Cosa Nostra.

'Shortly before the arrest of Totò Riina there was a clash, and he worked out that the sickness of Cosa Nostra came from there, from the *pentiti*: Totò Riina wanted to kill their children to the twentieth degree of kinship. I've thought a lot about this. Those words of his got my brain going. He said the *pentiti* were the worst threat to Cosa Nostra because, if it wasn't for them, even if the whole world was united against the Cosa Nostra, it couldn't touch us. That's why he wanted to kill their relatives to the twentieth degree of kinship, starting with the six-year-olds.

'Totò Riina turning *pentito*? I'd sooner believe in a flying donkey than Uncle Totò spilling the beans. But if it did happen it would be like setting off an atomic bomb. With all the secrets he knows, it would take out half of Italy . . .

'The judiciary are scared of the *pentiti*. Only the honest ones want the collaboration of the *pentiti*; the ones with skeletons in their cupboards have done everything they can to show them up as liars. So even if they catch Bernardo Provenzano Cosa Nostra won't be finished: everything will stay as it was before.

'To get to me, Totò Riina would do anything. I'm the one who harmed him. I mean that he's looking for me. At the massacres trial, in Florence, he threatened me. He said, "Don't be scared, Signor Cancemi, don't be frightened . . . go on, go on . . . I'm thinking about you" . . . I don't know when another man of honour who belongs to the *Commissione* will decide to collaborate again, someone who sits beside Totò Riina, who eats with him. I've brought Cosa Nostra to its knees, but the state refused to deliver the *coup de grâce*.'

'That word says a lot, it says everything, it says lots of things'*

Totò Riina

Magistrate Pier Luigi Vigna: 'What's the subject I want you to address, the one I'd ask you to think about? It's this: there's a huge number of rulings, and among other things they say Cosa Nostra exists . . . there's a considerable number of people saying you are the head of Cosa Nostra . . . So what I thought was, if you were willing to talk . . .'

Totò Riina: 'Please, don't even say those words.'

Vigna: 'If you were willing . . .'

Riina: 'Please, Dr Vigna, stop there.'

Vigna: 'No, I'm going to finish.'

Riina: '*Dottore,* please stop there.'

Vigna: 'You can't interrupt the record . . .'

Riina: 'Let's stop there and not go any further.'

Vigna: 'Excuse me, Riina, let me finish my thought, because I have the impression . . .'

Riina: 'You've got the wrong person.'

Vigna: 'You don't know . . .'

Riina: 'You and Dr Caselli have the wrong person!'

---

* Questioning of Salvatore Riina by the prosecutor of Florence Pier Luigi Vigna and the prosecutor of Palermo Giancarlo Caselli, 22 April 1996.

Vigna: 'You don't know what I was going to say. So there's no point shouting. Why on earth are you shouting like that?'

Riina: 'Because you have the wrong person.'

Vigna: 'If you don't let me finish talking you can't tell whether I've got the wrong person or I haven't got the wrong person. You imagine that I've come here to ask you if you might be willing to collaborate? Is that what you thought?'

Riina: 'You, Dr Vigna . . . that word says a lot, it says everything, it says lots of things . . .'

Vigna: 'I've told you there are people pointing the finger at you . . .'

Riina: 'Don't worry, don't worry about me.'

Vigna: 'I'm not worrying, certainly not about you, I'm only worrying about how the investigations are going. So what I was talking about was only if you were willing to talk about the reality of Cosa Nostra . . .'

Riina: 'Please spare your breath, Dr Vigna . . .'

Vigna: 'So you're refusing to listen to a hypothetical argument . . .'

Riina: 'I don't have to listen to anything, because I've already understood what you're talking about. I was expecting you; in fact I've been expecting this matter to come up for some time.'

Vigna: 'What matter would that be?'

Riina: 'The matter that you're talking to me about this evening.'

Caselli: 'Let's use this expression, even if they aren't your exact words . . . the so-called *pentiti*, walking arm in arm and so on . . .'

Riina: 'Sorry, *dottore*, you'll have to forgive me, I'm not talking. I don't want to seem rude and I would ask you, I would ask you to leave me in peace and let's finish this as if nothing has happened.'

Vigna: 'What do you mean, nothing? . . . An interrogation has happened. So you have no intention of addressing these issues. Would you care to tell me why?'

Riina: 'I will keep my reasons to myself.'

Vigna: 'Why won't you talk? [*to Caselli*] We could also use the video recording, because he's shaking his head, so I've got to record it . . . and that gives us an opening hand. Fine. So we can stop the interrogation and put together some minutes by way of summary.'

'Mutolo, you're a great nark'

Totò Riina

Insults, threats and slander.

Tommaso Buscetta

'Totò Riina is a man who's sick with *sbirritudine*. He's always behaved like a cop, going to the police to eliminate his enemies if he couldn't kill them. No, he wasn't trustworthy. He had the little vice – let's put it like that – he had the little vice of anonymous letters . . . God, the number he wrote!'

Gaspare Mutolo

'We've always seen anonymous letters as a bad thing to do.'

Totò Riina

'Mutolo, you're a great nark.'

Michele Greco

'I was ruined by anonymous letters. A blind, bad anonymity.'

Arguments between the capo *of the family of Marsala Mariano Licari and another Mafioso from the Trapani region*

Mafioso: 'You're a cop.'
Licari: 'If I'm a cop, you're a cop on horseback.'

Tommaso Buscetta

'A man of honour mustn't be offended or slapped . . . with a man of honour you can talk to him or in extremis shoot him.'

Tommaso Buscetta, confronting Pippo Calò in court

Calò: 'You've ruined me, I'll not get out of jail now, thanks to you I've got 120 charges and sixty-nine murders.'
Buscetta: 'If you really insist, I'd also like to add the murder of Giovanni Lallicata . . . and that makes seventy.'

John Gotti

'If someone offends me I crush him, I finish him off . . . and that's him fucking done with. That's Cosa Nostra.'

Totò Riina and Tommaso Buscetta

'When you talk about the Corleonesi you have to wash your mouth out with vinegar.'

Pietro Zanca

'Slander began with the first men who appeared on earth. And it has always led to atrocious consequences.'

Tommaso Buscetta to Pippo Calò
in the bunker court in Palermo

'Hypocrite. Liar. Peasant. Mafioso!'

'You, Signor Riina, are the one who killed Cosa Nostra'*

Tommaso Buscetta

His eyes are slits, his face a waxen mask. Frozen, Totò Riina is trembling with fury, but he says nothing. It's the day of the great *pentito*'s return to Italy. Almost ten years since the first revelations, and Giovanni Falcone and Paolo Borsellino are no longer alive. But Tommaso Buscetta is still in court giving evidence.

The bunker in Rebibbia is surrounded by hundreds of police; there are also armoured vehicles to protect Don Masino Buscetta. And dogs trained to sniff out explosives, snipers on the roofs. The *pentito* is facing the man he hates the most. The much-talked-about 'American-style' confrontation is about to begin, the face-to-face between Tommaso Buscetta and Totò Riina.

Their eyes meet, then Uncle Totò anticipates everything. He whispers: 'I'm not talking to anyone with low morals . . . My grandfather was left a widower at the age of forty with five children and he never looked for another wife. My mother was widowed at thirty-six. In our village, Corleone, we have high morals.'

The president of the Court of Assizes is about to say something; Buscetta interrupts him: 'Please let me, let me explain something about my morals . . . From which pulpit is this man speaking, this man of all people? He's making accusations to me

* 'American-style' questioning of Tommaso Buscetta and Salvatore Riina, bunker court in Rebibbia, Rome.

about women, about having several wives – the man responsible for the deaths of my children and my dear ones, he who was responsible for killing so many innocent people, directly or indirectly.' The *pentito* stops and catches his breath. He hisses: 'It's true, I thought about other women while you always went to bed alone with your wife because all the time you were only for Cosa Nostra.'

Totò Riina is pale, he twists his neck, he is trembling for the first time. He is furious, he feels outraged by those words, by those words mentioning Ninetta. His wife, the mother of his children. No one has ever dared to do that. Totò Riina lowers his eyes, he clenches his fists.

The president asks: 'Buscetta, how many deaths – as far as you know – were carried out on the orders of Salvatore Riina?' And he replies: 'That's the most ridiculous question I've ever been asked. He was the star of Cosa Nostra. You, gentlemen of the court, didn't realize the character you had in front of you, and in my heart I hope that you will come to realize it.'

Tommaso Buscetta talks about Totò Riina and his Corleonesi. Since the 1950s, when they machine-gunned their *capo* Michele Navarra. Since the 1970s, when they came down from La Rocca Busambra* to Palermo to conquer the city. Since the 1970s, when they slipped their poison into the Mafia throughout the whole island of of Sicily.

Buscetta starts talking about his enemy again: 'I want to make you understand, your honours, and above all to those of you who are not magistrates, who this man Riina is. I have to make you know who this man is who brought Cosa Nostra to its ruin. I could write science fiction novels about what I know about the two of them, about him and Bernardo Provenzano. I'm here talking now, but there's a whole tide of people talking now. But they, the

* The hill overlooking the town of Corleone.

'collaborators with justice', aren't the ones destroying Cosa Nostra. Here before you, sitting on that chair, is the man who helped the Italian state to destroy Cosa Nostra.'

Tommaso Buscetta looks straight into Shorty's eyes. And he shouts at him: 'You, Signor Riina, are the one who killed Cosa Nostra.'

SILENCE

After the capture of Totò Riina on 15 January 1993, Cosa Nostra no longer has its Commissione, *but it does have a very narrow summit. Some people call it a Directory, and it is coordinated by Bernardo Provenzano.*

Bernardo Provenzano (Corleone family)
Antonino Giuffrè (Caccamo family)
Salvatore Lo Piccolo (San Lorenzo family)
Benedetto Spera (Belmonte Mezzagno family)
Matteo Messina Denaro (Castelvetrano family)

It's a path in the middle of the countryside around Corleone, on the side of the Montagna dei Cavalli, right next to the cottage where Bernardo Provenzano was captured after almost forty-three years in hiding. A road sign, a road named after a date: Via 11 Aprile 2006.

'Seventy-three holy pictures showing Christ'*

Items from the inventory discovered in Bernardo Provencano's hideaway

– One weighing scales with an sky-blue footboard, 'Maross' brand; one rough wooden ladder with nine rungs; two 1 kg packets of Barilla pasta 'mezzi canneroni n. 48', one opened; one 500 ml bottle of water bearing the label 'San Benedetto Acqua Frizzante'; a cardboard packet containing four 1.5 volt AA batteries, 'Superpila' brand; ten ballpoint pens; one correction pen; one plastic bag containing six rolls of Sellotape; one felt-tip pen.

– Three paper holy pictures showing 'Madonna of Sorrows Sanctuary Corleone'; one paper holy picture showing 'Madonna of Grace of Corleone'; one paper holy picture showing 'Cardinale Pietro Marcellino Corradini'; one painting in a brown wooden frame captioned 'Weeping Madonna of Syracuse'; one small painting, unframed, on cardboard showing a woman and with the caption 'Madonna Queen of Hearts Madonna Queen of Families'; two holy pictures showing respectively one 'Madonna of the Rosary of Tagliavia' and the other 'B. Bernardo of Corleone Capuchin'; seventy-three holy pictures showing Christ with the caption 'Jesus I trust in you'.

---

* Inventory of the material found in the hideout of Bernardo Provenzano, report of the mobile unit of Palermo dated 11 April 2006 and passed on to the deputy prosecutor of Palermo Giuseppe Pignatone and his assistant prosecutors Michele Prestipino and Marzia Sabella.

– One book entitled *Health at the Table with Imco Waterless,** inside which is seen a cardboard crucifix bearing the words 'Jubilee, 2000'; a packet of breadsticks 'Mulino Bianco', containing two unopened packets; three 500 g packets of biscuits, 'Mulino Bianco' Grancereale classico brand, one open and missing several biscuits; a box of 'Riso Flora Parboiled'; a box of *bacetti*, 'Perugina' brand, containing one 'Perugina' chocolate in the shape of a heart and one 'Pocket Coffee Ferrero'; two boxes of chocolates 'Cuorenero, cholesterol and sugar free', one empty and the other partially empty.

– One electric radiator, 'De Longhi' brand'; one halogen stove 'Caldo casa'; one wooden table measuring 73 x 28.5 cm; one double mattress, beige patterned, 'Saninflex' brand, measuring approximately 190 x 185 cm'; one plastic bag containing a brown-coloured sweater with a label reading '100% cashmere', 'Ballantyne' brand, size 112 cm 44; a pair of red-and-grey-coloured pyjamas, 'Timonier' brand, size four; a claret-coloured sweater, 'Drumohr' brand, with a label reading '100% cashmere', size 107 cm 42; a blue-coloured cashmere sweater, 'Heritage' brand; a reddish-purple sweater with the label 'Ballantyne Giovanni Alongi Palermo 100% cashmere'; a pair of blue-coloured cloth trousers with the label 'Excelsior Giovanni Alongi size 50'.

– One device for intravenous infusion sealed in its individual packet; five syringe needles, 'Microlange 3' brand; one pair of sunglasses, 'Lotto' brand; one small bottle, partly used, with individual box of 'Eau de Toilette Roland Garros'; one unopened 50 ml bottle of after-shave with box, 'Armani' brand; three flat caps of various colours; one CD player; one CD by Mario Merola; one CD a compilation of Claudio Villa and another with a compilation by Mina; the soundtrack of *The Godfather Part II*; the album *Songs of the Smurfs*.

---

* A cooking system using stainless steel pots.

‘Curiosity is the antechamber of *sbirritudine*’*

Totò Riina

The man of honour doesn’t talk much; he listens a lot and he never asks questions. Cosa Nostra have never been keen on chitchat. An old Sicilian proverb says as much: *A megghiu parola è chidda cca nun si dici*. The best word is the one left unsaid.

If reservation and circumspection are the strength of every Mafioso on the island, for the Corleonesi discretion and prudence are obsessions. They are a special breed, a tribe apart, who come down from the woods of La Rocca Busambra and conquer Palermo with plots, *tragediamenti*, lies, silences. In Cosa Nostra there is an obligation always to tell the truth; for men of honour it is one of the commandments. They always tell the truth, all of them apart from the Corleonesi. They know who the affiliates of the other families are, but the others don’t know the names of the Corleone family’s affiliates. Totò Riina invents his own Cosa Nostra – a ‘Cosa Sua’; he makes his own men of honour, ‘reserved’ only for him. And for his brother-in-law Leoluca Bagarella. And for the other grand old man of Corleone, Bernardo Provenzano.

Secret. Everything’s secret for Uncle Totò.

The place where the *Commissione* holds its meetings is secret. The name of the next victim is also secret, the hitman finds it out

---

* Questioning of Antonino Giuffrè by the deputy public prosecutor of Palermo Michele Prestipino, 30 January 2004.

only a moment before leaving to *astutarlo*, to whack him, kill him. His hideaway is secret, his inner world is secret. His paranoia is as great as his crazed desire for omnipotence. No one can ask him any questions.

'Uncle Totò, what is it?' one of the Gancis of La Noce asks him. The Corleonese withers him with a glance. Even today, the men of honour can't work out how the man is still alive. Totò Riina speaks and everyone else stays silent. All mute. They never ask.

'Curiosity is the antechamber of *sbirritudine*,' Salvatore Riina hisses at the end of a *mangiata* in the country house of Antonino Giuffrè, the new *capomandamento* of Caccamo. Uncle Totò is at the head of the table. On his right, Raffaele Ganci, Nino Madonia and Michelangelo La Barbera. On his left Giovanni Brusca, Nenè Geraci and his host, Antonino Giuffrè.

'Provenzano wasn't there that evening. When Totò Riina was present he never came for fear of an attack of some kind: one of the two of them always stayed far from trouble,' Giuffrè would begin his statement when he turned *pentito*.

The bosses discuss the balance of power in the *mandamento* of Caccamo, after the arrest of the old *capo* Ciccio Intile. They talk about what is happening in the province of Caltanissetta, the feud with Gela, the clan of shepherds who want to command more than Cosa Nostra. And they also nod to Totò Riina's fugitive status. Uncle Totò is hidden in a villa surrounded by kitchen gardens in Borgo Molara, dry stone walls and brooks running behind the new prison of I Pagliarelli.

'I pretended to be distracted, because as far as going and asking where Riina was hiding, I hadn't the authority and frankly – you get me? – I didn't have the motive either,' Giuffrè told the chief prosecutor Pietro Grasso and his deputy Michele Prestipino.

The *mangiata* in the cottage is coming to an end; the *capomandamento* of Caccamo stands apart, far from the discussions of the others. About the hiding-place, Riina's movements, his bodyguards.

'Uncle had just said that curiosity was the antechamber of *sbirritudine*; he had just told everyone that being too curious got you killed.'

'I was careful and I wasn't careful . . . I was keeping an eye on him, in inverted commas'*

Giovanni Brusca

State prosecutor: 'After January 1992, how many times did you meet Bernardo Provenzano?'

Giovanni Brusca: 'Once in the garage . . . in Francesco Pastoia's warehouse in Villabate . . . a few times in a house in Belmonte Mezagno belonging to a certain Tanuzu, who is the man who was killed a year ago in the zone of Ciaculli . . . and then in Belmonte in 1994–1995 . . .'

State prosecutor: 'What do you know about the places where, from the 1980s onwards, Provenzano spent his time in hiding?'

Brusca: 'I met Provenzano when I was a little boy, perhaps fourteen, fifteen, maybe thirteen . . . sometime around 1973 and 1974. Or perhaps much earlier – Calogero Bagarella was still alive . . . I brought him food when the two of them were both in hiding in San Giuseppe Jato, with a certain D'Anna. My father filled bags up with fruit, with food, and I brought them to them. After which Bernardo Provenzano was in hiding in Palermo, in Monreale. Then I found out that he'd moved to Casteldaccia and the last time I know about, I don't know the exact house, but he moved between Belmonte, Marineo and Casteldaccia. That was the area where he was hiding out. I met

* Questioning of Giovanni Brusca by public prosecutor Antonino Di Matteo, trial of Simone Castello + 5, 12 December 2000.

him lots of times in Bagheria and Palermo in the 1980s. I didn't have regular contact with him, because my regular contact was with Salvatore Riina.'

State prosecutor: 'Do you remember any of the episodes when you met Provenzano in Bagheria?'

Brusca: 'Well, I met him once with Giuseppe Piddo Madonia for a work problem I was dealing with . . .'

State prosecutor: 'Was there anybody else there?'

Brusca: 'I met him in a villa that was at the disposal of Antonino Gargano; he took me there himself, but I don't know who owned it . . . Gargano's nephew was there as well. Then I met him twice in Bagheria or perhaps more in Leonardo Greco's iron warehouse, I brought him some notes, messages from Salvatore Riina. If I remember correctly I also went there once with Antonino Ferro from Canicatti . . .'

State prosecutor: 'Now I'd like you to remember if there were any reasons for suspicion, after Riina's arrest, between you and Provenzano . . .'

Brusca: 'After Riina's arrest, I stayed in direct contact with Leoluca Bagarella. He told me they'd come together as a family, meaning the Corleone family, and that the man who took the job of *mandamento* was Provenzano. So I said in front of them, "So when I need to talk, I just have to talk to Bagarella, I don't need to meet with you?" He replied, "Fine, fine." I just know that after the arrest of Bagarella I met Provenzano and he started complaining – Nicola Di Trapani was there too – about a whole series of things that his fellow villager had done . . . I said to him, "Make sure we know about everything that Bagarella does." Provenzano acted stupid, so much so that I worked out that he wasn't being straight, and all those signs that my father had warned me about, how he had different faces, and so on, started to put me on the alert . . .'

State prosecutor: 'And then what happened?'

Brusca: 'Provenzano started closing up, closing up . . . closing up . . . so I no longer felt at ease with him, and he didn't like me. At that point I was careful and I wasn't careful – that is, I was keeping an eye on him, in inverted commas.'

'You've got to be straight, correct and consistent'*

Bernardo Provenzano

He never talks on the phone. He hasn't got a mobile. His voice is in the *pizzini*, rolled-up pieces of paper wrapped in transparent tape, notes that he sends to all the corners of Sicily. In ungrammatical Italian, in his own words – words that can be wise and measured, or allusive and threatening – he sends messages to the people of Cosa Nostra. He has messengers everywhere, who come and go from his hideouts. He's Bernardo Provenzano's 'minister of post and communications'. With the uncertainties of technology – phone-tapping and bugging – for at least fifteen years the last godfather of Corleone has entrusted all his personal communications and 'public relations' to the notorious *pizzini*.

You've got to be straight, correct and consistent

'As regards mm. I have been told of things that PP has denyed, in a convinsing way, and now you must meet mm for clarifications since I dont know much, either to you, or to mm, it seems to me

* *Pizzini* shown at the custodial sentence against Bernardo Provenzano + 20, trial no. 4668/96, and the custodial sentence against Salvatore Rinella + 13, trial no. 7106/02 (prosecutor Antonio Caputo). All misspellings deliberate.

that mm is a good person, and maybe very simple, and a bit inexperienced in our bad ways, and if you need someone to drive he's good, and he can go on: you'll forgive me, I've only seen you once, and I can't tell you anything, just ask you to be calm, and straight, correct and consistent, know how to exploit the experience of suffered pain.'

You always need three pieces of evidence

'Don't disbelieve everything they tell you, and don't believe everything they tell you, always seek the truth before speaking, and rember that it isn't ever enough to have just one piece of evidence to confront a *ragionamento* to be absolutely certain in a *ragionamento* you need three pieces of evidence, and correctness, and consistency. I like to hear some of your words, because of their wisdom if you like, and because unfortunately there isn't any. Now I hear that they've also introduced this Antonio to you . . . I seem to understand that it's good to be very careful about what you say, if it's consistent with what you do, as you're very young . . .'

The vegetable identified as chicory

'Listen, can you tell us, your *compare*, that we joined in the spring, and he must know, the vegetable identified as chicory, if he could find some, the point where this chicory carries earth, if he could make a bit of seed, when it's seeded, and keep it for me? He can tell you that they sell it in bags, no that's not it in the natural state in which we know it, I wanted the natural one, the seed.'

Observe well

'Take a look, if around the farm they'd been able to put up one or more video cameras, near or far, you have to be careful to observe well. And that means you don't speak, either inside, or close to the cars, or at home, you don't speak out loud, not even deputies speak at home, whether your house is sound or falling down around your ears . . .'

'M', 'MM', 'MMM'

Accused of external involvement in Mafia association, on 11 December 2004 Marcello Dell'Utri is condemned in the first instance in Palermo to nine years' imprisonment. The appeal began in 2006. In 1994 the state prosecutor's office of Gian Carlo Caselli opens a file showing three coded names in the list of those under investigation: 'M', 'MM' and 'MMM'. The first is Silvio Berlusconi, the second Marcello Dell'Utri and the third Vittorio Mangano. The reference to Berlusconi is immediately crossed out and the judge in the preliminary investigations shelves the case 'for lack of sufficient corroboration'.

'Alfa' and 'Beta'

At the state prosecutor's office in Caltanisetta in 1994, two men are recorded in the investigation files as 'Alfa' and 'Beta'. One is Silvio Berlusconi and the other is Marcello Dell'Utri. After two years the case is shelved on the grounds of the 'weakness of the circumstantial evidence'.

'Autore 1' and 'Autore 2'

At the state prosecutor's office in Florence, responsible for investigating the Mafia massacres on the mainland in 1993, the names of Berlusconi and Dell'Utri are recorded in the investigation files under the heading 'Autore 1' and 'Autore 2'. The judges find no circumstantial evidence for the revelations of the pentito *Salvatore Cancemi, who talks – on the basis of hearsay – about mysterious negotiations between Totò Riina and 'the guys from above'. The reference is to 'business circles in Milan'. Berlusconi and Dell'Utri are definitively eliminated from the investigation in 1998. The inquiry into the principals of the massacres 'with covered faces' continues for another nine years. At the end of December 2007 inquiry number 3197/96 is shelved.*

'We're a single body: bandits, police and Mafia. Like the Father, the Son and the Holy Spirit'*

Gaspare Pisciotta

The report that reaches Washington bears the following title: 'The High Mafia fights crime in Sicily'. It is signed by Agent Bullfrog and dated March 1945. Over the past two weeks twenty-one corpses have been found in the countryside between Caltanissetta, Palermo and Agrigento. They are all petty thieves, kidnappers of aristocrats and landholders, shepherds devoted to cattle-rustling.

Agent Bullfrog of the Office of Strategic Services – the predecessor of the CIA – stationed in Sicily since the beginning of the year, keeps the top brass in Washington in detail. He informs his superiors:

'(1) Public Security and the *carabinieri* broadly welcome the High Mafia's unexpected interest in the law. (2) The police forces are deliberately avoiding the investigations. (3) The various 'Dons' and their deputies meet to make provisions against raids by brigands and criminals.'

In a dispatch dated 5 April of the same year, also sent to the American consul in Palermo and the Office of Naval Intelligence, the OSS agent lists the people 'executed' in the three provinces of the island and reports on what his informants have told him.

'Calogero Vizzini, the head of the High Mafia, said, "That's

* Documents made public by the Office of Strategic Services on 'Italy 1943–1948', National Archives, College Park, Maryland.

enough, now. Sicily needs its peace and quiet. A few delinquents have already been eliminated. But another hundred still have to fall. Today Sicily must be seen by the Americans as a jewel in the Mediterranean." . . .'

The OSS papers already contain the proof of this pact between the state apparatus and the men of honour which will shape events in Sicily over the decades to come. Until the fall of the Berlin Wall and even afterwards. From the massacres in Portella della Ginestra on 1 May 1947 to the slaughter in Capaci and Via D'Amelio in 1992, and from the death of the bandit Salvatore Giuliano to the mainland bombings in 1993.

The Sicilian Cosa Nostra has been negotiating with the other side for half a century. It's a discussion that never ends. Sometimes the manoeuvres are kept secret, and sometimes they manifest themselves violently in the open in the most unpredictable ways.

The Court of Assizes in Viterbo, 1951. Gaspare Pisciotta, cousin and lieutenant of his betrayer Turiddu Giuliano, is becoming agitated in his cage. All of a sudden he gets to his feet. He shouts at the Portella della Ginestra massacre trial: 'We're a single body: bandits, police and Mafia. Like the Father, the Son and the Holy Spirit.' A shout that will be his death sentence. On 9 February 1954 he is poisoned in the Ucciardone. Coffee laced with strychnine. He had been talking about 'agreements' between the *carabinieri* and the state, and Mafia families. Protection, the use of informers, promises of amnesty. A conspiracy.

The Court of Assizes in Florence, June 1998. Fifteen Cosa Nostra men of honour are sentenced to life for the 1993 attacks in Florence, Rome and Milan. For five years the best Italian investigators go in pursuit of hidden leaders. They don't find them.

Unlike all the other Mafias in the Western world, the Sicilian Cosa Nostra was never content with wealth. They always wanted something more. They were always pursuing a political goal.

'Those guys were shit scared'*

Totò Riina

These are the conclusions of the Court of Assizes in Florence in the trial for the slaughter on Via dei Georgofili.

'The record of what the witnesses and collaborators said demonstrates beyond question that in the second half of 1992 "contact" occurred between the ROS† of the *carabinieri* and the heads of Cosa Nostra via Vito Ciancimino. The personal and temporal terms of that "contact" are practically certain, as they have been related by two qualified witnesses, General Mario Mori and Captain Giuseppe De Donno . . . It is said that these events are interesting because they allow us to understand the ways in which, for the Mafia *capi* of the time, the massacre was made worthwhile.

'It's all too clear, in fact, that the responsibility of today's accused would not change at all if there were ministers, MPs, masons, the secret services or whoever the most suspicious mind might imagine standing behind [the witness] General Mori. Such an eventuality would enable us to understand who it was who was pulling the strings of some of the events of the last few years, but not to understand the role of Riina, Bagarella and the rest in the massacres of 1993–1994. Equally, the knowledge of whether

* Quotations from the sentencing documents on the Georgofili Massacre, Court of Assizes, Florence, 13 February 2001.

† Special Operational Group.

Ciancimino induced the arrest of Riina and whether the price paid by the state was that of substantial concessions to the Mafiosi could have no effect on the present ruling. This eventuality is very concerning, it makes every shrewd person shiver, but it is inappropriate to influence that judgement . . .

'ROS's initiative (because that is the organization we are talking about, given that a captain, the deputy commander and the commander of the department himself were involved) had all the characteristics of a 'negotiation'; the effect that it had on the Mafia *capi* was that of convincing them once and for all that the massacre was apt to bring advantages to the organization. In view of these profiles there can be no doubt whatever, not just because Captain De Donno has expressly talked about 'negotiation' and dialogue (General Mori, more careful with his words, has almost always avoided those two terms), but above all because the suggestion does not deserve to be called anything else . . . to contact the leadership of Cosa Nostra to understand what they wanted in return for the cessation of massacres . . .

'Brusca, for his part, declared that he had learned from Riina about requests condensed in a long *papello*.* Personally he understood that Riina was referring to the judicial institutions during that period: 41-bis, the law on collaborators, the reopening of trials . . . All of that leads us to conclude that Brusca is telling the truth when he asserts that the request to negotiate, formulated by an organization unknown to him (today we know that they were the men of ROS), led Riina to think (and communicate to his acolytes) that 'those guys were shit scared'. It led him, that is, to maintain that the massacres in Capaci and Via D'Amelio had completely disarmed the men of the state; they had convinced them of the invincibility of Cosa Nostra, they had led them to renounce the idea

* A long record sheet, or list.

of gridlock and make substantial concessions to the criminal organization.

'That conviction represents the most "reasonable" conclusion of the ROS initiative . . . and certainly had a detrimental effect on institutions, confirming the megalomania of the Mafia *capi* and laying bare the impotence of the state. Witness that as soon as the Corleonesi glimpsed difficulties in the conclusion of the "negotiations", they came up with another murder to "stir up" their opposite number: killing the magistrate Pietro Grasso.'

'I presented them with a *papello* that size'

Giovanni Brusca

'After the Capaci attack some facts were checked, and these are in some way, to my mind, the cause of the crimes and massacres that followed. I had a few meetings with Riina after the murder of Dr Falcone. The first time I asked him the reactions of all the *capimandamento* to the massacre: "Are they happy or are they not happy about what happened?" He always infiltrated all the families with trusted men who, for us Corleonesi, acted as a thermometer to gauge the most underground moods of the organization . . .

'He suddenly said to me very smugly: "They were shit scared. I presented them with a *papello* that size containing all our requests." He didn't tell me who he had given the *papello* to, or what was written on it. At that point he had a channel he wasn't telling me about. I didn't ask any questions for the time being because I knew I'd work it out sooner or later. I thought, who knows, it might be some Palermitan magistrate of politician; those were the first deductions. By now we'd ruled out the Andreotti tendency, so there must have been genuinely new channels . . . A few weeks later Riina told me the reply to his requests had come through . . . It said: "You're insane. We can't negotiate on this basis." I don't know who gave it to him.

'The decision to kill Borsellino, in my view, was taken in great haste. Cosa Nostra got things off to a bang with Borsellino to strike home another blow in the attempt to overcome the resistance that the "outcome of the negotiations" was facing. In the end, after the killing of Ignazio Salvo, Riina sent me to talk with Biondino: "We need another big bang. Who do you have to hand?" He knew I had my eye on judge Pietro Grasso, who at that point was going to his sister-in-law's house in Monreale . . . Grasso struck me as the right man at that moment: a man of the state, of the institutions, very well known, a target to strike.

'The people we wanted to force to the negotiating table were the ones who presented themselves on behalf of the state. We wanted them to say: "Fine. We've got it. What do you want in return for stopping?" . . . I could tell you more. Riina was convinced that he could come back to Corleone whenever he felt like it. His aim was a revision of the Maxi-Trial; that was in the *papello* too. Let's not forget that Riina's first convictions came in at that very point; he hadn't had any other definitive convictions before. We knew Riina was ready to go back to his village. He was already sending his children ahead, and he was going to keep his youngest daughter with him. He wanted to go back as a free citizen, and he already wanted to do that after the Capaci massacre. I knew that, my father knew that, Bagarella knew it . . . Then the project collapsed. The channel closed. And it closed in August 1992. That was why, since the *carabinieri* had no way of arresting him, they were negotiating like mad . . .

'If you go and see the images of my statement in the Capaci massacre trial, right when I'm talking about the *papello,* you can see Riina turning towards me and doing the cuckold's horns. He was making that gesture in a good sense, as if telling me: look at this wretch tossing out the facts . . . I know he's glad that the matter of politics is coming out, and the external instigators of the massacres . . .'

‘Of course, then, when the Berlin Wall comes down . . .’*

Antonino Giuffrè

‘In some villages you start breathing Mafia air as a child, leading to a single tight bond with politics, and with the Christian Democrats. So basically our work was also made that bit easier because the ordinary people were scared of the Communists, they were seen as the devil. We had holy water, on the other hand, which was the DC. Of course then, when the Berlin Wall comes down, the Communists stop eating babies, and they aren’t the devil any more; the subject is out of the picture. And we, who had been the ones who had guaranteed order for the Christian Democrats, started being sidelined. Unacceptable.

‘The Mafia doesn’t give anything for nothing, it always has to gain something. So I give something to you as a politician and you give something to me as a Mafioso. I give you some power, I get you to Rome, you have to guarantee me immunity, favours, earnings. Until all our affairs are in equilibrium.

‘Don’t think that we are the ones controlling Sicily politically; it would be a great mistake to imagine that. We’ve always been shrewd enough to side with the winners. In 1987 we worked out that they were the socialists. In 1994 Forza Italia. We didn’t cause

* Record of the questioning of the *pentito* Antonino Giuffrè, court of Termini Imerese, 16 October 2002, and in the trial of ‘Mafia and contracts’, 8 and 9 September 2002.

the rise of Forza Italia. It was people being fed up with DC. The ordinary people were fed up with politicians. Anybody you talked to, there was just one party to vote for, Forza Italia, as if it was the rock of ages.

'Provenzano said some politicians had come forward of their own accord. But Provenzano had exchanged words with us . . . He didn't say, "Let's do this," but he said, "I think . . . what do you say?" He was the one who made the decision. He's a master of manners, a diplomat, a true politician. He also said that he had good contacts for getting to the guys at the top of the party.

'When I get out of jail in 1993, I find a recycled Provenzano, from the fighter that he had been to a man showing signs of holiness. The massacres of 1992 had been madness – a lot of damage had been done and remedies had to be sought. Because we couldn't do without politics. Provenzano said: you don't have to make a lot of noise to attract attention, you have to move stealthily.

'Let's say we get midway through 1993, always in an atmosphere of tension, when finally on the horizon we see the birth of political situations that are slightly different from the traditional ones. We were watching this matter with very great interest because even when they were talking about new, about new men . . . we came from a pretty horrible past, we were rightly *scannaliati* – frightened – and what we especially wanted were some guarantees.

'So you could say that we espoused the cause of Forza Italia to some extent . . . an initial phase when you ask the representatives of the movement for some guarantees, then it's a matter of choosing those people from the various constituencies in Sicily, the most serious we could find, the cleanest we could find. That's part of Provenzano's subtlety . . . It's also established that Cosa Nostra has to steer clear of politicians, because otherwise, as Provenzano puts it, *a 24 ore l'abbracciamu*. Let me explain myself. The moment

I sponsor a politician, within twenty-four hours that politician is finished, because he'll be attacked by enemy forces, by a whole network of problems . . .'

'We have launched a civil, peaceful protest . . .'*

Leoluca Bagarella

Bagarella: 'In the name of all the prisoners held in this district penitentiary in L'Aquila, subject to Article 41-bis, weary of being exploited, humiliated, oppressed and used as bargaining counters by various political forces, we wish to inform this most excellent court that since 1 July we have launched a civil, peaceful protest that consists of reduction in exercises . . .

'Effectively we will only exercise for an hour. All that will stop the moment the responsible authorities, in a serious and careful manner, devote rather deeper attention to the problems imposed by this prison regime, and which have been exposed several times over the last ten years . . .

'The same people complain about the way in which the minister of justice is extending the particular regime of 41-bis every six months – a way of bypassing the law according to which the restrictive provisions of penitential treatment can only be temporary . . .

'And being plagued every three months by extensions of quite oppressive provisions is in stark contrast with Article 3 of the Constitution, of the Constitutional Court . . .

'Mr President, I have finished. I just wanted to add one thing. As the newspapers have spoken . . . "Ascoli Piceno, Salvatore Riina

---

* Record of the hearing of 12 July 2002, Court of Assizes, Trapani.

has begun a hunger strike . . ." I don't know whether he's at Ascoli Piceno . . .

State prosecutor: 'Mr President, I would like to understand the relevance of this. The spontaneous declarations always have to be pertinent to the subject of the trial.'

President: 'Listen, Bagarella . . .'

Bagarella: 'So what are you telling the politicians, what are the journalists saying, what are the—'

President: 'Bagarella, the state prosecutor objects to your continuing. You have read this kind of—'

Bagarella: 'This peti . . . let's say . . . this petition . . .'

President: 'We have taken note of it, that's sufficient.'

Bagarella: 'Fine, thank you, Mr President . . .'

State prosecutor: 'Mr President, I request that the minutes of the statement that Bagarella has just given be sent to my office as possibly falling under my jurisdiction.'

President: 'Fine, all right, we'll see to that.'

'United against 41-bis. Berlusconi is forgetting about Sicily'

Banner shown at a football match

The Favorita stadium is in party mood, pink and black balloons fly in the sky. The players are warming up on the pitch. On the terraces 26,000 spectators are waiting for the game to start. It's the penultimate Serie B fixture before the winter break: Palermo versus Ascoli. In the rowdy southern curve someone unrolls a twenty-foot banner, and the television cameras home in on it: 'United against 41-bis. Berlusconi is forgetting about Sicily.' The game ends in a draw: two all.

It's 22 December 2002, just a few months after the proclamation read by Leoluca Bagarella in the Court of Assizes and just a few weeks after a report from the secret service on the 'dangers' of a vendetta by the men of Cosa Nostra. All the Corleonesi are in jail, serving multiple life sentences. Ten years have passed since the Sicilian massacres of Capaci and Via D'Amerlio.

Almost all the men who killed Falcone and Borsellino are locked up in Spoleto, in Novara, in Sulmoni and in Terni. Totò Riina. Pietro Aglieri. The Graviano brothers from Brancaccio. Leoluca Bagarella. The Madonias of Resuttana. All buried away in the special wings of 41-bis. The analysts of SISDE (Intelligence and Democratic Security Service) write: 'Between March and July, the response of the political class to the authorities of Cosa Nostra has been entirely negative . . . on 41-bis all political forces, almost unanimously, have spoken out against its abolition and have advocated its being made even harsher. Thus we see the *capi* of Cosa Nostra facing the frustration of their hopes, a situation to which in all likelihood they intend to react . . . '

The bosses in jail are ready to strike. Who? The secret service has heard two names on the grapevine. One of those is Marcello Dell'Utri, the other the deputy Cesare Previti, both senior Forza Italia politicians.

There are also the prisoners in Novara jail, who send a letter addressed to the 'parliamentary lawyers'. It's also signed by Giuseppe Graviano and Salvatore Madonia. They accuse those lawyers who have become deputies – many are Sicilian – of having betrayed them over 41-bis.

Palermo trembles. The fear of another massacre returns, of deaths at the hands of people from Corleone.

SISDE also records the prison 'protest' in Novara: 'The warning addressed to the Palermo criminal lawyers who have become members of parliament, accused of disregarding the hopes of many of the defendants who had previously been defended in court, is interpreted in the relevant interest groups as indicative that the prisoners in jail for Mafia crimes are planning criminal actions against them.'

For the first time in many years, Sicilian Cosa Nostra seems to be divided in two, to be split down the middle. On one side the *capi* in jail, on the other major fugitives commanded by Bernardo Provenzano. The prisoners are itching to go, they want to see the special regime cancelled, they're still aiming at the revision of the trials. And they are issuing threats. The ones outside opt to go 'underground'; they choose silence, invisibility. But then there's also the 'party' of Pietro Aglieri, who speaks 'directly' to God but also tries to negotiate with the prosecutors.

Prison and trials are the problems of Cosa Nostra at the start of the new century. And they will remain so in years to come.

LAW OF 13 SEPTEMBER 1982, NO. 646

Article 416–bis – 'Mafia-type association'

Any person participating in a Mafia-type unlawful association including three or more persons shall be liable to imprisonment for three to six years. Those persons promoting, directing or organizing the said association shall be liable, for this sole offence, to imprisonment for four to nine years.

Article 110–416 bis – 'External participation in Mafia association'

According to some, it's a 'handy' instrument of investigation which too often proves incapable of sustaining a prosecution case to conviction. For others, it's an expedient that brings together two articles of the code to investigate figures whose responsibilities oscillate between something more than aggravated aiding and abetting and something less than Mafia association. The issue is hotly debated in Italy. According to research carried out by the National Anti-Mafia Unit, over the last sixteen years 7,190 people have been investigated for external participation. But the number of trials already completed – whether they resulted in conviction or acquittal – comes to only 542. Of the origins of external participation in crimes of association there are traces in two verdicts from very long ago. Verdicts by the Court of Cassation in Palermo. In 1875.

'Vittorio Mangano . . . is a hero, in his own way'

Marcello Dell'Utri

'The farmer Vittorio Mangano,* sentenced to life in the court of first instance†, died, and I was to blame. Mangano was suffering from cancer when he went to jail, and he was reputedly invited to make statements against me and the president [of the Council of Ministers], Silvio Berlusconi. If he had done, he would have got out of jail and been handsomely rewarded, and he would have saved himself. He is a hero, in his own way.'

That was how Marcello Dell'Utri remembered the 'farmer' of Arcore to *La Repubblica* on 8 April 2008, the eve of the political elections that would return Silvio Berlusconi to Palazzo Chigi.

This is how Marcello Dell'Utri, twelve years previously, explained his relations with Vittorio Mangano to the prosecutors of Palermo.

'I met him in Palermo in the early 1970s. I was a trainer with Bacigalupo, a youth football team. He was a kind of *tifoso* – a football hooligan. He traded in horses. I remembered that in 1975. I had moved to Milan, I'd become an assistant to Berlusconi, who

---

* Cosa Nostra member and former stable-keeper at Silvio Berlusconi's villa in Arcore.

† Italian criminal trials can go through at least two courts of appeal. Mangano was sentenced to life before appeal.

had been a college-mate of mine. Silvio Berlusconi gave me the job of finding an expert in farm management. So I called Mangano. He stayed in Arcore for two years. And he behaved extremely well. He negotiated with the peasants, he looked after the horses.

'Vittorio Mangano was taken into Dr Berlusconi's employment at my suggestion. In fact, immediately after I arrived in Milan, Berlusconi had bought Villa Casati and gave me the task of finding staff to run the villa. As regards the farmer, I remembered that Vittorio Mangano knew about horses, dogs and also about crops. So I introduced Mangano to Dr Berlusconi, who approved of the choice.

' . . . A threatening letter arrived, as well as anonymous phone-calls in which someone said he was about to kidnap or kill Berlusconi's son. I don't remember if there were any specific requests for money, or how much. That all happened after Vittorio Mangano went away, so late in 1974 or early in 1975. Berlusconi was extremely worried; he went to Spain with his family. I went to Spain too; I organized that trip. But I didn't do anything at all, nor did I know where those threats were coming from. The first threats received by Berlusconi in the early 1970s stopped as they had begun . . . I mean there was no intervention to make the threats stop . . . But Berlusconi's grave concern was not caused simply by the tenor of the anonymous threats, but by the connection we immediately made with Mangano, in that after the investigations into the kidnapping of Prince D'Angerio* we knew that Mangano had previous convictions. He was dismissed immediately after that kidnapping.

'As regards my acting as mediator for the Mafiosi, I would have to say that I just said those things to Filippo Rapisarda. I said I'd mediated between the people issuing those threats and Berlusconi,

* Sixteen-year-old Prince Luigi D'Angerio was kidnapped after dining at Berlusconi's villa on 7 December 1974.

but I only said it to boast. Rapisarda boasted of knowing various people in the criminal milieu, so I did more or less the same thing. Rapisarda boasted that he knew the Bono family, so I told him, by way of competing, "I know more important people than you do."

'I had good relations with Mangano, I'd go so far as to say that they were excellent . . . Even after the end of 1975 he visited Arcore, more specifically the stables where he kept a horse called Epoca. And he also hung around at a riding-school run by someone called Pepito. Once he was out of jail, between the late 1980s and the early 1990s, Vittorio Mangano came to see me in Milan a few times.'

Title of the film The Godfather, *length: 175 minutes, genre: drama, format: Technicolor, from the novel of the same name by Mario Puzo, produced in 1972 by Albert S. Ruddy of Paramount Pictures, directed by Francis Ford Coppola.*

Cast and characters: Marlon Brando (Don Vito Corleone), Al Pacino (Michael Corleone), James Caan (Sonny Corleone), Richard Castellano (Clemenza), John Cazale (Freddy Corleone), Richard Conte (Barzini), Robert Duvall (Tom Hagen), Corrado Gaipa (Don Tommasino), John Marley (Jack Woltz), Tony Giorgio (Bruno Tartaglia), Morgana King (Carmela Corleone), Al Lattieri (Virgil 'The Turk' Sollozzo), Diane Keaton (Kay Adams), Al Martino (Jonny Fontane), Lenny Montana (Luca Brasi), Talia Shire (Connie Corleone), Simonetta Stefanelli (Apollonia).

Story by Robert Towne, screenplay Francis Ford Coppola and Mario Puzo, cinematography by Gordon Willis, music by Nino Rota, edited by William H. Reynolds, Marc Laub, Murray Solomon and Peter Zinner, special effects by Paul J. Lombardi, production design by Dean Tavoularis, costumes by Anna Hill Johnstone.

'Certain films have been the ruin of mankind'

Michele Greco

'Giuseppe, my son, was never inclined towards the countryside like I was, and the rest of my family has been for many generations. Never, Giuseppe never. He has always been inclined towards the artistic life, since he is gifted in that direction. To cut a long story short, one day they got it into their heads to make a film. Giuseppe took part; he did well the first time he picked up a film camera. But now, rather than pursuing an artistic career, the slanders of the *pentiti* have made him pursue a prison career like the others.

'I can tell you one thing, Mr President – that certain films have been the ruin of mankind: violent films, pornographic films. They really are the ruin of mankind, Mr President, because . . . because if Totuccio Contorno had seen *Moses* and not *The Godfather*, for example, he wouldn't have slandered anyone, and that's the absolute truth. Instead Totuccio Contorno unfortunately saw *The Godfather* . . . I protest my innocence. This is the tragedy of the century.

'They described me as a Nero, as a Tiberius, but never in my life have I had so much as a parking ticket, because I've always had the good manners to know where to park my car. They call me the Pope, but I can't compare myself to the popes in terms of intelligence, culture and doctrine. But in terms of my serene conscience and the depth of my faith I can feel their equal, if not their superior . . . I always have hopes for the future. I have inner peace, a great inner peace. I get it from that great and illustrious guest who dwells within me and whom I received on the day of my christening. Even if they take me to the dungeons, with chains on my feet, I will always burst with serenity. I have read a great deal, Mr President, especially the Bible. And I know only such men as repent before God. The others, the ones used by the legal system, are only failed criminals who, to be honest, exist only to tell falsehoods. Like Contorno, who has seen *The Godfather*. Mr President, I am outside of everything.'

'A famous notable'[*]

Umberto Castagna, aka Enzo

In his archive there are files on 20,000 film appearances. All from Palermo, walk-on parts in films from *The Godfather* to the Italian Mafia-based mini-series *La Piovra 11.* Every producer and every director who comes to Sicily has to meet him. He says of himself: 'I'm the greatest organizer in Italian cinema, although some would say world cinema.' He's the owner of a funeral parlour, but anyone who wants to shoot a Mafia film in Palermo has no option but to turn to him: Umberto Castagna, aka Enzo.

His slang is a mixture between the Palermitan of the suburbs and some other language as yet unknown. A rich vocabulary, sometimes even bordering on genius. Pasolini is Pasolino, Francis Coppola is Franz Coppola, public opinion is public union, Roberta Torre is Roberta Torres. And Umberto Castagna aka Enzo is 'a famous notable'.

On the big wall of his drawing room – in Via Monfenera, in the Zisa district of Palermo – Al Pacino smiles at Michele Placido. Two huge posters. Two of 'his' actors. They face a chest of drawers. 'It used to be full of 100,000 lire notes, but then that *infamone* Aurelio Neri came along . . .'

---

* Interview with Umberto Castagna by the author, Palermo, March 2000.

A *pentito*. Aurelio Neri 'names him'; accuses Umberto Castagna, aka Enzo, of acting as a lookout in the billion-lire raid on the post offices of Palermo in 1995: the 'famous notable' ends up spending two and a half years in the Ucciardone. It's when he manages to get himself put under house arrest that he starts to ponder his revenge. Not with bullets, but with a screenplay. 'I'm diabolical, I'm truly diabolical,' he says. It's the film he's been dreaming about since he was arrested and convicted, a film about Aurelio Neri, the man who betrayed him. The script is in the chest of drawers that was once 'full of 100,000 lire notes', a pile of pages crammed in at random.

The last scene is set in the Ucciardone, on an unspecified day in an unspecified year. There's a frightened prisoner and a prison warder who seems like a sadist. The former asks fearfully, 'Where are you taking me to?' The other man, who is dragging him by one arm, replies: 'I'm taking you to Section Six.' The notorious sixth section of Palermo prison, the jail of the lowest, the outcasts. Where Aurelio Neri must sit out his sentence. The end of the film and the end of the history of cinema in Italy and perhaps in the world.

'*Weellll*, it'll be a masterpiece. That rat fink fraud Aurelio Neri gets seven years in solitary in my film, as much as the judges dumped on me . . .'

Cinema and local festivals, long live Santa Rosalia, Neapolitan songs, the music of popular performers like Gianni Celeste and Mario Trevi, the big fireworks known in Palermo as *masculiate*, a crowd of people queuing up on Via Monfenera to request a walk-on part in the latest film. And he recalls:

'I was born in 1941. My father was a builder – we were ten siblings, seven boys and three girls, a fine family, all working. Pippo, the oldest of the brothers, immediately emigrated to Rome, where he has always worked in cinema. It was Pippo who taught me everything.'

Pippo. Franco Rosi and Visconti. The Taviani brothers. Damiano Damiani. Sofia Loren. Risi and De Sica and Peppuccio Tornatore. Little Totò Cascio. Gianni Amelio. Aurelio Grimaldi. 'All my creations,' says Umberto Castagna, aka Enzo.

'Dom, if you've killed for the government you can do it for the family too'*

Nino Gaggi

That bastard Winnie Mook doesn't deserve to live. One way or another he has to die. The task is assigned to Dom, the most accurate when it comes to certain 'little jobs'. Dom organizes a plan. He checks Winnie's movements, he discovers where he leaves his car every night, he slips a stick of dynamite into the engine of his Cadillac. The explosion shatters all the shop windows in Hester Street, but somehow Winnie gets away. He loses both legs, but he survives. A week later Dom is celebrating his wife's birthday at home, he gives her a kiss, cuts the cake, gives her a clock encrusted with precious stones, he says goodbye to his two sons with a ruffle of their hair and then runs towards the hospital to which Winnie has been admitted. He takes out his revolver – a blow to the back of the neck. The bastard is dead at last. Dominick Dom Montiglio – an American from Brooklyn, his father born in Palermo and his mother born in Sciacca – has killed his ninety-fourth man. 'Ninety-three when I was a soldier in the jungle, and after that just Winnie,' he says when recalling his 'career' in New York, at the service of the Gambino family.

Ten thousand dollars a week to extract the *pizzo* from the shopkeepers fleeced by his uncle Nino Gaggi. His uncle, just back from

---

* Interview with Dominick Montiglio, the nephew of Nino Gaggi, by the author, New York, June 2005.

Vietnam, said to him: 'Dom, if you've killed for the government you can do it for the family too.' Thus begins Dom Montiglio's *wiseguy* story in the streets of Brooklyn, someone who knew old Gaetano Badalamenti and visited the houses of the Sicilians in Cherry Hill. A first life as a Mafioso and a second life as a Mafia stuntman. Dom is the shining example of the criminal America that still speaks a 'betwixt and between' form of Italian, surviving on its past.

After the joyriding, after all the money earned with Uncle Nino, after the murder of Winnie Mook, he ended up in the FBI's witness protection programme and then in a film on Cosa Nostra. As an actor. A docudrama produced in 2005 for the National Geographic Channel, in memory of the state prosecutor of Palermo, Paolo Borsellino. Real ex-bosses and fake ex-bosses, former undercover anti-drugs agents and Hollywood stars, all together on the set. A clack of the clapperboard and the memory of a murder, a crime scene and a smile for the press. Dom has set up a small industry around his previous existence as a Mafioso. Today he even has a PA, called Ross. They met at the Manhattan Correctional Center in the 1980s. Ross finds him contacts with film producers, organizes appointments for him with the journalists who want to know about the 'brutal events' on Hester Street in the old days, fixes up TV interviews for him. In 1992 Ross introduced Dom to Jerry Capeci, the most famous American journalist in the field of organized crime. A year later their book *Murder Machine: A True Story of Murder, Madness and the Mafia* came out in bookshops.

In the evening Dom strolls through SoHo in search of his favourite restaurants; he loves Thai food. By day he paints, he meets artists. And plays the bass. That's how Dominick Montiglio, the 'terrible' nephew of Uncle Nino Gaggi, has remade his life.

THE FUTURE

THE HEIRS, 2008

Giuseppe Salvatore Riina (Corleone)
Matteo Messina Denaro (Castelvetrano)
Gianni Nicchi (Palermo, suburb of Pagliarelli)
Giovanni Inzerillo (Palermo, suburb of Passo di Rigano)
Francesco Paolo Augusto Calì, aka Franky Boy (New York)

Legends flourish about them from the early 1980s onwards. They're all in hiding in Venezuela. They're reorganizing for a mass landing in Sicily. They're in Miami. Some nights, people swear they've spotted them behind the dilapidated church of San Ciro in Maredolce. Or in the lemon orchards of Santa Maria del Gesù, among the paths leading from the Conigliera to Mezzo Monreale.

In Palermo they repeat their names obsessively. And with considerable fear. Then, after a quarter of a century, 'the runaways' suddenly come back.

'Not so much as a seed must be left of those Inzerillos'*

Totò Riina

In those days they were the only ones who got away. They found refuge in New Jersey, with their American 'cousins'. It's the spring of 1981, the official beginning of the big Mafia war. The Inzerillos of Passo di Rigano, the Castellanas, the Di Maggios and the Di Maios, the Gambinos, their relatives from Torretta and the other ones from Bellolampo and l'Uditore, escaped from Totò Riina's hitmen, who pursued them into their suburbs. They reappear a whole lifetime later.

One at a time, and only every now and then. In 2000 there are fifteen or perhaps twenty Inzerillos who have survived the wipe-out of the Corleonesi, who go back to Passo di Rigano. They live in the same houses that they had abandoned, they frequent the same places, meet up every day, all move around together.

The first to come back is Francesco Inzerillo, aka *ù truttaturi.*† And then Tommaso. And Rosario. And Giuseppe, the son of Santo. The last to return is Giovanni. He's the son of the boss Totuccio, the one who was first to be killed on Via Brunelleschi with the Kalashnikovs. Giovanni, an American citizen born in New York in

---

* Quotations recorded in arrest documents for trial no. 2474/05 against Antonino Rotolo + 51, 20 June 2006.

† 'The trotter'.

1972, is the youngest brother of Giuseppe. 'Not so much as a seed must be left of those Inzerillos,' roars the killer who hacked the boy's right arm off twenty-five years before.*

Now all the Inzerillos are in Palermo. A discussion begins within Cosa Nostra about their fate. The survivors were 'spared' by the intercession of their relatives in Cherry Hill; it was old Charles Gambino who personally requested this 'kindness' from Totò Riina. And the *capo dei capi* of Corleone accepted. On one condition: that the Inzerillos never set foot in Palermo ever again. And that they kept Rosario Saruzzu Naimo informed about their every movement – journeys, changes of residence, even short trips lasting only a few days. Cosa Nostra gave Saruzzu the job of keeping a constant check, in perpetuity, on the lives of the Inzerillos.

It's late in 2000 when they start to repopulate Passo di Rigano. Their return unsettles some and delights others.

There's Salvatore Lo Piccolo, who devotes himself passionately to making sure they can stay and who forges alliances with three or four families which – in his head – would take him to the top of a new Sicilian Mafia organization. Antonino Rotolo, Totò Riina's right-hand man, is against it. Terrified of vendettas, of the power that the Inzerillos could still acquire. As usual, Bernardo Provenzano is ambiguous, two-faced. He is in favour, but cautiously so; he is hostile, but cautiously so.

Everyone is agitated, but no one can decide on their fate. Every Sicilian man of honour knows what these 'runaways' represent. They are blood relatives of the Gambinos of New York, the wealthiest Mafiosi on the other side of the Atlantic Ocean.

The much hated and envied Inzerillos offer new business prospects, an extraordinary opportunity for a Cosa Nostra undergoing a crisis of liquidity, and which hasn't been a leader on the interna-

---

* A reference to the killing of Giuseppe Inzerillo in 1981. He had vowed to avenge his father's murder, and was kidnapped, tortured and killed.

tional crime scene for many years. So it's the 'topic' of the Inzerillos that dominates discussions among the Sicilian Mafia in the first few months of the new millennium.

'The moment we're sound asleep it could be that we don't wake up'*

Antonino Rotolo

'If we don't reach an agreement with one another, the world will end. Is that right? And then how can we stay calm when somebody . . . Lo Piccolo . . . tells the Inzerillos' sons, "Don't worry, because good weather and bad both pass" . . . How can we be calm? These Inzerillos were children and now they've grown up, they're about thirty now. If they have to go . . .

'Right now, the situation is that we can't sleep soundly because the moment we're sound asleep it could be that we don't wake up. *Picciotti*, you see . . . nothing's finished, nothing's finished. We've always got those dead people before our eyes, there are always anniversaries, they sit down at the table . . . they sit down at the table and this one's missing and this one's missing, these are things we can't forget . . . They've got to get out . . . they've got to get out of Italy . . . the deal is that they can't stay in Italy.

'In fact, I'll tell you the truth – if they get out of Italy it's better for all of us, because that way we always know where they are. We're free of them, we can forget about them . . . Basically here in Passo di Rigano, when I came back I found Franco Inzerillo waiting in the car to shoot me . . . my brother-in-law Pino told me when I was in jail, he informed me that it was Franco Inzerillo . . .

---

* Quotations recorded in arrest documents for trial no. 2474/05 against Antonino Rotolo + 51, 20 June 2006.

Totuccio's brother, the runaways, let's say . . . and I said to him, "And who authorized this, from America, coming here?" In the end I told him, "If I go out tomorrow and find him in the street I'll fire two rounds at him."

'The pledge was that they had to stay in America, those runaways, all of them. And they had to turn up for Saruzzu Naimo's roll-call . . . Saruzzu whistled and they had to come running: "Signore Saruzzu, present!" "Fine, you're all here? Then off you go." So that was the deal. If they came back to Italy, that was the pledge. And nothing has changed, nothing has ever changed.

'Franco Inzerillo is supposed to be the brother of Masino, the one who was the *sottocapo* . . . the one who set up Totuccio's brother, so that he could make his own getaway. So you see the kind of man he is; the one they found in the boot of the car in America . . . What am I saying, what am I saying? He got out on one condition: either you or me . . . And are we able to trust this guy? He took his father's brother, he took him away and had him drowned and he shot his own cousin. Can we trust him? He's betrayed his own blood to us and you think he has respect for us?

'We have to keep a special eye on him. You see what we've got to do, if we need people we can trust. Listen carefully and take care because we've reached a point of no return, so we've got to get out, because apart from anything he could do some damage . . . We can't forget, because if these guys gain a hold they'll crack all our skulls open.'

'You're not here because you're you, you're here because you're him'*

Antonino Rotolo to Sandro Manino

'First I want to say I'd never have expected to meet you or have you in my house, but since Nicola is a friend and he's also a nephew of Pietro, who you know and who's a brother of mine . . . Nicola is very fond of you, so much so that he's persuaded me to bring you here today. And that's why you're here. You're not here because you're you, you're here because you're him.

'Now, before we talk, there's something I want to tell you: unfortunately between you and me there's a precipice, there's a great gulf, so we need a bridge to get across and since I'm used to plain speaking, I'll speak to you plainly today . . .

'You're the nephew of Totuccio Inzerillo, who . . . along with others, for no reason, for no reason at all, came looking for us to kill us, when no one had done anything to them. They looked for us and they found us. We didn't go looking for them. And that's how we got into this situation of conflict and prisons. And it's their own fault, your uncle's and his companions' fault, if they're dead or in prison. So I'll tell you that there's no difference between you with your dead and the families who have people in jail for ever, because either they're the living dead or they're just dead . . .

'If we like, there's another gap between us too. Because you've

---

* Quotations recorded in arrest documents for trial no. 2474/05 against Antonino Rotolo + 51, 20 June 2006.

been left with your property and all of ours has been taken away. But I'm telling you this to tell you that you're here, but between me and you there can't ever be . . . You're you and I'm me, you lot are you lot and we're us . . . Unfortunately these things that you didn't create – because after all you were just a boy – your relatives created them and left them to you as a legacy. So the situation is this . . . Listen, from this minute onwards, given that Nicola has this pleasure, you tell me and if I can do something I'll do it. But this is a personal relationship, not an official relationship, because I can't have an official relationship with you . . .

'Now I'll tell you something more. It's not as if these deaths happened because they were cops or because they were bad people . . . the operation was carried out by the cops because they wanted to carry out an operation that hadn't been agreed upon but, in fact, I couldn't say that they're bad people. We did it, unfortunately, but they were to blame. We were all calm, we were all in our houses, and now we're all ruined. Because the ones with dead relatives and the ones with people in jail are all in the same boat. Don't you feel that you're to blame, because it wasn't bad people in the operation? Because when a person is bad, in this Cosa, he sits down, he brings his arguments and, if he's bad, everyone lowers their heads for the axe. So, obviously, those arguments didn't amount to much.

'Your uncle came looking for us at home to crack our heads open even though we hadn't done anything, over a matter of money and power. Personally I have one issue with your relatives: that they'd put me on the list as well. Everybody who'd put me on the list and everyone who was on the list was facing the same fate. But because Niola told me I was a good person, a good boy, you know you've got to stay where you are. You've got to stay *nna to casedda*,* you've got to stay *nna to casedda* without ever leaving it

* 'In your place'.

. . . between you and me there's a great valley . . . and it was your uncle, not us, who built that valley. So we can't unite: because your name might not be Inzerillo, but you are an Inzerillo.'

'Unlucky guys'*

Salvatore Lo Piccolo

Pizzino sent on 19 June 2005 to Bernardo Provenzano

'Dear Uncle, I was delighted to receive your letter, I'm glad to know you are in the best of health as indeed I am myself. Dear Uncle, I thank you as ever for the honour that you're doing me, and ask you to forgive me if I talk again about these poor wretches as you call them. I just hope I will be able to explain myself and make you understand my state of mind.

'Uncle, this is a matter of a decision and a pledge made at least twenty-five years ago, between then and now many people have died and many things have changed and many are still to change. We have reached the point at which we are almost all ruined, and the *pentiti* who have destroyed us walk around unmolested. Unfortunately we are in a sad situation and don't know how to hide. However, we're still here, keeping the *cosa* going.

'These guys who are are fully under control – and I can assure you that they won't get off track – are members of our family, who all take responsibility for the case (the *unlucky guys* have already been informed). I tell you that this case has been taken into

* *Pizzino* used as evidence in Trial no. 38/08, Palermo District Anti-Mafia Office, against Alamia Pietro + 20, 16 January 2008.

consideration by our *sotto*, who isn't here at the moment, so he was the one who assumed responsibility, but I don't know who with . . .

'Dearest Uncle, I should also like to ask you to risk the little bit of peace that we have in our family. If you can come back with a solution to make them stay here I won't pull unhappy faces: however, at any rate, whatever decision you take will be done. Ever your servant, I will stop writing, may God protect us. Wishing you, dearest Uncle, great patience and a world full of blessings.'

Memorandum found in Provenzano's hideaway on 5 November 2007

'Where the Inzerillo brothers are concerned – a week before he was arrested, Uncle had informed me that the matter of the Inzerillos is still open – to the extent that Rotolo took it upon himself to make them leave . . . But Uncle said that if they stayed here it was better because they could be checked. And also because if they ask for mercy it is right that they should be given it.

'Uncle also told me that since it was his village that wanted them, none of us could oppose it! Because they automatically assume responsibility.'

'My dearest one, you need more besides my opinion'*

Bernardo Provenzano

Pizzino sent in the spring of 2005 to Salvatore Lo Piccolo on the return of the Inzerillos.

'As regards the INZ brothers. And not only they but you too ask if I could put a stone on top of this matter. Listen, you know that it doesn't depend either on me alone or on you alone . . . Of course we don't all agree, you and I could say yes, or no . . . You, by God's will and given what's possible, are to do what you can for the guys from Bocca Di Falco, to make them persuade 25 [Antonino Rotolo], and if 25 would care to come to me, I am willing to see him, to tell you what 25 thinks, but you and I are a bit far away. You can try this out and then we will see how things are, and see if we can find a good solution. There's no longer anyone here (like the INZ brothers) to give the OK to change or reverse the situation we are the ones who are needed . . .

'Let's state it clearly: if they can't take this responsibility why should we claim to be angry with the others, who don't even know the INZ brothers? I am minded to speak to weigh things up and in the meantime we'll find some solution by listening to

---

* *Pizzino* used as evidence in Trial no. 38/08, Palermo District Anti-Mafia Office against Alamia Pietro + 20, 16 January 2008. All mistakes deliberate.

the opinions of the others. We always see to it that we are going around in search of a good solution. Even if they had to leave right now and then we made them come back . . . My dearest one, you need more besides my opinion. My heart wanted peace, and tranquility for everyone if such a thing was only possible . . . But we must either create right conditions or wait for the conditions to come right.

'Now tell me, if I want to know who the ones are taking the responsibility for the INZ brothers. You want me to tell them about you asking, it was all good to know but if this request was interpreted as being hopeful for responsibility, we won't be flattering anybody. So by the will of God right or wrong I have replied to your dear letter.'

'[Franky Boy's] everything over there'*

Gianni Nicchi

If there are no killings in Palermo it's down to that guy. Everybody's looking for him. They're leaving Sicily to see him, queuing up to talk to him. He's American, but it's as if he were Sicilian, very Sicilian. He's a son of Ballarò, the working-class district of Palermo famous for its colourful market. His father was born in Via Candelai, the road that comes down from Via Maqueda, crosses Via Capo and comes out on the other side of Via Papireto. The guy's full name is Francesco Paolo Augusto Calì, but everyone knows him as Franky Boy. Franky Boy is a big shot.

'He's everything over there,' says young Gianni Nicchi to his *capomandamento*, Antonino Rotolo. 'Over there' is New York. It's America.

The same America where Franky Boy became a made man. They made him a *wiseguy*, a man of honour. He grew up on 18th Street, in Brooklyn. Where Jackie D'Amico was in charge, John Gotti's right-hand man. He married Rosaria, the sister of Inzerillo, one of the ones who left the suburb of Passo di Rigano in 1964 and moved to Cherry Hill. And Franky Boy started climbing his mountain: the mountain of Cosa Nostra in the United States. In 1997 he looks like one of many *siciliani* at the court of the Gambinos. In

* Quotations recorded in Trial no. 11059/06 against Casamento Filippo + 29 (Old Bridge), Palermo, 7 February 2008.

2007 FBI agents discover that he has the 'character' to become the boss of bosses of the five big New York families. The feds have sources inside Cosa Nostra. One of those is Frank Fappiano, the other Michael Di Leonardo. He's the rising star of the Mafia in America.

Everybody prays for him, everybody gives him respect. In Palermo and in New York. He's young – born in 1965 – but his fate seems to be sealed. He's linked to the Inzerillos of Sicily and the Gambinos of America. Even the Corleonesi cross the Atlantic and go running to him.

The 'journeys' begin in 2003. Nicola Mandalà of the Villabate family and Gianni Nicchi of the Pagliarelli family, the former on a mission from old Bernardo Provenzano and the latter on the orders of Antonino Rotolo, who hates the Inzerillos, but who is now in business with the Inzerillos. Giovanni goes there too, the most Inzerillo of them all, Totuccio's son, accompanied by Filippo Casamento. Enemies in Palermo, in New York they're partners in the new *bisinisso*.* They deal in drug consignments, they drive in cars registered to Haskell International Trading Inc. and Circus Fruits Wholesale, to Two Brothers Produce Express Ltd and Bontel USA Corp., all food and construction companies registered to Francesco Paolo Augusto Calì or his nominees.

It's a route that's known to the feds. Since the days of the Pizza Connection, the vast heroin trade between Sicily and the States run by the Adamita, Catalano, Bono and Badalamenti families. It's their sons and nephews and brothers-in-law who are travelling down the same road. There's a certain 'Silvio' who's Franky Boy's right-hand man. His real name is Silvestre Lo Verde and his father is Leonardo, a greengrocer from Palermo who's related to the Gambinos and who emigrated to new York in 1988. Just a few years after Franky's father, Cesare Augusto, opened a video store on 18th Street.

---

* 'Business'.

New York suddenly turns into what it has always been for the Palermo bosses: a market, and an embassy. Cosa Nostra's dream is to rediscover America. In the face of so much money they're willing to forget everything – the Corleonesi and the others too. Grudges. Rights and wrongs. Conflicts. But things don't go as the men of honour imagine they will.

‘We have to get out. Not just out of Sicily, not just out of Italy – we have to get out of Europe’*

Francesco Inzerillo

Palermo, 345 Via Castellana – a high wall, a road that leads to the bottom of the mountain. At the end of it lies the property of the Inzerillos of Passo do Rigano. A black cloud darkens the sky, smoke from the Bellolampo rubbish dump. They're all there. They're waiting. To come back like the big guys they once were, to walk around Palermo without feeling the Corleonesi breathing down their necks, without looking over their shoulders at traitors. Now they've got Franky Boy in America. They're still alive as far as he's concerned. And with him they can make themselves rich, richer than their fathers ever were.

Giovanni Inzerillo, Totuccio's son, meets everybody he's supposed to meet. The old friends of his family who live up in Torretta, the others who live in Piano dell'Occhio, the cousins who are scattered around the streets of L'Uditore and Cruillas. The Inzerillos are ready. They're ready to take over Palermo again.

But they've been following them for two years and two months, the crime-fighters and the federal agents. In Sicily and the United States of America. They film their every movement, they tail them day and night, they bug their homes. The young members of the Passo di Rigano family think they've got the whole world in their

* Conversation recorded by the mobile unit of Palermo state police headquarters.

hands. They feel strong, there are lots of them, they're starting to see the money coming in from New York. From Franky Boy. They don't suspect that they're already 'marked'; they think they're still living in the Sicily of their fathers and grandfathers, the Palermo of thirty or forty years ago. Only one of them, the oldest one, warns of the danger. He's Francesco Inzerillo, the one they call *ù truttaturi*, 'the trotter', and the first of the 'runaways' to have come back. The father of the same Rosario who married Franky Boy on 18th Street in Brooklyn.

At the time Francesco is locked up in jail. On 30 August 2007 Giovanni Inzerillo and his cousin Giuseppe go to talk with him. A bugging device records their concerns.

'We can't stay here, we have to get out. Not just out of Sicily, not just out of Italy – we have to get out of Europe. We can't work freely, morally any more. There's no future for us here any more. I'm sorry about that, it's a beautiful part of the world, but there's no future. If you want a bit of peace, you've got to get out . . . If it was enough just to get out of Sicily, you could head north, but as soon as you pick up the phone to your mother or your sister, or your brother or your nephew, you're already under surveillance . . . you've got to go to South America, to Central America, and that's it.

He's worried; he's sure it will never again be as it used to be. 'Even if the goods are registered to third parties, even if you're eighty years old, if they have to confiscate your stuff they will, just because you're a friend of, because you're an acquaintance of . . . So the best thing is to get out, you just have to be charged under Article 416-bis and that's enough for them to start confiscating your properties. And there's nothing worse than having your property confiscated. We Inzerillos all have to get out.'

Six months later, early in February 2007, all the Inzerillos are in jail. One raid in Sicily and another in New York. A hundred arrests. The Gambinos, the Manninos, all their relatives in Cherry Hill. The first on the FBI's list is Francesco Augusto Calì, aka Franky Boy.

Eight years have passed since the Inzerillos dreamed of reigning over Sicily again. But this time America hasn't brought them good luck.

According to the rules of Cosa Nostra, he's still the one: Totò Riina. Since he was arrested early in 1993, the Commissione *hasn't actually met again, and has never chosen another new* capo. *For thirteen years the leading role was inherited by Bernardo Provenzano, the other godfather in Corleone. But since his capture in the spring of 2006 Cosa Nostra has been rudderless. In November 2007 Salvatore Lo Piccolo, a boss accredited as a possible leader of the criminal association, is also sent to jail. More than being in search of a* capo, *Cosa Nostra now seems to be in search of itself and its future.*

'Duties and prohibitions'*

Salvatore Lo Piccolo

'Commandments' confiscated in Salvatore Lo Piccolo's hideaway.

Composition of the family

Capofamiglia
Sottocapo
Consigliere
Capodecina
Soldati

The head of the family is elected by votes from all members of the family. As is the *consigliere.*

The *sottocapo* is appointed by the *capofamiglia.* As is the *capodecina.*

The *capofamiglia* has the final say.

The *sottocapo* stands in for the *capo famiglia* in the absence of the *capo famiglia.*

The *consigliere* has the role of keeping everybody united in the family – and to give advice for the good of the family.

---

* Evidence used in Trial no. 38/08, Palermo District Anti-Mafia Office, against Alamia Pietro + 20, 16 January 2008.

The *soldati* are the ones who take care of the family's needs under the orders of the *capodecina.*

The *mandamento* is a family with a seat on the *Commissione.* And which is at the head of several families.

Composition of the Commissione

The *Commissione* is composed of all the *capimandamenti.* Where the *capo di Commissione,* plus the *sottocapo di Commissione,* plus the secretary are elected. Whereby the secretary is responsible for the appointments of the *Commissione.*

The role of the Commissione

It is constituted to act as a balance within the families and in Cosa Nostra. And to deliberate the most delicate facts and the decisions to be taken.

I swear to be true to Cosa Nostra. If I were to betray it my flesh must burn – as this picture burns.

Duties and prohibitions

You can't be introduced to another of our friends except through a third party.

You shall not look at the wives of our friends.

You shall not consort with the cops.

You shall not frequent pubs or clubs.

It is your duty to be available to Cosa Nostra at all times, even if your wife is about to give birth.

Appointments are to be respected categorically.

You shall treat your wife with respect.

When you are called upon to provide information about something you must tell the truth.

You cannot appropriate money belonging to others and other families.

Those who cannot be a part of Cosa Nostra

Anyone with a close relative in the forces of law and order.
Anyone with emotional betrayals in the family.
Anyone who behaves badly and does not comply with moral values.

'It'll take time, you teach me'*

Giuseppe Lipari and Salvatore Miceli

Miceli: 'Better like this though . . . and yet everything has changed.'

Lipari: 'It's changed but . . .'

Miceli: 'There's a friend of mine . . . who says the toy is broken . . .'

Lipari: ' . . . the toy . . .'

Miceli: 'This friend has got away . . . he's from Marsala, he's in a fix, too, and we met and he says, "Get out – the toy is broken!!!"'

Lipari: ' . . . it's basically a stalemate situation . . . Because . . . Bino [Bernardo] Provenzano . . . you know Bino?'

Miceli: 'No, never met him.'

Lipari: 'I said that . . . There was a moment of stalemate . . . there was me, Bino, Nino Manuzza . . . Benedetto Spera . . .'

Miceli: 'You know "Uncle" Benedetto . . .'

Lipari: 'He got arrested too. Gaetano Cinà, and Lo Piccolo, in fact . . . do you know him? Have you perhaps heard of Lo Piccolo?'

Miceli: 'Yes, yes . . . I don't know him but I've heard of him.'

Lipari: 'So we've got Bino himself, saying, "Gentlemen, let's get this toy back on its feet" . . . which happens, if I, if I don't get instructions to do it from jail . . . because it means that I've got to go against them . . .'

Miceli: 'Of course.'

---

* Evidence used in the preliminary hearings by the court of Palermo in the trial of Lipari + 16, 12 December 2003.

Lipari: 'Against Totuccio Riina . . . against Bagarella . . . the situations were what they were. At that point I said to him, "Listen, Bino," I said, "we haven't got more than two years left here." I said, "Don't get annoyed, Bino, I'm taking this liberty because we know each other." I said, "Neither everything can be protected, nor everything can be swallowed up, nor everything can be shared of what has been done, because in the past right things have been done and wrong things . . . you have to have a bit of patience" . . .'

Miceli: 'Right, yeah . . .'

Libari: 'And when I said that Benedetto came and kissed me . . . I said to him, "No, we can't say everything was done right" . . .'

Miceli: 'That you've made mistakes, yes.'

Lipari: 'We did some things that were, were pretty murky . . .'

Miceli: 'Because . . . however . . . there is a complaint going around . . .'

Lipari: 'I know, I know . . .'

Miceli: 'A complaint from some people on that side, though . . .'

Lipari: 'There are people who feel disappointed, perhaps, that's what's happening! In fact, when we're reorganizing, it might be a bit better to say, "Gentlemen, it isn't as if someone takes all the mistakes and paints the bigger picture on that basis" . . .'

Miceli: 'Of course . . .'

Lipari: 'Just to say: "Yes, yes, it's wrong. Sorry" . . . '

Miceli: 'It'll take time, you teach me, it'll take time.'

Lipari: 'It will.'

'The toy is broken'

Salvatore Miceli

It's less illegible, as if it has lost the mystery that always made it seem different. It has become more Italian, as if something or someone had finally brought it closer to the other big cities of the country. In some way 'de-customized'. After the 1992 massacres Palermo has changed. And it's heading towards a *normality* that's never been seen before. It's both more beautiful and uglier. Freer and more predictable.

Its Mafia has changed as well. From the old bosses of the 'happy' 1970s to the Commandments of the Lo Piccolo family of San Lorenzo. The men of 2007 are elevated to the rank of major crime bosses; father Salvatore and son Alessandro even keep a manual for the perfect Mafioso in their fugitive hideaway, a kind of crib-sheet, the list of rules to be observed by men of honour. A generational leap and a leap into the void. A sign of the times, the decadence of a world that seemed immutable.

Cosa Nostra has entered a deep crisis. An economic one above all: it's out of *piccioli*. Much of its property has been confiscated, *pentiti* and investigations have broken down its military structure. And then there's the crisis in vocations. There's no longer a queue to join up; in the suburbs there's no longer any status attached to becoming a man of honour. Once upon a time it took five, ten or even twenty years to make someone a man of honour; today the new affiliates are picked up and recruited from amongst the drug-dealers, the kidnappers, from amongst *malacarne*, the lowlifes, of any kind. In some ways it's the end of a secret association born more than two centuries before. Its decline seems unstoppable. For fifty years it's been the most powerful criminal organization in the West; today it's destined to become one Mafia among many.

It's a break-up that began with Totò Riina's megalomania: the massacres, the attack on institutions, the idea of submitting the Italian state to the will of the peasants of Corleone. It was Uncle Totò who brought the Sicilian men of honour to ruin.

'The toy is broken,' confesses Salvatore Miceli to another boss as they remember the errors of ten years before, the season of bombings, the killing of Giovanni Falcone, the death of Paolo Borsellino. The strategy of massacres drove them up a blind alley. The police came down on them with extreme and unstinting violence, for the first time without being on the alternating current of a state of emergency.

It's a war that's still being fought in Italy. If the state goes on as it began to do in the 1990s, Cosa Nostra could one day become what it is in America: just business. More money, perhaps. But less power.

The heirs of the big Sicilian families face a difficult existence. The only son of Totò Riina still at liberty will spend the rest of his life under special surveillance; the sons of the Inzerillo family were stopped before their rise could begin. The myths have crumbled. The myth of invincibility above all. The next in line will be left with uncertainty and fear.

'Pick a fight with whoever you like, but you leave the state alone'*

Conversations picked up by bugging devices in a driving school in the centre of Palermo.

Unknown speaker

'The first thing was sacred. First you had to see who his *mamma* was and whether for some particular reason, for some trifle, he couldn't be *made*. A trifle, you get me? For a piece of crap, kids having a drink from the wrong glass of water couldn't be *made* for that reason. Now, on the other hand, they just have to bring money. Business, I tell them . . . like the Americans. But what are we doing? Are we mucking about? That world is over. There are kids who won't listen to a thing. And they have to belong to a particular family . . . Because it's not just a matter of pulling the trigger . . . kids now have a different mentality. They're only interested in one thing: money.

'No one paid Uncle Leopoldi a cent. All the tax-collectors were in our district. And there was no half-ways. Now there's nothing. To

* Bugged conversations used as evidence in the preliminary hearings of the court of Palermo by the judge Roberto Binenti, in the Trial against Lipari + 16, 12 December 2003.

tell the truth, in my brief history I've never been treated badly by anyone . . . today they're bothering the shopkeepers; they're asking exorbitant sums from those poor guys who are just trying to earn a crust. One million, three million. In the end a *picciotto** said, "People change and times change." I looked at him and I said to him, "In my day you'd have met a horrible end" . . .'

Carmelo Amato and Giuseppe Vaglica

Amato: 'Because, remember, for as long as the world has existed, you can pick a fight with whoever you like, but you leave the state alone. The state, if you like, "gets on your wick". Mistakes get made. Unfortunately you can't talk about them these days. Because if you go and talk to someone somewhere they might say to you, "This is bollocks." . . . You get me?'

Vaglica: 'That's true, that's true. Let me tell you, mistakes are made in life, but wouldn't it have been better if Falcone hadn't ended up like that?'

Amato: 'Mistakes have been made. But unfortunately, what can we do? . . . Am I right? . . .'

Vaglica: 'Oh, nothing . . .'

Amato: 'I bought the anti-bugging device. I'll keep it a bit and you keep it a bit . . . I'll check the cars every three days as well . . . you do the office, check everything, check your car and then bring it back to me. But you mustn't forget that I always need it . . .'

Vaglica: 'OK, fine . . . fuck, this is how you're making sure I'm safe . . .'

Amato: 'There's a war on, *compare*. You have to be careful and keep your eyes open. I've been told to be careful, because the place is swarming with cops.'

---

* 'Kid'.

Carmelo Amato and Gaetano Cinà

Amato: 'Tanino, forget it . . . you've behaved well in your life. Don't worry, because you always keep your head above water. Tanino, I've set out my case. I'm at your complete disposal for anything you want.'

Cinà: 'I'm still on trial.'

Amato: 'Anything at all, at your disposal for anything at all.'

Cinà: 'Carmelo, Carmelo, you see that I'm *combinato* like you are . . . wherever I go I've got friends in high places.'

'Unfortunately life isn't always a bunch of roses'*

Sandro Lo Piccolo

Quotations and words found in one of Sandro Lo Piccolo's notebooks. Eight pages, his 'dictionary'. Phrases to be used from time to time in his *pizzini*.

'In life there's a human value that's worth more than freedom, which is honour and dignity.'

'There's a proverb that says you can take the leaves off a tree, you can cut off its branches, but when the roots are strong and big, you can rest assured that both the branches and the leaves will grow back.'

'Roll up those sleeves . . . doing up my shoelaces . . . the Creator . . . I'm firmly convinced . . . Until. Slithers like an eel. But with preconditions. That's why I feel, I tell you I've been saddened (or am saddened) . . . I formulated various questions, but even today I have had no answers. Luckily everyone is his own arbiter.'

'Extremis; for extreme evils extreme remedies. I don't tolerate tolerance. I don't want to get moralistic or deliver lectures. Determinant.

---

* Evidence used in Trial no. 38/08, Palermo District Anti-Mafia Office against Alamia Pietro + 20, 16 January 2008.

Elucidations. He doesn't agree, they agree. He ponders things well. You have been very wearing. Through unofficial channels. Through confidential channels. I can't act the Franciscan friar . . . just to do them a favour.'

'Of course, the matters have stirred within me the deepest feelings of bitterness, suffering and pain, but they have not affected my dignity, which I preserve intact.'

'I try to pace out my day as best I can.'

'There is no need to thank me, when things are done with the heart it's all already included.'

'Meanwhile that is a problem with which, against my will, I must unfortunately burden you. Understandably. Don't even mention it. Unfortunately life isn't always a bunch of roses. We reached an agreement . . . I, for example, would do . . . or tried desperately – hopelessly . . .'

'I want something more – visceral – deeply rooted, along the lines of love.'

'But let's keep it to ourselves and reveal nothing of what I have just said to you. If this is the only way for x to get close to him, so be it!'

'Panic is the enemy of reason.'

'I tell you from now on . . . I'll pay you in advance from now on . . . till now I haven't managed to . . . in safeguarding my safety . . . It's good that you should know from now on . . . then I wanted to inform you that where you were concerned.'

'On the quiet – excuse – this is not a reproach, I would be very careful. Potential difficulties.'

'In my view, you're acting stupid on purpose.'

'In my modest experience . . . I will immediately begin by asking your forgiveness for having forgotten . . . While I am here, you must never. Don't let it be an exorbitant sum.'

'Throughout these years I have learned to live with him, accepting his defects and his requests. Probably – of course – because – since – in fact – so that – deliberately – who . . . factotum – chip in – curriculum. Arbitrarily.'

'Unfortunately fate has put me to a sore test.'

'We must try to leave nothing untried. You must bear in mind. In my view, this guy is the kind who always likes to sow discord . . . punctuality with regard to the personality.'

'Freudian, Freud the philosopher.'

'I . . . unscrewed it and found it'*

Antonino Rotolo and Gianni Nicchi

Rotolo: 'I've . . . I've got them plugged in . . .'

Nicchi: 'I'm coming, I'm coming with a guy . . .'

Rotolo: 'That guy from over there, the radio engineer?'

Nicchi: 'No, he's a guy who's crazy about that kind of thing. I don't know if he's a radio engineer or not . . .'

Rotolo: 'Well, he might be up to finding them or putting in these things that are put there to cancel out . . .'

Nicchi: ' . . . the waves . . .'

Rotolo: ' . . . because they were going to make one for me, and when I plugged it in, for a radius of forty metres, even outside . . . it cut off the waves, all the waves . . .'

Nicchi: 'Let's get organized first. First, I'll send him all the equipment and then I'll send him this guy, who has these two machines – ten minutes, twenty minutes . . . *peep, peep, peep, peep, peep, peep* . . . and he can spot, what do I know, a video camera, directional microphones, bugs in the sockets . . . He says: "The only ones I can't check are the ones put directly into the phone cable . . . Those ones don't give off any signals." And this is a hard-working guy . . .'

Rotolo: 'I've got one in a radio . . . That made me realize that they

* Quotations from the arrest document for trial no. 2474/05 against Antonino Rotolo + 51, 20 June 2006.

were putting in bugs, because the evening before the lawyer came I'd forgotten that the plug was in . . . they had the detector and another signal, you see what I mean? And they put it in front of me, so when I got home I immediately went over there, unscrewed it and found it. Not least because, before I left, I said it right in my wife's ear. I said to her: "They've put bugs in!" Because I'd worked it out.'

Nicchi: 'And yet this guy is making himself available . . . he has an office with video cameras, all those things. You saw him, you went in, you came out and you had all these products and these things . . .'

Rotolo: 'You get this guy and you put in the plug, you sit down, you speak . . . but – 100 per cent! Because this thing has to happen even if there's nothing there. Because if I'm not there today and they put them in at night and I'm there the next morning, you can't feel safe because now there aren't any . . .'

Nicchi: 'Fine . . . by the doorway, whether it's here or there, just show him.'

Rotolo: 'It would be good to have a day to do this week, or maybe Saturday . . . or any day. I'm interested, at this point I'm interested . . . But are we sure about this guy? Does anyone know him from before?'

Nicchi: 'Nicola, he's a friend of Nicola and Paccarè . . .'

Rotolo: 'He's a friend . . . he's a friend . . . I get it, that's fine . . .'

'But how I loved you (asshole)'*

Maria, lover of Sandro Lo Piccolo

'Today, 5 March, I am very happy that at last I have had news from you. I know it's not your fault if you haven't written to me before but, believe me, apart from being worried, I can no longer live without your writings and this is due to all those years of absence from you. I wrote to you two months ago but our interlocutor told me not to for now . . . I miss you so . . .

'With regard to what people say about you it's that you had plastic surgery and that's why you're still wanted, and that you're an unscrupulous person because of all the murders they accused you of, but those bastards don't know that they're speaking ill of you and that 70% of what they write in the journals is nonsense.

'Then forgive me if I wanted to know a bit more about you . . . I would never want to get you into trouble (things are bad enough for me!!!). For the work I will wait. I know that sooner or later you will find something. Apart from the fact that Di Maio is a wonderful person he put me through moments of thoughtlessness on the boat . . . with regard to the photographs I hope he told you that I promised him never to say a word to anyone because it's a secret (not that they are hardcore pictures, but it's still a married woman;

---

* Letter used as evidence at Trial no 38/08, Palermo District Anti-Mafia Office, against Alamia Pietro + 20, 16 January 2008.

they're just photographs of a happy summer day in the company of the friends we have in common) . . .

'With regard to the father of my little girl, I assure you once more on the contrary apart from San Lorenzo he is really allergic to the cops until a few days ago he killed one beating him up only because he showed him his ID to make him move the van that he'd parked a bit badly, he said you're a fucker and a cop and I'll kill you right now with my fists do you get it!! . . .

'In the letter I wrote you I said that given that you've told me you will always be at my complete disposal I forced you to write to me because I miss you so much and I was very sad (and now you've written to me too) then I told you that on Christmas Day I had the little girl christened. About the shoes for my children thank you I really needed them I'm thinking of going next week because the little one has a temperature . . .

'Don't forget that you are one of the few reasons that I still have for living, a few days ago I remembered how many sandwiches we ate in Montepellegrino do you remember? But how I loved you (asshole). Forgive me but sometimes I get angry however they are the best memories I am left with, and I have never regretted anything of all that we did together because as regards this love it was and remains a film that will never be erased.

'Now I say goodbye even though there are many things I would like to say but you will get big headed (joke!!). Wishing you a happy Easter and don't remember that if one day you should need anything (in my small way) I will be glad to help you. I send you a big smacker my love look after yourself and always remember that I have loved you and will love you forever.

'PS you will always be in my thoughts, in my dreams that will go with me until the end of my days.'

F. A. is the mysterious hand that signed the pictures of the faces of the Mafioso Matteo Messina Denaro which appeared in January 2007 on the walls of Palermo. Brightly coloured faces in the style of Andy Warhol. One of the murals is in front of the cathedral, the other a few steps away from the grand square of Quattro Canti. The anti-Mafia associations are outraged. They protest about this 'hymn' to Cosa Nostra and ask for the murals to be removed. Censorship breaks out: white paint on the faces of the last* Capomafia *still in hiding. The artists reveal themselves a few weeks later; they are two architecture students. F. is Filippo Bartoli and A. is Alessandro Giglio. Their 'artistic provocation' puts fear into a suspicious Palermo that is a prisoner of its own shadows.*

---

* After Provenzano's arrest, Denaro was widely considered to be one of the new bosses of Cosa Nostra.

'I belong to you'*

Matteo Messina Denaro aka Alessio

Letters to Bernardo Provenzano.

'I am addressing you as a guarantor of everyone and everything so your contacts are the only ones I am at ease with; that is, I don't recognize anyone else's, anyone who is your friend is and will be my friend, anyone who is not your friend not only is not my friend but will be an enemy of mine, about this there is no doubt . . . Thank you for taking the trouble to ensure harmony and peace for all of us . . . Before getting to the nub of the matter I wish to tell you that I am in favour of dialogue and pacification as you have asked me, and I respect your will for the way it has always been. I know that you have no need of any recommendation because you are our master, but it is my heart that is speaking and I ask you to listen very carefully. I love you very much.

With unchanged esteem and my affection as ever,
your "nephew" Alessio.'

'Dearest Z,

I hope this finds you well as it leaves me. I received your news. Sorry if my mail always travels a bit late, it is all due to a security problem, I

---

* Letters included in the report by the Palermo mobile unit sent to the deputy prosecutor of Palermo, Giuseppe Pignatone, and to assistant prosecutors Michele Prestipino and Marzia Sabella, 11 April 2006.

think you will understand me, besides who can better than you, but let us leave it at that, I am replying to yours . . . Thank you for the lovely words you used for me about them and I am honoured, but I would humbly like to say that I am no better than you. I prefer to say that I belong to you, as has also incidentally always been the case, I always had a life that is yours, I was born that way and I will die that way, that much is certain.

'Now I entrust myself fully to your hands and to your decisions, everything that you decide I will accept without problems and without creating problems, that is honesty as far as I'm concerned.

'Because I trust in you and only in you; (2) because I have sought you out to resolve this matter and now I cannot see a reason why anyone else would be interested; (3) because I am only acknowledging the authority that is your due; (4) because we both understand each other even if we don't see each other.'

'My dearest,

I hope this finds you well as it leaves me, I recently received your letters and I am replying straight away . . . As regards the methane supply, the villages in question were six in number, I know exactly which villages they are, the missing money was about 250 million lire, because even before they were sent you had made a discount of around 300 million lire, but the 250 million lire they were supposed to give us which never happened. In fact after a while you told me you didn't know what to do and that they didn't want to pay and that was how it was left. After a while I discovered that in fact the 250 million did go out but they never reached us because they were stolen by one of the sons of your late fellow villager, that son is in Rome. I never said anything of that to you because I understood that the only result of the matter would be mortification and so I preferred to let the subject die. Now I am telling you that because you yourself are asking otherwise I would have said nothing, basically each one of us replies with his own name and his dignity, this son of your dead fellow villager knows that he has stolen money that wasn't his and certainly he has enjoyed himself in Rome seeing as how he lives there, what he doesn't know is that that money was destined for families of prisoners who need it, but I still consider the matter closed, let him deal with his own conscience . . .'

'I am an enemy of Italian justice that is rotten and corrupt'*

Matteo Messina Denaro, known as Alessio

Letter to Suetonius (the ex-mayor of Castelvetrano, Antonino Vaccarino†), 1 February 2005.

'My dearest one,

. . . I have known despair as well and have been left alone, I have known hell and I have been alone, I have fallen many, many times and have got back on my feet alone, I too have known ingratitude from anyone and everyone and I have been alone, I have known the taste of dust and in my solitude I have fed upon it. Can a man who has endured all this in silence still have faith? I think not. Today I expect my fate to fulfil itself along the lines of this thought: I have seen what life has given me and I have not been afraid and I have not averted my eye from there and I have not forgiven what cannot be forgiven.

'In Italy about fifteen years ago there was a coup, white tinted with red, carried out by a number of magistrates along with some political bigwigs, and even today we are living on that wave. There are no first-rate politicians now; the only one I can remember is Craxi and we saw what happened to him. Today, to be a good politician you just have be anti-

* This letter was published in the Sicilian weekly magazine *S*, issue no. 5, in 2008.

† Vaccarino was fully acquitted of Mafia association in the 1990s.

Mafia – the more he shouts the further ahead he gets, and the most abject politicians are the Sicilians, who have always sold this land of ours to those currently in charge. It's too simplistic for the Italian state to consider the phenomenon of Sicily as a horde of criminals and a hotbed of felons. It isn't like that, we have more history than the Italian state. If I had been born two centuries ago, with the same experience as today, I would already have led a revolution against this Italian state and I would have won; today, affluence, progress and globalization are taking the world in a very different direction and my methods are old-fashioned, so all I am now is a disappointed idealist and we both know what happens to idealists.

'When a state resorts to the most wicked kinds of torture for the purposes of revenge and even more forcing the weakest to inform, tell me what state it is? Certainly informing will have made the careers of certain individuals, but as an institution the Italian state has failed. They have practised and continue to practise torture in jails . . . they introduced 41-bis; let them do it and let them add 82-quarter, there will always been men who won't sell off their own dignity . . .

'I am an enemy of Italian justice that is rotten and corrupt to its foundations. Toni Negri says that and I think he means it . . . For the abolition of life terms I think we'll get there with time but all of those things will happen by themselves with the process of civilization, and yet we two will no longer be of this earth because they will be long processes that take their time. As regards retrials I don't think that will ever happen, I told them we aren't interested in that any more. I've had ridiculous convictions without a shred of objective evidence. The law says that two collaborators with the law saying the same thing is evidence, but I have many convictions with only one collaborator with the law and without any corroboration . . . I get convictions anywhere and everywhere because it's the name that they're convicting. I can say I've been at the mercy and the laughing-stock of lots of little Torquemadas . . .

'I think I've told you everything . . . I'm very pragmatic and I've managed to disappoint even my own expectations, which is saying a lot. But if speaking uninhibitedly like this has caused you annoyance, I humbly ask your forgiveness.'

His birth certificate calls him Giuseppe Salvatore; at home they call him Salvo; in the village he is ù picciriddu.[*] *Born at Pasqualino e Noto hospital in Palermo on 3 May 1977, vaccinated at Local Health Authority no. 58 with a certificate issued by the 'medical director' Antonio Rizzuto, he is the third son of Salvatore Riina and Ninetta Bagarella, and the only male member of the Corleone family not to have received a life sentence.*

Salvo has one brother and two sisters: Giovanni Francesco, born 21 February 1976; Maria Concetta, born 19 December 1974; Lucia, born 11 November 1980. Giovanni, Maria Concetta and Lucia were also born at the Pasqualina e Noto hospital on Via Dante; they too were vaccinated at Local Health Authority no. 58, with certificates issued by Dr Antonio Rizzuto. The children of Totò Riina and Ninetta Bagarella were all born during their father's long period in hiding: twenty-four years and seven months. A ghost family haunting Palermo.

* 'The kid'.

'You've always been *catu e corda*'[*][†]

Antonina Bagarella, known as Ninetta

Ninetta Bagarella and her sons Giovanni and Salvo

Ninetta: 'You've always been *catu e corda* . . . both of you, you remember? But it was always Giovanni pulling . . .'

Giovanni: 'No, we took it in turns . . .'

Salvo: 'No, Papa said you were the one who pulled in the sense . . . the one who was more, more . . .'

Ninetta: ' . . . more tough and hard . . .'

Giovanni: 'Papa once said something to me that I've never forgotten, he said, "You do the talking! You're always right as far as I'm concerned, so what's the problem?" . . .'

Ninetta: '"He takes care of my affairs," he says . . . "that *picciutteddu* takes care of my affairs" . . . because if you were another, bad brother, he'd have said, "He does the talking, and he takes care of his own affairs" . . .'

Giovanni: 'Yes, he's said that to me.'

Ninetta: 'Well done, well done, Salvo, always the same, it gives me real pleasure.'

Salvo: 'Mamma, who are you talking to?'

---

* 'Bucket and rope'.

† Recorded conversation used in Trial no. 13100/00, Palermo District Anti-Mafia Office.

Antonietta: 'Both of you . . .'

Salvo: 'You see I'm from the school of Corleone . . .'

Ninetta: 'Well thank goodness, thank goodness . . .'

Salvo: 'My father's from Corleone, my mother's from Corleone, what other school and blood could I have?'

Ninetta: 'Pure Corleone blood.'

Giovanni: ' . . . but I knew . . .'

Ninetta: 'But it's beautiful.'

Ninetta and Salvo

Salvo: 'Mamma, you're always going on about these things . . . I don't want property, they'll confiscate it from me.'

Ninetta: 'Sorry, Salvo, but where are we going to have to go?'

Salvo: 'To a rented house, so that when they confiscate it they won't be confiscating it from us, they'll be confiscating it from the landlord. And what are they going to do to us? That's the modern ideology, Mamma. Properties can't be bought any more.'

Salvo and Giovanni

Salvo: 'Petrol strike . . . Chaos . . .'

Giovanni: 'What do you mean? I thought of you and I said: "You'll have no problems in Corleone" . . .'

Salvo: 'There's work going on in Corleone . . . there are queues and queues . . .'

Giovanni. 'It's hell . . .'

Giovanni: 'And who doesn't know you in Corleone?'

Salvo: 'On Wednesday evening I saw the chaos at Vito's pumps . . . the guy at the petrol pumps says to me, "There's no petrol left."

I call him over and I say, "Vito, come here, how are things looking?" He says: "I've got 200 litres in the pump but they're all for the forces of law and order." So I tell him: "Vito, I'm your forces of law and order – stop and fill me up . . ." There was one 40 litre barrel and I nicked a 40 litre barrel and made him fill it up, and I filled up my car . . .'

Giovanni: 'So we can assume that you paid for the petrol?'

Salvo: 'The petrol was paid for by the "international community".'

‘The decision was this: let’s kill them. And they were killed.’*

Salvo Riina

He is talking to Salvatore Cusimano as they drive down the Capaci bypass.

‘They paid the consequences, but in the end they were men. Hard-line. You see, it smarts with me even more . . . They’re hanging wreaths on this thing . . . there was too much obstinacy, and then the ball got dropped, in ’92, in May. It really didn’t end well, things were on the way out . . . That massacre, the other one in July, and then in January they arrested my father . . . I don’t know how things would have gone if he hadn’t made the state lower its horns.

‘Telling the state: we’re in charge. And instead his foot slipped . . . because we were being disloyal to all our comrades and saying to them: here in Sicily there’s us, maybe up there there’s you, but down here we’re in charge. Whoever replaced him didn’t have the balls to take things forward. A colonel always has to make the decisions and he always has the responsibility. He can’t go: “What am I saying? What’s going on?” . . . He has to take a decision, and the decision was this: let’s kill them. And they were killed. It led to bad things because there were prison restrictions . . . but they did four or five years, in jail the *cristiani* never got a thing to eat. The Paler-

---

* Recorded conversation used as evidence in Trial no. 13100/00, Palermo District Anti-Mafia Office.

mitans are weak . . . fuck, now they've got 41-bis . . . only my uncle and my father had 41-bis, and that's enough!!! . . .

'If you think what my father's done, with all the fantastic things my father did in terms of the *pizzo*, today we couldn't make as much as one per cent of that. But I'll tell you why – there was more wealth around in those days, you could make money then, nowadays, as you see, you can't make money any more . . .

'Now when one of those bastards turns up – forgive me for talking like that – when one of those bastards turns up and takes all our wealth away, he confiscates our properties, our commodities and our money, our cars, one of those kids . . . sadly you need those things with this shitty state. But you know what's going on, you declare a [BMW] 740 and then you can buy, you can afford to buy . . . And if they ask you, "How did you buy this?", "Oh, I make fifty million a year, do you mind?" . . . Unfortunately now we need to justify things. You have to be able to recycle money, illegal money – you can have it ticked off as "original". You have to make it look legal; if it's illegal you have to fill your bags . . .

'You've got it, this is the government we have! Now anyone who goes to the appeal court now is going to get thirty years, life, when they would have been acquitted before. Bad . . . all of them. Because they're shutting everything down in a great hurry. It's never been like this with the courts of appeal. They're confirming sentences, they're going to pick up acquittals . . . but the important thing is that the fish rots from the head! Let's go to Rome, and then we'll see what needs to be done. Once general headquarters are in Rome, you immobilize Rome and then, fuck, you can start talking . . . The judiciary, things . . . in fact all the tricks they've played . . . that anti-Mafia guy Vigna, then you have to start talking in a different way . . .'

'Please do not disturb'*

Maria Concetta Riina

'I don't bear the scars of a hopeless childhood, and neither do my brothers. We didn't think: God, they're going to get us, because we weren't aware that anyone was after us. We were born into circumstances that already existed, and in a sense it was normal not to be able to do certain things, so they didn't seem like deprivations to us. When they arrested Papa, it was even more traumatic: it was as if the world had collapsed on top of us.

'I feel constantly judged, besieged by journalists. I feel I'm being observed as if I'm a strange phenomenon, a guinea-pig. Everyone expresses judgements about me, even though no one knows me. I would like to go around with a sign around my neck with the words "Please do not disturb". If people think I want to hide, that I'm scared of speaking, they're wrong. The only thing I'm really afraid of is being exploited. Every detail about me is inflated and twisted. If I go to that film about the life of Falcone they want to know why I went; if I don't go they say I refused to. Do you want to know what I felt? Even though I didn't know Judge Falcone, I felt the dismay that any human being would feel when faced with scenes of such cruelty and violence.

'All we ask is to be forgotten and to be allowed to live a normal,

---

* Interview with Maria Concetta Riina by Sandra Amurri, *Panorama*, 7 December 1995.

dignified life. There seems to be an endless appetite for journalistic scoops about the facts inherent in our private lives, different and separate from the judicial facts pertaining to other parts of the Riina family. Starting a legal occupation can hardly be scandalous. I want to live like an Italian citizen who sees her rights respected and doesn't wish to shirk her duties, with a love that is a beautiful thing, with new friends that I can go for a walk with or go for a pizza with on a Sunday.

'Mafia is violence, injustice, intimidation. My father always taught us not to commit acts of violence, or injustice, or to show the slightest disrespect towards our fellows . . . a father who always gave me affection and love, and whom I miss very much . . .

'He always told us that the most important thing is to have the courage to fight for what we believe in and always rebel against injustice. Then to have respect for people, even if that means disregarding what they represent. Always to be yourself, to be honest, and not judge people you don't know. And then he taught us to display our feelings without fear of seeming weak.

'I read what Dr Boccassini* wrote. I felt anger and a sense of infinite dismay because she took the liberty of judging me without knowing me. What am I supposed to distance myself from? From the affection and love that Papa gave me from the time of my birth? How could I stop going to see him, knowing that after every meeting he would be counting the days until the next one? And how, again, could I help loving him? . . . Dr Boccassini, who also stresses the sacrifices that her children were required to make because of her professional commitment, is urging a daughter to deny her father. I don't know how she would behave if her father or her daughter made a mistake one day. Would she erase them from her life, or would she forgive them and go on loving them? I don't think her message is a good one for young people.'

---

* Ilda Boccassini, a notorious anti-Mafia judge, known for her flame-red hair.

His focaccias with spleen and lights and caciocavallo cheese were eaten by politicians like Francesco Crispi and writers like Luigi Pirandello, and by the royal families of Italy, Spain and Belgium. It was in 1902 that the shop first assumed the name of Antica Focacceria San Francesco. The owners, five generations on, are still the Conticellos. Like everyone in Palermo, they have to 'fix themselves up' – they have to pay the pizzo. *Vincenzo Conticello rebelled; he denounced the messenger-boys of the racket; at the trial he identified them to the judge of the third penal session. In court, on 12 October 2007, one of the Mafiosi he accused of extortion is also heard. He is Francolino Spadaro, the son of Tommaso, king of the Kalsa. At the end of his questioning he shouts, 'The Mafia is disgusting.' Francolino isn't the first person in Palermo to use the phrase. And he won't be the last.*

‘Sleep, sleep, Godfather’*

Constanzia Corleone, known as Connie

Cannoli. The most poisonous are the ones that choke the treacherous Don Altobello in the Teatro Massimo, Palermo. Murder at the opera.

In the closing images of *The Godfather III*, Eli Wallach – playing Don Altobello – is given a box of cakes by Connie, Michael Corleone’s sister. The lights go out. Then a hand slips into the darkness and picks up a *cannolo*. Don Altobello sniffs it, sinks his teeth into the creamy ricotta that spills from the pastry, closes his eyes and sighs in ecstasy. His fingers reach back into the box, feel for the roughest crust, delicately pick up another *cannolo* that then disappears into his mouth. He hasn’t time to swallow it down before Don Altobello has gently died. ‘Sleep, sleep, Godfather,’ whispers Constanzia Corleone, known as Connie. It’s the eighth scene, ‘*Hanno ammazzato compare Turiddu*’ – They have murdered Turiddu – the show-stopper in Mascagni’s opera *Cavalleria Rusticana.*

Sicily’s most famous *cannoli* are the huge ones from Piana degli Albanesi and the cinnamon-flavoured ones from Caltanissetta, *Kalt El Nissa*, ‘castle of women’, in Arabic. According to some people, the origins of the *cannolo* actually lie on the opposite shore of the Mediterranean, in the skilled hands of the concubines of a

---

* *The Godfather, Part III.*

harem who wanted to win the favours of their sultan. According to others, they were born in the cloistered cells of some highly mysterious nuns in a convent clinging to the ridge of a mountain. A Sicilian-Arab cake or a Sicilian-Sicilian cake, the *cannolo* – with *cassata* – is the triumph of the island's pastry-making. The ricotta has to come from sheep's milk; in eastern Sicily it's decorated with chopped pistachios, in the west with bits of bitter chocolate and candied orange peel.

The most treacherous *cannoli* are the ones that arrived at the Palazzo d'Orléans, in the splendid halls of the presidency of the region of Sicily, in January 2008. *Cannoli* in honour of the Sicilian president, Totò Cuffaro. Thirty-two of them, big and fresh, just prepared in a pastry-works in Castronovo di Sicilia, a village on the border between the provinces of Agrigento and Palermo. They had been thoughtfully sent by Vincenzo Bonaccolta, a friend of Cuffaro, his schoolmate at the Salesiani. The *cannoli* are to 'celebrate' a ruling by the court of Palermo against the governor: five years' imprisonment. Simple criminal association rather than the Mafia association that the state prosecutors requested. For Totò Cuffaro it's almost an acquittal.

Someone sets out the tray of those *cannoli* from Castronovo di Sicilia on a circular table where Cuffaro is about to announce that he is going to stay on as governor. 'I'm staying, I'm staying because the majority of Sicilians have asked me to stay.' He sees the tray of cakes and picks it up to pass it to a clerk, just for a moment: *click*, a photographer immortalizes Totò Cuffaro with the *cannoli* in his hands. The photograph goes around the world with the caption: 'Sentenced and celebrating, out of public office and greedy as ever'.

A week later, the most powerful Sicilian politician, elected with 1,600,000 votes, is no longer governor. The Sicilians can forgive him his five-year sentence. And his dangerous relations with the

Mafia. But those *cannoli* betray him. 'You've ruined me,' Totò apparently mutters to the photographer Michele Naccari, when he has ceased to be governor of Sicily for a night and a day.

'The Mafia is disgusting'

Advertising campaign for the region of Sicily

Three years earlier, the billboards are striking – blue, with the coat of arms of the region of Sicily. The writing is big and black: 'The Mafia is disgusting'. They appear on the walls of the buildings, in squares, on the corner of every street on the island. It's a counter-offensive by Totò Cuffaro. While being investigated for Mafia association, he launches a slogan against the Mafia. It's November 2005, and Cuffaro has been under investigation for three years. The state prosecutor's office in Palermo is divided. Some people would like to charge him with external involvement in Mafia conspiracy, while chief prosecutor Pietro Grasso – more pragmatically – requests that he be charged with Mafia association. The governor defends himself both inside and outside the court.

He declares: 'I'm the first to believe that anti-Mafia work can't be done through slogans, but that what matters is acts of government . . . I feel like a "second Andreotti" . . .' He goes on: 'If they think they can open an electoral campaign in Sicily by presenting a book with allegations against me in front of State Prosecutor Gian Carlo Caselli, and even a few prosecutors who have investigated me, it all gets worrying. If these people are trying to put the wind up me, they're making a bad mistake: I'm not intimidated by anybody.' He explains: 'We are waging a genuine struggle, encouraging development and work, governing, just to get out of this damned, disgusting Mafia culture.'

'The Mafia is disgusting.' It's written up everywhere in Sicily. During these days the governor is accused of receiving from his 'moles' confidential information from the Palace of Justice. Of having some sort of dealings with the *capomandamento* of Brancaccio, Giuseppe Guttadauro, and eluding investigation. Of helping the Sicilian health mogul Michele Aiello, the prime tax contributor in the province of Palermo and a suspected figurehead for Bernardo Provenzano.

But 'The Mafia is disgusting' is an advertising slogan that finds favour with the Mafia as well. Gone are the days when the word was never uttered; on the contrary, the men of honour can now sometimes demonstrate their 'anti-Mafia' allegiances. They try and infiltrate anti-racket associations, they organize conventions, sometimes they are the first to sponsor demonstrations 'against' Cosa Nostra.

At Villabate, the friends of Bernardo Provenzano – authorized by the family – give an award to the actor Raoul Bova for his role in the television mini-series *Ultimo*, in which he plays the policeman who captured Salvatore Riina. In Enna, the president of the businessmen who take to the streets to demonstrate against the *pizzo* ends up being arrested. In Palermo, the heads of Sicindustria rage publicly against their bosses, but they are their secret associates. In Altofonte, a man of honour even puts on a painting exhibition 'dedicated to Falcone and Borsellino'.

The journey from 'the Mafia doesn't exist' to 'the Mafia is disgusting' has only taken twenty years. This is a less brazen Mafia, still tribal in its rites and rules, but, when it looks outside itself, also more modern, more sophisticated. Adapting, ready to follow each new development in society. A Mafia that hides behind the slogans of its own enemies. 'Anti-Mafia' has become a source of capital even for Cosa Nostra. The modern anti-Mafia Mafia: the absolute limit.

Sources

Below is a list of the sources from which the quotations in this book are taken. For secondary documentation and books consulted, please see the Bibliography.

p. 11: 'He saw the world and his brain exploded'
Interview by the author with Gaetano Riina, Corleone, May 1993

p. 17: The *Commissione* 1960–75
Court ruling against Abbate Giovanni + 706, Palermo, 8 November 1985 (investigating magistrates Antonino Caponnetto, Giovanni Falcone, Paolo Borsellino, Giuseppe Di Lello and Leonardo Guarnotta)

p. 21: 'As paper I burn you, as a saint I worship you'
Examination of Leonardo Messina at the Parliamentary Anti-Mafia Committee, Rome, 4 December 1992

p. 24: 'The oath is like the Ten Commandments'
Testimony of Salvatore Contorno at the Maxi-Trial in Palermo, hearings on 11 and 17 April 1986

p. 27: 'He's like us'
Examination of Tommaso Buscetta at the Parliamentary Anti-Mafia Committee, Rome, 17 November 1992; verdict, 8 November 1985 against Abbate Giovanni + 706, Palermo (investigating magistrates Antonino Caponnetto, Giovanni Falcone, Paolo Borsellino, Giuseppe Di Lello and Leonardo Guarnotta)

p. 30: 'We are men of honour, we're the elite of the crime world . . . We're the worst of all'
Pino Arlacchi, *Gli uomini del disonore*, Milan: Mondadori, 1992

p. 32: 'We mustn't talk about Mafia: we talk about friendship'
Gaetano Savatteri and Pietro Calderoni, *Voci del verbo mafiare,* Naples: Pironti, 1993

p. 34: 'Did you see him in the paper today, that Gina Lollobrigida?'
Pino Arlacchi, *Gli uomini del disonore,* Milan: Mondadori, 1992

p. 39: 'You Feds take care of the citizens' virtues, I'll look after their vices'
National Archives, College Park (Maryland), record 170, file 71-3555 on Lucky Luciano, portfolio Drug Inforcement Administration/ Federal Bureau of Investigation

p. 41: 'I'm the Gianni Agnelli of Palermo'
Legal judgement against Abbate Giovanni+ 706, Palermo, 8 November 1985 (investigating magistrates Antonino Caponnetto, Giovanni Falcone, Paolo Borsellino, Giuseppe Di Lello and Leonardo Guarnotta)

p. 44: 'The smuggling milieu was . . . not respectable enough for a man of honour like me'
Record of the questioning of Francesco Marino Mannoia by the deputy state prosecutor of Palermo, Giovanni Falcone, 9 November 1989

p. 47: 'For me four kilos is a modest amount'
Hearing of Gaspare Mutolo, at the Parliamentary Anti-Mafia Committee, Rome, 9 February 1993; Antonio Di Stefano and Lino Buscemi, *Signor giudice, mi sento tra l'anguria e il martello,* Milan: Mondadori, 1996

p. 53: 'That's it, that's what I'm saying: the damage'
Testimony of Salvatore G. to the trial in the Court of Assizes for the murder of Nené Geraci, 'the young one', Palermo, 6 November 1999

p. 55: 'Strangulation, what they usually did'
Questioning of Giuseppe Marchese, trial of Mariano Agate + 51, fifth penal session of the Palermo tribunal

p. 58: 'Kill the puppy'
Saverio Lodato, *Ho ucciso Giovanni Falcone,* Milan: Mondadori, 1999; Vincenzo Vasile, *Era il figlio di un pentito,* Milan: Bompiani, 2007

p. 61: 'Always fire two or three shots . . . then you can spray him in the head'

Detention of suspects, procedure no. 2474/05, 20 June 2006 (Gotha), concerning Antonino Rotolo + 51, Palermo (deputy prosecutor Giuseppe Pignatone and assistants Michele Prestipino, Domenico Gozzo, Maurizio De Lucia, Nino Di Matteo and Roberta Buzzolani)

p. 65: The *Commissione*, 1979
Legal judgement against Abbate Giovanni + 706, Palermo, 8 November 1985 (investigating magistrates Antonino Caponnetto, Giovanni Falcone, Paolo Borsellino, Giuseppe Di Lello and Leonardo Guarnotta)

p. 69: 'This is how tall Salvatore Riina is'
Transcription of the questioning of Salvatore Riina on 1 and 4 March 1993 in the trials for 'cross-linked crimes' and 'political crimes', bunker court, Rebibbia, Rome

p. 71: 'I love him because the Corte de Assise in Bari told me that Salvatore Riina . . . did not have blood on his hands'
Interview with Antonina Bagarella by Mario Francese, in *Il Giornale di Sicilia*, 27 July 1971

p. 74: 'I've never seen him angry'
Hearing of Gaspare Mutolo, Parliamentary Anti-Mafia Commission, Rome, 9 February 1993

p. 76: 'They look like two people but they're just one person'
Documents from the trial of Giuseppe Agrigento + 17, Capaci massacre, 10 October 1993 and 2 November 1993

p. 83: 'The tax-collectors aren't monsters'
Panorama, 5 July 1982

p. 86: 'Too much envy, too much betrayal, too many murky things'
Intercepted conversation, 12 June 1981, in the files of the legal judgement against Abbate Giovanni + 706, Palermo, 8 November 1985 (investigating magistrates Antonino Caponnetto, Giovanni Falcone, Paolo Borsellino, Giuseppe Di Lello and Leonardo Guarnotta)

p. 89: 'That magistrate did some crazy things'
L'Espresso, 4 July 1982; *Panorama*, 5 July 1982; *Corriere della Sera*, 17 September 1982

p. 93: 'Jesus, Jesus, another *parrino* in Cosa Nostra'
Attilio Bolzoni and Giuseppe D'Avanzo, *Il capo dei capi*, Milan: BUR-Rizzoli, 2007

p. 96: 'Cosa Nostra likes to trace itself back to the Apostle Peter'
Questioning of Leonardo Messina, Parliamentary Anti-Mafia Commission, Rome, 4 December 1992

p. 99: 'A lot of confusion . . . between sins and crimes'
Interview with Pietro Aglieri by Salvo Palazzolo, *La Repubblica*, 14 March 2004

p. 101: 'Don Pino smiled and said: "I've been expecting this"'
Francesco Anfossi, *E li guardò negli occhi. Storia di Padre Puglisi, il prete ucciso dalla mafia*, Milan: Edizioni Paoline, 2005; interview with Salvatore Grigoli by Salvo Palazzolo, *La Repubblica*, 8 September 1999

p. 103: 'These are the murders that give you satisfaction'
Files from the trial of Gaspare Spatuzza + 4, second Court of Assizes, Palermo, 14 April 1998

p. 107: 'An unforgettable *mangiata* in Section Seven'
Files from the trial of Giuseppe Albanese + 54, penal court of Palermo, Section 4, 1 December 2005

p. 109: 'Talking about cells is just a manner of speaking'
Questioning of Gaspare Mutolo, Parliamentary Anti-Mafia Commission, Rome, 9 February 1993

p. 111: 'I had half the *Cupola* in hospital'
Files from the trial of Giuseppe Albanese + 54, Penal Court of Palermo, Section 4, 1 December 2005

p. 114: 'The land draws us Sicilians, fugitives or non-fugitives'
Questioning of Gaspare Mutolo, Parliamentary Anti-Mafia Commission, Rome, 9 February 1993

p. 116: 'When you're in the middle of that stuff, the more you eat the more you like it'
Gruppo Abele, *Dalla mafia allo stato. I pentiti: analisi e storie*, Turin: Ega, 2005

p. 121: '[They] had lovers . . . they had no morals'
Questioning of Gaspare Mutolo, Parliamentary Anti-Mafia Commission, Rome, 9 February 1993

p. 123: 'I couldn't marry the daughter of a separated couple, but I could marry an orphan'
La Stampa, 10 January 1993

p. 125: 'Bagarella decided to suspend the killings because he was in mourning'
Antonio Di Stefano and Lino Buscemi, *Signor giudice, mi sento tra l'anguria e il martello*, Milan: Mondadori, 1996

p. 128: 'Her husband even killed children. That was why God was punishing her'
Record of the questioning of Tony Calvaruso by deputy public prosecutor of Palermo Teresa Principato, 23 October 1996

p. 130: 'Women are drawn to the Mafia, until they're stung by the pain'
Pino Arlacchi, *Gli uomini del disonore*, Milan: Mondadori, 1992

p. 132: 'For a great love I had to do a great thing'
Interview by Francesco La Licata for *Storie di mafia*, produced by RaiDue; Liliana Madeo, *Donne di mafia*, Milan: Mondadori, 1994

p. 137: 'All disappeared, disappeared for ever'
Records of the questioning of Salvatore Contorno by the investigating magistrate Giovanni Falcone, November and December 1984

p. 139: 'That day in Palermo we washed our feet'
Record of the questioning of Calogero Ganci by the deputy public prosecutor of Palermo Giuseppe Fici, 13 February 1996

p. 142: 'We had to take this bitter decision'
Trial no. 5464/05 of the Palermo District Anti-Mafia Office, requested for the application of custodial measures against Antonino Rotolo, Antonino Cinà and Diego Di Trapani

p. 147: 'If there's democracy in Italy today, you've got me to thank'
Il Messaggero, 16 April 1986; *Corriere della Sera*, 16 April 1986

p. 150: 'The Mafia is a democratic organization'
Questioning of Leonardo Messina, Parliamentary Anti-Mafia Commission, Rome, 4 December 1992

p. 153: 'And then his hand went up'
Documents from the trial of Giuseppe Agrigento + 51, ruling of the Court of Assizes of Palermo, 12 July 1997

p. 155: 'He's the dictator of everything and for everything'
Files from the trial of Giuseppe Agrigento + 51, ruling of the Court of Assizes, Palermo, 12 July 1997

p. 159: 'Your honour, if the Anti-Mafia exists . . .'
Antonio Di Stefano and Lino Buscemi, *Signor giudice, mi sento tra*

l'anguria e il martello, Milan: Mondadori, 1996; interview with Marcello Dell'Utri by Michele Santoro, *Moby Dick*, Italia 1, 11 March 1999

p. 161: 'Viva la Mafia, viva Ciancimino'
The words of Massimo Ciancimino are taken from Leo Sisti, *L'isola del tesoro*, Milan: BUR-Rizzoli, 2007

p. 163: 'OK, call it Mafia, because that suits everybody'
Interview with Vito Ciancimino by Massimo Martinelli, *Il Messaggero*, 9 June 2000; Leo Sisti, *L'isola del tesoro*, Milan: BUR-Rizzoli, 2007; files from the ruling in the sentence of Vito Ciancimino + 4, fifth penal section of the Court of Palermo

p. 166: 'He was more dangerous as a spiteful pensioner than as a prefect with special powers'
Questioning of Vito Ciancimino on 17 March and 11 June 1993 in the files of trial no. 3538/94, 'brought against Andreotti Giulio'

p. 169: *The members of Cosa Nostra*
Mobile unit and field section of the carabinieri of Palermo, Centro Dia Roma

p. 173: 'He shoots like a god but has the brain of a chicken'
Judicial report no. 2734/116-1977, Palermo police working group concerning the report against Riina Salvatore + 25 and containing the declarations made by the known Mafioso Di Cristina Giuseppe

p. 176: 'Where is this Mafia, these days?'
Marina Pino, *Le Signore della droga*, Sicilian Documentation Centre 'Giuseppe Impastato', Palermo: Editore La Luna, 1988

p. 179: 'The shame was too great'
Ansa News Agency, 30 June 1995

p. 181: 'We're on the outskirts of Mafiopolis'
The record of the Impastato murder is taken from the files of the Sicilian Documentation Centre 'Giuseppe Impastato'.

p. 184: 'He got himself killed because he couldn't bear all this'
Felicia Bartolotta Impastato, *La mafia in casa mia*, Sicilian Documentation Centre 'Giuseppe Impastato', Arci Donna, Palermo: Editore La Luna, 1986

p. 189: The *Commissione*, 1992

Ruling no. 12/98, 15 July 1998, against Riina Salvatore + 31 (Lima murder), Second Court of Assizes of Palermo

p. 193: 'They fired sixty-three shots into my back, but I'm sure it was by mistake'
L'Ora, 20 December 1967

p. 196: 'I've talked to the judge . . . That's the adjustment of a trial'
Questioning of Tommaso Buscetta, Parliamentary Anti-Mafia Commission, Rome, 17 November 1992

p. 198: 'No one says: I want money. Things just happen like that . . .'
Questioning of Antonino Calderone, Parliamentary Anti-Mafia Commission, Rome, 11 November 1992

p. 200: 'The jury was contacted for an "adjustment"'
Documents from the first-degree murder trial of Giuseppe Madonia, Armando Bonanno and Vincenzo Puccio, Court of Assizes, Palermo, 31 March 1983; record of the questioning of Francesco Marino Mannoia by deputy prosecutor Giovanni Falcone, November 1989

p. 203: 'No door is ever closed'
Questioning of Leonardo Messina, Parliamentary Anti-Mafia Commission, Rome, 4 December 1992

p. 207: 'I hold the Noce family in my heart'
Record of spontaneous declarations delivered by Leonardo Vitale to the mobile unit of Palermo, 30 March 1973

p. 210: 'They walk arm in arm . . . and they tell lies, the *pen-ti-ti*'
Testimony of Salvatore Riina in the trials for 'indirect' and 'political crimes' in Palermo, bunker court of Rebibbia, Rome, 1 and 4 March 1993

p. 212: 'There's times when I remember and times when I don't remember'
Testimony of Stefano Calzetta at the Maxi-Trial in Palermo, 4 July 1986

p. 215 'A handful of rogues'
Gruppo Abele, *Dalla mafia allo stato. I pentiti: analisi e storie*, Turin: Ega, 2005

p. 217: 'Cosa Nostra is over, Totuccio. You can talk'
Camilla Cederna, *Casa nostra. Viaggio nei misteri d'Italia*, Milan: Mondadori, 1983

p. 219: 'Why should they keep quiet?'
Antonio Di Stefano and Lino Buscemi, *Signor giudice, mi sento tra l'anguria e il martello*, Milan: Mondadori, 1996

p. 225: 'I wish you all eternal peace'
Record of spontaneous declarations made by Michele Greco, Maxi-Trial, Palermo, 14 December 1987

p. 228: 'Tell me where I'm supposed to have "Mafiaed"'
Corriere della Sera, 12 June 1986

p. 231: '[Socrates is] someone I admire because he never wrote anything'
Gaetano Savatteri and Pietro Calderoni, *Voci del verbo mafiare*, Naples: Pironti, 1993

p. 233: 'It wasn't us'
Hearing at the Maxi-Trial Palermo, 7 October 1986; Francesco Marino Mannoia's statement is taken from *La Repubblica*, 7 December 1989

p. 236: 'It was a political trial; we had to pay the price'
Record of the questioning of Gaspare Mutolo in the records of court case no. 3538/94, 'brought against Andreotti Giulio'

p. 238: 'As far as I'm concerned Judge Carnevale is as righteous as Pope John' Interview with Pieruccio Senapa by the author, February 1991

p. 241: 'Things are getting more and more *trubbole*'
Intercepted phonecall between Giuseppe Joe Gambino and person unknown, files from the drug-trafficking trial (Iron Tower), ruling of the Tribunal of Palermo, 30 January 1991

p. 247: 'The Anti-Mafia shouldn't play the Mafia's game'
Il Diario, 11 September 1980; *Il Giornale di Sicilia*, 28 June 1987, 23 March 1988

p. 249: 'They're coming back'
'Details and course of investigation of the custodial sentence against Salvatore Riina and others for the murder of Salvo Lima', 11 October 1992

p. 251: 'Judge Carnevale was also somebody who felt . . . the tug on the reins'
Documents deposited by the public prosecutor of Palermo in court case no. 3538/94, 'brought against Andreotti Giulio'

p. 253: *The Court acquits . . .*
I sentenza Andreotti, quinta sezione penale di Palermo, 23 ottobre

1999; II sentenza Andreotti, prima sezione Corte d'appello di Palermo, 2 maggio 2003; III sentenza Andreotti Corte di Cassazione, 15 ottobre 2004; I sentenza Carnevale, sesta sezione penale di Palermo, 8 giugno 2000; II sentenza Carnevale, terza sezione Corte d'appello di Palermo, 29 giungo 2001; III sentenza Carnevale, Corte di cassazione, 30 ottobre 2002

p. 255: 'Totò Riina . . . greeted all three men with a kiss'
Files deposited by the public prosecutor of Palermo in trial no. 3538/94, 'brought against Andreotti Giulio'

p. 258: 'They could use at least one man like him on every street in every city in Italy'
Questioning of Tommaso Buscetta on 11 Septemeber 1992 by the state prosecutors of Palermo, files in case no. 3538/94, 'brought against Andreotti Giulio'

p. 261: 'Once upon a time I called him Masino; now I'd say: Signor Buscetta'
Interview with Gaetano Badalamenti by Stefano Zurlo, *Il Giornale*, 18 October 1999

p. 267: 'The meat's arrived'
Files in the ruling on the Capaci massacre, Court of Assizes, Caltanissetta, 26 September 1997

p. 269: 'I didn't even get to hear the bang'
Record of the questioning of Gioacchino La Barbera in the Capaci Massacre trial, 2 December 1993 (magistrates Giovanni Tinebra, Carmelo Petralia and Ilda Boccassini)

p. 271: '*Minchia*, the way the young men walk around in Palermo . . .'
Files in the trial of Giuseppe Agrigento + 17, Capaci Massacre, 10 October 1993 and 2 November 1993 (magistrates Giovanni Tinebra, Ilda Boccassini, Carmelo Petralia, Fausto Cardella)

p. 274: 'I represent the end of everything'
Files in the trial of Giuseppe Agrigento + 17, Capaci Massacre, 10 October 1993 and 2 November 1993 (magistrates Giovanni Tinebra, Ilda Boccassini, Carmelo Petralia, Fausto Cardella)

p. 276: 'These people are the lowest in the world since the days of Nero'
Attilio Bolzoni and Giuseppe D'Avanzo, *Il capo dei capi*, Milan: BUR-Rizzoli, 2007

p. 281: 'In Palermo . . . the people are very polite about paying'
Questioning of Gaspare Mutolo, Parliamentary Anti-Mafia Commission, Rome, 9 February 1993

p. 284: 'That's how I fixed things up'
Ruling, custodial sentence in Tommaso Lo Presti + 5, case no. 5847/03, court of Palermo

p. 286: 'Even Garibaldi paid the *pizzo* to land at Marsala'
Questioning of Antonino Patti by magistrate Massimo Russo, Court of Assizes, Trapani, 14 October 1998

p. 288: 'With a litre of petrol, boom . . . you can set the whole world alight'
Report from Monreale police headquarters to the state prosecutor's office of Palermo, 3 December 1997

p. 291: 'We're putting on the glue'
Record of the questioning of Aurelio Neri by state prosecutor Maurizio De Lucia, 6 July 1996; statement of solidarity taken from Tano Grasso and Aldo Varano, *'U pizzu. L'Italia del racket e dell'usura*, Milan: Baldini Castoldi Dalai, 2002

p. 293: 'Because those guys eat everything'
Custodial sentence issued by prosecutor Marcello Viola against Luigi Adamo + 37, Palermo 27 April 2004

p. 297: 'We're hostages of these gentlemen'
Interview of Filippo Salamone by Attilio Bolzoni, *La Repubblica*, 23 September 1997

p. 300: 'Work in peace'
Pino Arlacchi, *Gli uomini del disonore*, Milan: Mondadori, 1992

p. 303: 'The eye of respect'
Interview with Angelo Siino, *Sette*, 20 January 2000; interview with Angelo Siino by Gianni Barbacetto, *Diario*, 26 May 1999

p. 306: 'The politicians went mad: because a kind of protection money was being imposed on their bribes'
Interview with Angelo Siino by Gianni Barbacetto, Diario, 26 May 1999; record of the questioning of Angelo Siino by deputy prosecutor of Palermo Maurizio De Lucia, 23 July 1997

p. 309 'Angelo Siino could end up like Ciancimino if he gets involved in things like that'

Questioning of Baldassare Di Maggio in the trial 'Mafia and contracts', Palermo, 14 September 2003

p. 313: 'Somebody might turn cop'
Files of the Capaci massacre trial, Court of Assizes of Caltanissetta, 26 September 1997

p. 316: 'Totò Riina wanted to kill their children to the twentieth degree of kinship'
Gruppo Abele, *Dalla mafia allo stato. I pentiti: analisi e storie*, Turin: Ega, 2005; Salvatore Cancemi, *Riina mi fece i nomi di . . .*, ed. Giorgio Bongiovanni, Bolsena: Massari, 2002.

p. 318: 'That word says a lot, it says everything, it says lots of things'
Questioning of Salvatore Riina by the prosecutor of Florence Pier Luigi Vigna and the prosecutor of Palermo Giancarlo Caselli, 22 April 1996

p. 321: 'Mutolo, you're a great nark'
Gaetano Savatteri and Pietro Calderoni, *Voci del verbo mafiare*, Naples: Pironti, 1993

p. 324: 'You, Signor Riina, are the one who killed Cosa Nostra'
'American-style' questioning of Tommaso Buscetta and Salvatore Riina, bunker court in Rebibbia, Rome

p. 329: The Directory, 2000
Ruling no. 12/98, 15 July 1998, against Riina Salvatore + 31 (Lima murder), Second Court of Assizes of Palermo

p. 333: 'Seventy-three holy pictures showing Christ'
Inventory of the material found in the hide-out of Bernardo Provenzano, report of the mobile unit of Palermo dated 11 April 2006 and passed on to the deputy prosecutor of Palermo Giuseppe Pignatone and his assistant prosecutors Michele Prestipino and Marzia Sabella

p. 335: 'Curiosity is the antechamber of *sbirritudine*'
Record of the questioning of Antonino Giuffrè by the deputy public prosecutor of of Palermo Michele Prestipino, 30 January 2004

p. 338: 'I was careful and I wasn't careful . . . I was keeping an eye on him, in inverted commas'
Record of the questioning of Giovanni Brusca by public prosecutor Antonino Di Matteo, trial of Simone Castello + 5, 12 December 2000

p. 341: 'You've got to be straight, correct and consistent'
Custodial sentence against Bernardo Provenzano + 20, trial no. 4668/96 (prosecutor Renato Grillo); custodial sentence against Salvatore Rinella + 13, trial no. 7106/02 (prosecutor Antonio Caputo)

p. 345: *'M', 'MM', 'MMM'*
Penal procedure. 4578/96, Palermo public prosecutor's office

p. 347: 'We're a single body: bandits, police and Mafia. Like the Father, the Son and the Holy Spirit'
Documents made public by the Office of Strategic Services on 'Italy 1943–1948', National Archives, College Park, Maryland

p. 349: 'Those guys were shit scared'
Sentencing documents on the Georgofili Massacre, Court of Assizes, Florence, 13 February 2001

p. 352: 'I presented them with a *papello* that size'
Saverio Lodato, *Ho ucciso Giovanni Falcone*, Milan: Mondadori, 1999

p. 354: 'Of course, then, when the Berlin Wall comes down . . .'
Record of the questioning of Antonino Giuffrè, court of Termini Imerese, 16 October 2002; record of the questioning of Antonino Giuffrè by prosecutor Michele Prestipino, trial 'Mafia and contracts', 8 and 9 September 2002

p. 357: 'We have launched a civil, peaceful protest . . .'
Record of the hearing of 12 July 2002, Court of Assizes, Trapani, in Saverio Lodato and Marco Travaglio, *Intoccabili*, Milan: BUR-Rizzoli 2005

p. 363: 'Vittorio Mangano . . . is a hero, in his own way'
La Repubblica, 8 April 2008; *Corriere della Sera*, 21 March 1994; record of the questioning of Marcello Dell'Utri by the state prosecutors of Palermo, 26 May and 26 June 1996

p. 369: 'Certain films have been the ruin of mankind'
Gaetano Savatteri and Pietro Calderoni, *Voci del verbo mafiare*, Naples: Pironti, 1993

p. 371: 'A famous notable'
Interview with Umberto Castagna by the author, Palermo, March 2000

p. 374: 'Dom, if you've killed for the government you can do it for the family too'
Interview with Dominick Montiglio by the author, New York, June 2005

p. 383: 'Not so much as a seed must be left of those Inzerillos'
Arrest documents, trial no. 2474/05, 20 June 2006 (Gotha), against Antonino Rotolo + 51

p. 386: 'The moment we're sound asleep it could be that we don't wake up'
Arrest documents, trial no. 2474/05 of 20 June 2006 (Gotha), against Antonino Rotolo + 51

p. 388: 'You're not here because you're you, you're here because you're him'
Arrest documents, trial no. 2474/05 of 20 June 2006 (Gotha), against Antonino Rotolo + 51

p. 391: 'Unlucky guys'
Trial no. 38/08, Palermo District Anti-Mafia Office, against Alamia Pietro + 20, 16 January 2008 (prosecutors Marcello Viola, Domenico Gozzo, Gaetano Paci, Francesco Del Bene, Annamaria Picozzi and Alfredo Morvillo)

p. 393: 'My dearest one, you need more besides my opinion'
Trial no. 38/08, Palermo District Anti-Mafia Office against Alamia Pietro + 20, 16 January 2008 (prosecutors Marcello Viola, Domenico Gozzo, Gaetano Paci, Francesco Del Bene, Annamaria Picozzi and Alfredo Morvillo)

p. 395: '[Franky Boy's] everything over there'
Trial no. 11059/06, decree of arrest against Casamento Filippo + 29 (Old Bridge), Palermo, 7 February 2008 (prosecutors Michele Prestipino, Domenico Gozzo, Maurizio de Lucia, Antonino Di Matteo, Roberta Buzzolani, Giuseppe Pignatone and Guido Lo Forte)

p. 398: 'We have to get out. Not just out of Sicily, not just out of Italy – we have to get out of Europe'
Report by the mobile unit of Palermo state police headquarters, trial no. 11059/06 issued by the Palermo District Prosecutor's Office

p. 403: 'Duties and prohibitions'
Trial no 38/08, Palermo District Anti-Mafia Office, against Alamia

Pietro + 20, 16 January 2008 (prosecutors Marcello Viola, Domenico Gozzo, Gaetano Paci, Francesco Del Bene, Annamaria Picozzi and Alfredo Morvillo)

p. 406: 'It'll take time, you teach me'
Ruling in the preliminary hearings of the court of Palermo by the judge Roberto Binenti, shortened ruling re. Lipari + 16, 12 December 2003

p. 410: 'Pick a fight with whoever you like, but you leave the state alone'
Ruling in the preliminary hearings of the court of Palermo by the judge Roberto Binenti, shortened version of ruling against Lipari + 16, 12 December 2003

p. 413: 'Unfortunately life isn't always a bunch of roses'
Trial no. 38/08, Palermo District Anti-Mafia Office against Alamia Pietro + 20, 16 January 2008 (prosecutors Marcello Viola, Domenico Gozzo, Gaetano Paci, Francesco Del Bene, Annamaria Picozzi and Alfredo Morvillo)

p. 416: 'I . . . unscrewed it and found it'
Arrest document, trial no. 2474/05 of 20 June 2006 (Gotha), against Antonino Rotolo + 51

p. 418: 'But how I loved you (asshole)'
Trial no. 38/08, Palermo District Anti-Mafia Office, against Alamia Pietro + 20, 16 January 2008 (prosecutors Marcello Viola, Domenico Gozzo, Gaetano Paci, Francesco Del Bene, Annamaria Picozzi and Alfredo Morvillo)

p. 423: 'I belong to you'
Report by Palermo mobile unit sent to the deputy prosecutor of Palermo, Giuseppe Pignatone, and to assistant prosecutors Michele Prestipino and Marzia Sabella, 11 April 2006

p. 426: 'I am an enemy of Italian justice that is rotten and corrupt'
Sicilian weekly magazine *S*, no. 5, 2008

p. 431: 'You've always been *catu e corda*'
Trial no. 13100/00, Palermo District Anti-Mafia Office

p. 434: 'The decision was this: let's kill them. And they were killed.'
Trial no. 13100/00, Palermo District Anti-Mafia Office

p. 436: 'Please do not disturb'
Interview with Maria Concetta Riina by Sandra Amurri, *Panorama*, 7 December 1995

p. 441: 'Sleep, sleep, Godfather'
The Godfather, Part III

Bibliography

Anfossi, Francesco, *E li guardò negli occhi. Storia di Padre Puglisi, il prete ucciso dalla mafia*, Milan: Edizioni Paoline, 2005.

Arlacchi, Pino, *Addio a Cosa Nostra*, Milan: Rizzoli, 1994.

Arlacchi, Pino, *Gli uomini del disonore*, Milan: Mondadori, 1992.

Bartolotta Impastato, Felicia, *La mafia in casa mia*, Sicilian Documentation Centre 'Giuseppe Impastato', Arci Donna, Palermo: Editore La Luna, 1986.

Bellavia, Enrico and Salvo Palazzolo, *Voglia di mafia*, Rome: Carocci, 2004.

Biagi, Enzo, *Il boss è solo*, Milan: Mondadori, 1986.

Bianconi, Giovanni and Gaetano Savatteri, *L'attentatuni*, Milan: Baldini e Castoldi, 1998.

Bolzoni, Attilio and Giuseppe D'Avanzo, *Il capo dei capi*, Milan: Bur-Rizzoli, 2007.

Bolzoni, Attilio and Giuseppe D'Avanzo, *La giustizia è Cosa Nostra*, Milan: Mondadori, 1995.

Bonanno, Joseph, *Uomo d'onore*, ed. Sergio Lalli, Milan: Mondadori, 1985.

Bongiorno, Giulia, *Nient'altro che la verità*, Milan: Rizzoli, 2005.

Cancemi, Salvatore, *Riina mi fece i nomi di . . .*, a cura di Giorgio Bongiovanni, Bolsena: Massari, 2002.

Cederna, Camilla, *Casa nostra. Viaggio nei misteri d'Italia*, Milan: Mondadori, 1983.

Ceruso, Vincenzo, *Le sagrestie di cosa nostra. Inchiesta su preti e mafiosi*, Rome: Newton Compton, 2007.

Deaglio, Enrico, *Raccolto rosso*, Milan: Feltrinelli, 1993.

De Francisci, Ignazio, 'Cosa Nostra a tavola', in *Slow Food*, July 2002.

Dino, Alessandra, *La mafia devota*, Rome-Bari: Laterza, 2008.
Dino, Alessandra and Teresa Principato, *Mafia Donna*, Palermo: Flaccovio, 1997.
Di Stefano, Antonio and Lino Buscemi, *Signor giudice, mi sento tra l'anguria e il martello*, Milan: Mondadori, 1996.
Falcone, Giovanni and Marcelle Padovani, *Cose di Cosa Nostra*, Milan: Rizzoli, 1991.
File of the Alto commissariato per la lotta alla mafia: 'ricoveri facili' all'Ospedale civico di Palermo, May 1987.
Grasso, Pietro, report on 'Il sistema di protezione dei collaboratori di giustizia, situazione attuale e prospettive di modifica 1996/2006', Direzione nazionale antimafia, Rome, December 1996.
Grasso, Tano and Aldo Varano, *'U pizzu. L'Italia del racket e dell'usura*, Milan: Baldini Castoldi Dalai, 2002.
Gruppo Abele, *Dalla mafia allo stato. I pentiti: analisi e storie*, Turin: Ega, 2005.
Lirio, Abbate and Peter Gomez, *I complici*, Rome: Fazi, 2007.
Lodato, Saverio, *Ho ucciso Giovanni Falcone*, Milan: Mondadori, 1999.
Lodato, Saverio and Marco Travaglio, *Intoccabili*, Milan: BUR-Rizzoli, 2005.
Lodato, Saverio, *Quindici anni di mafia*, Milan: Rizzoli, 1994.
Lo Verso, Girolamo, *La psiche mafiosa*, Milan: Franco Angeli, 2003
Lupo, Salvatore, *Storia della mafia*, Rome: Donzelli, 1993.
Madeo, Liliana, *Donne di mafia*, Milan: Mondadori, 1994.
Mignosi, Enzo, *Il Signore sia coi boss*, Palermo: Arbor, 1993.
Nania, Gioacchino, *San Giuseppe e la mafia. Nascita e sviluppo del fenomeno nello Jato*, Palermo: Edizioni della Battaglia, 2000.
Palazzolo, Salvo and Michele Prestipino, *Il codice Provenzano*, Rome-Bari: Laterza, 2007.
Pantaleone, Michele, *Mafia e droga*, Turin: Einaudi, 1966.
Pino, Marina, *Le Signore della droga*, Sicilian Documentation Centre 'Giuseppe Impastato', Palermo: Editore La Luna, 1988.
Renda, Francesco, *Storia della mafia*, Palermo: Sigma, 1997.
Savatteri, Gaetano and Pietro Calderoni, *Voci del verbo mafiare*, Naples: Pironti, 1993.
Sisti, Leo, *L'isola del tesoro*, Milan: BUR-Rizzoli, 2007.

Stille, Alexander, *Excellent Cadavers: The Mafia and the Death of the First Italian Republic*, London: Random House, 1996.

Torrealta, Maurizio, *La trattativa*, Rome: Editori Riuniti, 2002.

Turone, Giuliano, *Il delitto di associazione mafiosa*, Milan: Giuffrè, 2008.

Vasile, Vincenzo, *Era il figlio di un pentito*, Milan: Bompiani, 2007.

Index of Names